BIBLIOGRAPHY OF

AMERICAN PUBLICATIONS ON

EAST CENTRAL EUROPE, 1945-1957

BIBLIOGRAPHY OF AMERICAN PUBLICATIONS ON EAST CENTRAL EUROPE, 1945-1957

By
Robert F. Byrnes

INDIANA UNIVERSITY PUBLICATIONS

Graduate School

SLAVIC AND EAST EUROPEAN SERIES

Volume 11/12

Composed At The

INDIANA UNIVERSITY

RESEARCH CENTER IN

ANTHROPOLOGY, FOLKLORE, AND LINGUISTICS

PREFACE

I have sought in this volume to list in an organized way all scholarly or semi-scholarly works concerning East Central Europe published by Americans in books and journals from 1945 through 1957. The term East Central Europe, or the term Eastern Europe which is often used in its place, in this book refers to Albania, Bulgaria, Czechoslovakia, Finland, Hungary, Poland, Rumania, Yugoslavia, and the Baltic states now under Soviet rule, Estonia, Latvia, and Lithuania. Eastern Germany and Greece are not included, except when relationships involving states within this definition of East Central Europe are involved. The volume lists books and articles published in the United States (generally, but not always, written by Americans) from 1945 through 1957. It does not include book reviews, though it does list review articles. It does include the work of Canadians and books and articles published by Americans in Canada. It also contains a few articles published by Americans in German, Dutch, and English journals.

No bibliography is complete, but I have sought desperately to attain that goal. Even so, I am aware that some items were not identified. A few periodicals were not attainable; some books, I assume, were not found because they were privately printed, although the bibliography does list a number published in that way; some books and articles published abroad may have escaped our grasp, though we tried rigorously to identify and list such publications; some articles, I suppose, were printed in journals which did not attract the attention of our group or, indeed, of any of the scholars whose bibliographies and footnotes we reviewed in our final check; some books and articles dealing primarily with Russian history, or with minorities and displaced persons, may have evaded us; a few obvious items, I fear, slipped through our grasp through one mischance or other.

The organization of the bibliography is clearly revealed by the table of contents. As everyone knows who has ever engaged in research or made use of a bibliography, every bibliographical listing presents complex problems for which there is no ideal or permanent solution. In all cases, I have tried to reach the most sensible and useful solution. In every case, I have used the spelling adopted by the author. The technical system used throughout is that used in the annual bibliographies of the <u>Publications of the Modern Language Association of America</u>.

    This bibliography grew out of research undertaken in 1957 for a critical analysis of American scholarship on East Central Europe from 1945 through 1957. This paper, which is published in this book, was presented at a conference at Columbia University on "The American Concern with East Central Europe." The bibliographical research and analysis undertaken for that article were so considerable that I decided to make the collection complete and to publish it, particularly since this step will provide experience for another work in progress, an annotated bibliography of American scholarship on Russia and East Central Europe since 1945. I hope this will be a useful tool for both scholars and teachers and that it will serve as a measure of the achievements and shortcomings of the interest in and research upon this critical area by Americans since World War II.

    I have been generously assisted by the Indiana University Research Committee, whose support I gratefully acknowledge. The burden of much of the collecting and checking was cheerfully and skillfully undertaken by Joseph Backor, Matthew Downey, Janet Hawley, and Edward O'Day. My wife, in the midst of all her other duties, completed the index.

                                                     Robert F. Byrnes

TABLE OF CONTENTS

	Page
Preface	v
Journals Used and Their Abbreviations	xi
American Publications on East Central Europe, 1945-1957	xv

I. EAST-CENTRAL EUROPE

Bibliography	1
Area Studies	4
General	7
Geography and Population	14
History	15
Government and Politics	18
Propaganda	22
Law	23
Peace Treaties and International Affairs	24
Soviet Rule	26
American Policy	29
Federation Plans	32
The Economy	33
Agriculture	39
Trade	40
Forced Labor	42
Languages	44
The Arts	46
Literature and Folklore	47
Education	48
Philosophy and Religion	49
Sociology	50
Pan-Slavism	51
Minorities	52
Refugees	54
The Jews and Anti-Semitism	56

II. THE BALKANS

General	60
Geography	61
History	61
Government and Politics	62
International Affairs	62
The Economy	63
Literature	63
Philosophy and Religion	63
Sociology	63

III. THE BALTIC STATES

General	64
Geography and Population	65
History	65
Government and Politics	66
Law	67
International Affairs	67

	Page
Soviet Rule	67
The Economy	68
Languages and Literatures	69
The Arts	70
Education	70
Philosophy and Religion	71
Sociology	71

IV. SOME DISPUTED AREAS

Bukovina	72
Carpatho-Ukraine	72
Macedonia	73
Northern Epirus	74
Trieste	74

V. ALBANIA

General	76
Geography and Population	76
History	77
International Affairs	78
The Economy	79
Language and Literature	79
Education	81
Philosophy and Religion	81

VI. BULGARIA

General	82
Geography and Population	82
History	83
Government and Politics	83
Law	85
International Affairs	85
The Economy	86
Language, Literature, and Folklore	87
Education	88
Philosophy and Religion	88

VII. CZECHOSLOVAKIA

General	89
Geography and Population	91
History	91
1948 Coup and Soviet Rule	94
Government and Politics	96
Law	98
International Affairs	99
The Economy	100
Languages	103
The Arts	104
Folklore	104
Literatures	105
Education	106
Philosophy and Religion	107
Sociology	108

Page

VIII. FINLAND

    General 109
    Geography and Population 110
    History 110
    Government and Politics 112
    The Economy 112
    Language and Literature 112
    The Arts 113
    Philosophy and Religion 114
    Sociology 114

IX. HUNGARY

    General 115
    Geography and Population 117
    History 117
        1956 Revolution 120
        Hungarian Refugees 123
    Government and Politics 123
    International Relations 125
    Law 127
    The Economy 128
    Language 130
    The Arts 131
    Literature 132
    Folklore 134
    Education 134
    Philosophy and Religion 135
    Sociology 136

X. POLAND

    General 137
    Geography and Population 140
    History 141
        World War II 147
    Government and Politics 150
    Law 153
    International Affairs 154
    The Economy 155
    Language 159
    The Arts 161
    Literature 163
        Mickiewicz 165
    Folklore 167
    Education 168
    Philosophy and Religion 169
    Sociology 170

XI. RUMANIA

    General 172
    Geography and Population 173
    History 173
    Government and Politics 174
    International Affairs 175
    Law 176

		Page
	The Economy	176
	Language	178
	Literature	178
	Education	179
	Philosophy and Religion	179
XII.	YUGOSLAVIA	
	General	181
	Geography and Population	183
	History	183
	Government and Politics	185
	Law	187
	International Affairs	188
	Soviet-Yugoslav Disputes since 1948	189
	The Economy	193
	Languages	195
	The Arts	196
	Literature	196
	Folklore	197
	Education	197
	Philosophy and Religion	198
	Sociology	198

JOURNALS USED, AND THEIR ABBREVIATIONS

AA	American Archivist	BMC	Burlington Magazine for Connoisseurs
AAAG	Annals of the Association of American Geographers	BR	Baltic Review
AAAPSS	Annals of the American Academy of Political and Social Science	CAJ	Central Asiatic Journal
		CEF	Central European Federalist
AAnt	American Antiquity	CH	Current History
AAnth	American Anthropologist	ChH	Church History
		CHR	Catholic Historical Review
ABAJ	American Bar Association Journal	CHSQ	California Historical Society Quarterly
ACSR	American Catholic Sociological Review	CL	Comparative Literature
AER	American Economic Review	CLJ	Chitty's Law Journal
AHR	American Historical Review	CLR	Columbia Law Review
		Com	Commentary
AJA	American Journal of Archaeology	CP	Classical Philology
AJCL	American Journal of Comparative Law	DA	Dissertation Abstracts
		DD	Democratic Digest
AJIL	American Journal of International Law	DSB	Department of State Bulletin
AJS	American Journal of Sociology	DQ	Designers Quarterly
	America	EDCC	Economic Development and Cultural Change
	Anthropos		
AN	Art News		
APSR	American Political Science Review	EE	East Europe
		EEH	Explorations in Entrepreneurial History
Arch	Archaeology		
ARec	Architectural Record		
	(1) Arts	EEProb	(2) East European Problems
AS	American Statistician		
ASEER	American Slavic and East European Review	EG	Economic Geography
			Encounter
			Ethics
ASoR	American Sociological Review	FA	Foreign Affairs
ASp	American Speech	FAgr	Foreign Agricultural Monthly
	Athene		
AUA	Annals of the Ukrainian Academy of Arts and Science in the U.S.	FEQ	Far Eastern Quarterly
		FES	Far Eastern Survey
			Focus
			Fortune
		FPB	Foreign Policy Bulletin
BA	Books Abroad	FPR	Foreign Policy Reports
BBJ	Boston Bar Journal	FSJ	(3) Foreign Service Journal

(1) Arts Digest until 1955-56.
(2) Incomplete
(3) Also called American Foreign Service Journal (AFSJ).

GR	Geographical Review	JEccH	Journal of Ecclesiastical History
GWLR	George Washington Law Review	JFE	Journal of Farm Economics
HCLAME	Highlights of Current Legislation and Activities in Europe	JG	Journal of Geography
		JIA	Journal of International Affairs
HER	Harvard Educational Review	JMH	Journal of Modern History
HINL	History of Ideas Newsletter	JPol	Journal of Politics
		JPE	Journal of Political Economy
Hist	Historian		
HJAS	Harvard Journal of Asiatic Studies	JQ	Journalism Quarterly
		JSP	Journal of Social Psychology
HLB	Harvard Library Bulletin		
HMPEC	Historical Magazine of the Protestant Episcopal Church	KASP	Kroeber Anthropological Society Papers
HSS	Harvard Slavic Studies		Language
		LE	Land Economics
HudR	Hudson Review		Law and Contempory Problems
IC	International Commission of Jurists	LLJ	Law Library Journal
		LLR	Law Labor Review
ILR	International Labor Review	LQ	Library Quarterly
ILRR	Industrial and Labor Relations Review	MEA	Middle Eastern Affairs
IO	International Organization	MEJ	Middle East Journal
		MF (4)	Midwest Folklore
IRSH	International Review of Social History (Amsterdam)	MFL	Marriage and Family Living
		MFS	Modern Fiction Studies
ISS	Indiana Slavic Studies	MLabR	Monthly Labor Review
IUGSSEES	Indiana University Graduate School Slavic and East European Series	MLJ	Modern Language Journal
		MLQ	Modern Language Quarterly
		MP	Modern Philology
JAA	Journal of Asian Affairs	MQ	Musical Quarterly
JAAC	Journal of Aesthetics and Art Criticism		Nation
		NBIC	News From Behind the Iron Curtain
JAAUW	Journal of the American Association of University Women	NMQ	New Mexico Quarterly
JAF	Journal of American Folklore	NMR	National Municipal Review
JAOS	Journal of the American Oriental Society	NR	New Republic
		NTJ	National Tax Journal
JCEA	Journal of Central European Affairs	NWUSG	Northwestern University Studies in Geography
JEH	Journal of Economic History		
		NY	New Yorker

(4) Hoosier Folklore until 1949.

NYFQ	New York Folklore Quarterly		(Notre Dame)
		RRel	Review of Religion
NYSBB	New York State Bar Bulletin	RusR	Russian Review
		SAQ	South Atlantic Quarterly
OLR	Oklahoma Law Review	SatR	Saturday Review
	Onomastica (Ukrainian Free Academy of Sciences)	SEEJ	(5) Slavic and East European Journal
		SEER	Slavonic and East European Review
PacA	Pacific Affairs	SG	State Government
PAR	Public Administration Review	SJA	Southwestern Journal of Anthropology
PG	Popular Government	Spec	Speculum
PHR	Pacific Historical Review	SOAHJ	Society of Architectural Historians Journal
PNQ	Pacific Northwest Quarterly	SOF	(6) Südost-Forschungen
PoC	Problems of Communism	SocP	Social Problems
		SoR	Social Research
	Polish American Studies	SSRC	Social Science Research Council, Items
PolR	Polish Review		
POQ	Public Opinion Quarterly		
		SSSQ	Southwestern Social Science Quarterly
PPR	Public Personnel Review	Sym	Symposium
PQ	Philological Quarterly (Iowa City)		Thought
PR	Partisan Review		
PS	Pacific Spectator	UNR	United Nations Review
PSQ	Political Science Quarterly	UQ	Ukrainian Quarterly
	Psychiatry	USNIP	US Naval Institute Proceedings
PT	Physics Today		
QJCA	Quarterly Journal of Current Acquisitions of the Library of Congress	WAQ	(7) World Affairs Quarterly
		WHR	Western Humanities Review
QJE	Quarterly Journal of Economics	WO	World Oil
			Word
		WP	World Politics
Rept	Reporter	WPQ	Western Political Quarterly
RES	Review of Economics and Statistics		
RM	Review of Metaphysics		
RPol	Review of Politics	YR	Yale Review

(5) AATSEEL - American Association of Teachers of Slavonic and East European Languages Bulletin (1943-53); Journal (1954-56).
(6) Incomplete.
(7) WAI - World Affairs Interpreter until 1956.

AMERICAN PUBLICATIONS ON EAST CENTRAL EUROPE, 1945-1957

I am not a scholar on East Central Europe. I know none of the languages of the area, I have done no research on the area, and I do not intend to attempt any research on East Central Europe. Moreover, I cannot speak with equal interest and knowledge concerning all disciplines, for I am an historian. I have the knowledge of the basic problems of East Central Europe which any historian interested in Western Europe and in Russian history would have. I write not as a participant or specialist, but as an interested external observer, with all the advantages and disadvantages deriving from that position.

I do have one special source of knowledge concerning this area and recent American scholarship devoted to it, for I was for two years, 1954 through 1956, the director of the Mid-European Study Center, the research organization of the Free Europe Committee. This organization, founded in 1950 and incorporated into Radio Free Europe in 1956, was established to increase the fund of information available on this critical area to Americans and others in the free world and to provide refugee scholars and officials an opportunity to collect and publish objective and useful data concerning their native lands. Large numbers of American scholars worked closely with the center. Consequently, in two years I acquired some understanding of the principal problems involved in research in this area and of the people in the United States engaged in this study.

I have over the years compiled a bibliography on East Central Europe similar to that which any historian interested in modern European history would have collected. This, of course, was not adequate for this review. I have supplemented this bibliography by a systematic collection and analysis of the scholarly work published on this area since 1945, assisted significantly by a grant from the Indiana University Research Committee which enabled me to employ graduate student aids.

Some leading Americans, notably Mr. Adolf Berle, have argued that the failure of American policy in Europe after 1919 and our disasters again after the Second World War with regard to East Central Europe derive fundamentally from the lack of information which our policy makers and American informed opinion had at hand. Moreover, they have demonstrated that even today we rely very heavily upon journalists, travellers, and current affairs analysts for our basic information on this area and on other critical areas. Consequently, while our knowledge of current events is probably remarkably great, our understanding of the basic forces behind these developments is also extraordinarily shallow. One of the consequences of this is the flightiness of even informed opinion; another is the prevalence of great myths in our society concerning East Central Europe. I think it quite likely that informed Americans a century ago were better informed concerning the Hungary of Kossuth than we of today are concerning the Hungary of Horthy or Nagy or Kadar.

The American people in the last few years have awakened to the existence of several important foreign cultures, and the study of foreign areas has become increasingly significant in American education. In this situation, however, we have tended to study those foreign areas from which national states threaten our national interests and institutions or which have contributed significantly to the values and institutions upon which our society rests. Consequently, with this view of the world, we tend to ignore East Central Europe or to treat it as a satellite area of the Soviet Union, important only as an increment to Soviet power. Generally, even scholars view East Central Europe as an area of minor importance, a kind of football kicked about by various Great Powers. Moreover, the people from this area who are now citizens of the United States represent cultures which are considered inferior by many who live in our Anglo-Saxon society. They speak strange foreign languages, they have strong religious beliefs and traditions, their diet and dress seem exotic, their national histories seem full of chaos, confusion, and bloodshed, and they have a greater affection for their native country than many Americans think desirable or necessary.

In any case, we have tended to slight East Central Europe in our scholarship, in our educational systems, and in our general view of the world. The penalties for this in the past have been very great, and they will remain great unless we revise our attitudes.

East Central Europe in the United States is considered a part of the Slavic and East European area, and scholarship on this area has developed in large part in the last sixty or seventy years because of the increased interest in Russia and the Soviet Union. The first course on Russia or Eastern Europe in this country was introduced at Oberlin College in Ohio in 1885, to help train men for missionary work. Since that time, several rather striking spurts of interest in Russian and East

European studies have occurred. The first came about the turn of the century, with the establishment of Slavic language and literature courses at Harvard University and at the University of California at Berkeley. Men such as Professor Archibald Cary Coolidge at Harvard University devoted their lives to developing programs in their institutions and to creating significant library collections.

The second injection of interest in this area came immediately after the First World War, which began in the Balkans, thereby attracting the attention of Americans to the area. Several professors were members of the American delegation to the conference at Versailles, because President Wilson recognized the importance of experts for the process of reorganizing the map of East Central Europe. These men returned to their universities with their understanding, interest, and, it should be noted, their prestige increased. Moreover, other professors who were members of the delegation or whose interest had been stimulated by the First World War and the peace treaties following it, also increased the pressure within their universities for additional courses devoted to the languages and the history of the area. Consequently, in the twenties and thirties, an age of isolation generally, a new generation of scholars concentrating primarily upon Russia began to appear. Thus, the foundations were fairly solid by 1939, when World War II broke out.

The Second World War had a profound influence upon Slavic and East European studies in this country. While the government was drawing professors into its service, at the same time it also sponsored training programs on this area, and on other foreign areas, in many institutions. Consequently, by the end of World War II, the United States possessed a small band of devoted and skilled professors, with good academic training and with considerable government experience. It also had a rather substantial number of men and woman who had received language training, had acquired some knowledge concerning the area, and in some cases had worked in the area in the closing years of the war. Even more important, however, was the substantial general American interest in Russia and East Central Europe, stimulated by the violent and bloody events of the war, by the uncertainties concerning the peace and the future, by the rise of Soviet Russia as a hostile world power, and by the immense new responsibilities thrust upon the United States as it emerged as a major power.

Consequently, following World War II, Russian and East European studies flowered in an atmosphere of interest and concern. It was in this atmosphere that the great institutes and research centers which now dot the American academic landscape were established and flourished. These training programs are producing an increasing number of well-trained scholars, and these young scholars, under the leadership of their more established colleagues, are writing and publishing an increasing quantity of first-rate books concerning Russia and East Central Europe. In other words, with regard both to personnel and to information, our national situation with regard to this area is better than it has ever been before, although our needs have increased even more rapidly.

Fundamentally, then, research in the last ten or twelve years on East Central Europe has benefited from the heightened interest in the area brought by the Second World War, Soviet expansion, and the cold war. The area now has a high priority in the minds of all Americans, and everyone working in this field or preparing to enter it can proceed on the assumption that he is in an area of growing interest and in which he can enjoy a productive and useful career, which are immeasurable advantages.

Moreover, scholarship on East Central Europe has benefited from freedom from political and other pressures. While we all appreciate the enormous and indispensable benefits of freedom in scholarship, we sometimes fail to realize that scholarship on this area has not been affected by the same pressures, conflicts and penalties which have hampered those Americans working on the Far East, for example, or which hamper scholars in many other parts of the world.

Scholarship on East Central Europe has also benefited from rather considerable financial support. Indeed, a careful review of the circumstances under which scholars, especially young scholars, have worked in the last ten years reveals that never since the Renaissance has research been so lavishly and munificently financed. The foundations, particularly the Ford Foundation, the Rockefeller Foundation, and the Carnegie Corporation, have been very generous, both in providing support for research and training programs for some universities and also in providing fellowship funds which have enabled these programs to attract a rather substantial portion of the most able students in our society. When one compares the financial support available for the study of this area with that available for the study of other countries and other areas, such as France, Germany, or Latin America, one can appreciate the immense advantages under which scholars on Russia and East Central Europe have worked.

Financial support, of course, has not come solely from the foundations, or even in large part from the foundations. All of the universities engaged in this area have invested substantial sums of money. For example, the investment of Indiana University in faculty salaries for those now teaching in Russian and East European studies is about $70,000 a year, and in the academic year 1958-1959 will rise to considerably more than $100,000. Indiana now spends approximately $25,000 a year for books for these areas, and administrative and other expenses involve other large sums. Other universities have made substantially larger investments than this (for example, the University of California at Berkeley investment in 1957-1958 was about double that of Indiana University), and the sums involved rise each year.

Those working on East Central Europe also benefit from the wealth or riches of American university and institutional libraries, for the United States now has some of the best libraries on this area in the world. A generation ago, anyone interested in Russian or East Central European studies had to go to Europe to obtain access to the great libraries outside of Russia and East Central Europe; the great collections used to be those of the Bibliothèque Nationale and the British Museum. Now, in Russian studies alone, several American libraries (the Library of Congress, the New York Public Library, Widener Library at Harvard University, the University of California at Berkeley Library, and the Columbia University Library) individually have larger and better collections than all of the libraries of Western Europe together. These collections are excellent not only for the last twelve years, but also for earlier periods. Moreover, they are far better organized than most European libraries. Indeed, the gap between American libraries and the best West European libraries is constantly growing because of the funds our libraries have for the purchase of books and because of the skill with which these funds are spent.

Another very considerable advantage is the publication since 1951 by the Library of Congress of an immensely useful journal, the East European Index. For East Central Europe, this monthly publication lists all the acquisitions of the Library of Congress, as well as some of those of other libraries. No similar journal exists for France, Germany, the Far East, Latin America, or Africa, or other areas, except for a similar journal for the Soviet Union, the Monthly Index of Russian Accessions. Moreover, the staff of the Slavic and Central European Division of the Library of Congress provides expert assistance for scholars and also publishes a number of excellent bibliographies on this area.

Scholars working on East Central Europe profit also from the existence of several journals devoted fundamentally to the area, a circumstance which does not exist for many other fields of study. These journals include the Journal of Central European Affairs, the American Slavic and East European Review, the Bulletin of the American Association of Teachers of Slavic and East European Literature, and finally, East Europe, (formerly News Behind the Iron Curtain), an extraordinarily good monthly journal on current affairs which provides a remarkably efficient and thorough analysis of recent developments. Fundamentally, in other words, while scholars generally complain about the difficulty of having articles published, publishing is relatively easier in this field than in most other scholarly fields.

Moreover, some publishers in the United States are particularly interested in this area and eager to publish works devoted to it. One has only to look at the catalogue of Frederick Praeger, Inc., to note the high level of attention he gives to this area; this again is not the case for other fields. Finally, the Joint Committee on Slavic Studies has a substantial fund to help finance the publication of scholarly books in the Russian and East Central European area. Such a fund does not exist for scholars working in other fields.

Fundamentally, then, the circumstances of the last twelve years have been remarkably favorable for those working in East Central European studies. This point should be emphasized, because many working in this field feel neglected and scorned, and believe that they work in an atmosphere of hostility or indifference. While this may happen in a few cases, in the last twelve years those working in this area have labored in extraordinarily benevolent circumstances. There is no reason whatsoever for the kind of persecution complex which afflicts many of those engaged in scholarship and teaching on East Central Europe.

A review of the present state of scholarship on East Central Europe, or, more accurately, of the achievements of the last twelve years, should immediately emphasize very significant contributions. The most striking of these is the presence in the field of a large number of first-rate scholars, men who would be distinguished in any field. Moreover, a comparison of the relative number of distinguished scholars working in this field with that working in French history, German history, or Latin American history, reveals the high proportion in this small field of distinguished scholars, such as Philip Mosely, Cyril Black, Henry Roberts, Oscar Halecki, Otakar Odlozilik, Robert Lee Wolff, S. Harrison Thomson, Francis Dvornik, and Roman Jakobson.

Another of the great achievements, one which reflects

credit upon the American academic community and upon the visiting scholars as well, is the ease and efficiency with which many distinguished refugee scholars have been accepted and made at home within the American academic community. This is a non-recurring benefit for scholarship in this area, because we cannot expect another increment of this kind or magnitude. However, one need only review the list of contributors to the scholarship on this area over the last decade to note the extraordinary proportion of refugees of distinction. These include men such as Oscar Halecki, Jan Wszelaki, Jan Kulski, Nicolas Spulber, Theodore Brzezinski, Jozo Tomasevich, John Lukacs, Stephen Kertesz, and many others. All of these men have contributed mightily, not only to scholarship, but also to education and training. Moreover, their contribution has been unique, because they have an understanding of this area and of its problems which no native American can hope to attain.

The most striking achievement, of course, has been the quality of the scholarship itself and the number of scholarly publications which have appeared. About seventy-five good books have been published on East Central Europe since 1945 by men and women residing in America. The number has increased every year, so that the average for the last four or five years of this period is about eleven volumes a year, a very considerable achievement for a group of scholars which in a sense represents a first generation. Some of these books are particularly excellent, and would be accepted as examples of first-rate scholarship in any field of endeavor.

Analysis of these publications, however, indicates certain patterns. For example, most of the books published, and most of the best books produced, have dealt with history, government, and international relations. Moreover, there has been a fairly heavy emphasis upon three countries, Poland, Czechoslovakia, and Yugoslavia, with Hungary, Romania, Bulgaria, and Albania receiving relatively little attention. These patterns have become more and more clear as we have moved away from 1945. Finally, in general, the American scholarly community has concentrated almost entirely upon monographs and has neglected teaching materials and general texts.

While the achievements of American scholarship have been considerable, there are also a large number of gaps and shortcomings. Thus, there has been a very heavy overemphasis upon the modern period; indeed, more than half of the published books and articles deal with the period since 1945. This is a pattern which exists also in American scholarship on the Soviet Union, or on the history of Russia, where there has been a very heavy emphasis upon the last thirty or forty years. Earlier periods, which are particularly important for those who want to understand the basic problems of this area, are generally neglected. In the long run, if this pattern should be maintained, scholarship on East Central Europe would become even more shallow than it is now. The social sciences and humanities dealing with East Central European studies would be eliminating what one might call basic research or pure research on the area. Since academic communities tend to reproduce themselves, the scholars now working in the field who tend to concentrate upon the modern period will produce students who will also concentrate upon the modern period. Fundamentally, then, unless the trend is reversed, the overemphasis will become greater and greater as time passes.

A second gap or shortcoming has to do with weak disciplines or fields. A study published in 1956 by the Mid-European Studies Center listed all the work then in progress on East Central Europe in this country. This study demonstrated that more than half of the work in progress was in the fields of history and government. Only one-eighth of the projects were in economics; only one-twelfth in the arts and literature. Geography, population, science, religion, education, and sociology were almost completely neglected. A review of the published works of the last twelve years reveals the same pattern. Thus, little work has been done in geography or sociology, little work is being done in these disciplines, and presumably, unless the scholars change the pattern, little will be done in the future.

Finally, certain kinds of subjects are ignored, even in those fields where a substantial amount of work has been completed or is under way. For example, there are few studies of political parties. There are strikingly few biographies of distinguished or important individuals. As a matter of fact, the recent biography by General Marian Kukiel, Czartoryski and European Unity, published by the Princeton University Press in 1953, is almost unique. There are a vast number of important statesmen, political leaders, scholars, artists, generals, religious leaders, and outstanding men and women in many fields in even the last two centuries for whom no biography exists. Since biographies constitute one of the better methods for interesting students in foreign areas, this is a particularly serious gap.

Other significant gaps include studies of regions which have been critical problems throughout history. There is no good book in English concerning Galicia. There is none on Bessarabia, or the Banat, or Silesia. Indeed, the list of major problems which deserve study, but which have not drawn attention, is almost endless. While this is inevitable in a relatively new field of study, the gaps are rather striking and deserve attention in the very near future by those working on this area.

Another vital shortcoming is the definition of East Central Europe used by scholars and teachers. Generally speaking, the area is considered passive and is viewed from the outside. It is not considered an independent area, but a plaything of the major powers. It is treated as a kind of football kicked by the Turks, the Austrians, the Russians, the Germans. Thus, analysis of the books dealing with this area in terms of European diplomatic history reveals that even the best books view it from the outside and as a plaything of factors beyond the power of the people living in the area. The books by Langer, Sumner, Harris, and the many books which deal with Russian and German policy are good examples of this.

On the other hand, some scholars treat East Central Europe as though it were a geographical and cultural unity, which it is not, though it does have some elements of unity. Still others treat individual countries such as Poland, or sections of the area, such as the Balkans, as though the country or the section were an accurate reflection of the entire area, and as though he who understands Poland or the Balkans will have a basic understanding of East Central Europe. Still others, and this I think includes the majority, write and publish studies of individual countries, without placing those countries in any kind of area focus whatsoever. Thus, Poland often is treated as though it were in a vacuum.

Fundamentally, many of even the best scholars working on this area do not really understand or comprehend the area and are by no means specialists on the area as a whole. They are specialists on Poland, Czechoslovakia, or Bulgaria, but they do not know the area or its languages and do not try to put their own work in the perspective of the area and of Europe in general. This criticism is especially important because knowledge of East Central Europe has not been incorporated into our general body of knowledge. The principal reason for this may be the manner in which the specialists themselves treat East Central Europe. They have no pattern, coherence, or agreed rationale. We therefore cannot expect those who write general textbooks to incorporate information concerning individual countries or this area as a whole into the general body of knowledge if the specialists themselves are not of great assistance in defining the area and placing it in its European and world context.

Another important shortcoming of the scholarship on this area is the style in which many scholars write. We are all aware that American scholarship generally does not have a wide appeal. The quality of scholarly writing is one of the principal reasons for this, among a series of reasons. The style of those who have written on East Central Europe is perhaps the least distinguished and the least attractive of that of any group working in the social sciences and humanities. This may be because a fairly large number of those working in this area are new to this country and to the English language; it may reflect the haste to publish; it may derive from the heavy preponderance of recently-trained men in the field; it may be due in part to the high proportion of professors and the absence of literate amateurs; it reflects also in part the definition of the area, because a narrow or unclear vision has an effect upon the style of writing; it reflects also the sense of purpose. Fundamentally, scholars working on this area seem to write for other scholars and fail to keep in mind that they should seek a wider audience. The scholarship on this area is particularly narrow, and the style is especially cramped and unattractive. One of the major consequences of this is the extraordinary gap between the level of scholarship and the level of even informed thinking.

Another important shortcoming concerns the treatment of materials. Scholars in general consider the collection and preservation of materials the responsibility solely of librarians. A review of the history of Russian and East European studies in this country reveals that some of the greatest scholars— Archibald Cary Coolidge of Harvard University, Robert Kerner of the University of California at Berkeley, and Philip Mosely of Columbia University, for example—devoted enormous time and energy to the collection and preservation of books, journals, newspapers, and manuscripts. The great collections of Harvard, Berkeley, and Columbia would be much less distinguished and complete but for the immense effort of these men, all of them great scholars.

The present generation of scholars must be willing to devote that kind of effort to collecting and organizing materials if this field is to thrive. This is especially important because large quantities of materials are now being dissipated and will soon disintegrate. For example, the Free Europe Committee, which purchases more newspapers and journals on this area than any public library or academic institution, and perhaps even more than does the American government, destroys a large portion of its acquired materials. Even the New York Public Librar destroys significant quantities of newspapers, and many government agencies either destroy or withhold many of their acquisitions. Moreover, immense quantities of materials scattered around the country are badly handled and will soon disintegrate or be destroyed. Many collections are also unknown even to scholars.

Finally, scholars usually ignore the immense problem of cataloguing, and they fail generally to support our libraries in their campaigns for funds for cataloguing, although they are diligent and even aggressive in persuading universities to increase the funds for purchase of books.

Most colleges and universities consider East Central Europe a marginal field. Many people are teaching courses in this field who are not competent, and many are writing who lack sound training and deep interest. Consequently, in terms of quality, some books concerning this area published in the last twelve years are simply disgraceful. Moreover, when one compares the general level of work done in this field with that done in fields with a more established tradition in American scholarship, East Central Europe does not measure up to general standards. This may be in part because the field is relatively new to Americans; it may develop in part from the relatively large number of young men and women in the field; it may reflect the fairly high proportion of men who have only recently come to this country, who do not know our language well, and who have not received professional training. In any case, in those qualities which are most important for scholarly work— technical competence, accuracy and thoroughness, organization and style, and above all, insight and imagination— much of the scholarship in this area is quite inferior and does not even qualify as good journalism.

I would now like to turn to some positive and, I hope, useful suggestions so far as the future of American scholarship on East Central Europe is concerned. These suggestions reflect quite clearly my definition of the problems involved for American scholarship on this area. The first phase of the problem involves recognizing and overcoming the general neglect to which this area has been subject. The United States is now paying the penalty for the long age of isolation. However, we must not be too hasty, we must not lower standards in a general drive to overcome the neglect of the past and to prepare the American people to face the terrible problems of the future. We should seek simply to ensure that this area attains its proper position or role in American scholarship and education.

A second part of the problem involves strengthening weak periods and disciplines. There has been a heavy emphasis or concentration upon the twentieth century, particularly upon the last twelve years. In the future, scholars on this area must devote far more attention to earlier periods than they now do. Moreover, they must also concentrate upon those disciplines which were weak in 1947, so far as this area is concerned, and which are still weak today. In other words, a direct and determined effort must be made to improve the quality and quantity of the work in particular disciplines and periods.

A third factor involves improvement of research methods. Only a few disciplines are now well represented in American scholarship on East Central Europe. Consequently, our approach toward the area is somewhat unbalanced. We must, therefore, pay greater emphasis to quality in training. Students must not only be well trained in their own professions or disciplines, but they must have an increased understanding of the methods or techniques used by other disciplines, so that their scholarship will reflect advances made in all fields of scholarship.

Frankly, the most important suggestion I should like to make to scholars working in this field involves a new spirit or attitude. Many members of the scholarly community who work on East Central Europe are hampered by a kind of inferiority complex. They think that the area is of secondary importance; they give the impression that they are working in a minor league. This spirit or attitude must be changed. Everyone working in East Central European studies should recognize his immense advantages and opportunities. Everyone should recognize that this is an area of importance, an area which will inevitably be one of even greater significance in the future, a field of study in which scholars can lead useful and productive lives.

Those working on this area should also recognize the responsibility which they have to the field in general and to the American educational system in particular. If the spirit and attitude improve, if the scholars working in East Central European studies develop a spirit of confidence and determination, scholarship will improve and the field will rise in the general estimation within American education. Scholars must first respect themselves and their work if they expect recognition and attention.

Three points must be made with regard to the main lines for research in the foreseeable future. First, scholars working on this area should reach agreement concerning the main shortcomings of the last ten years or so and concerning the main lines which research should follow for the next decade.

In particular, scholars should recognize the overconcentration on the modern, should reduce this emphasis, and should restore balance to the field. In addition, they should create some conceptual framework in which all scholars might work, in particular eliminating the thesis or feeling that East Central Europe is a kind of football kicked hither and yon by various outside powers. They should also develop a conceptual framework in which works on individual countries, for example, could be produced against a background of the area in general, and not in vacuum.

The second point so far as guide lines for research are concerned involves training a new or different kind of scholar. Scholarship in this area reflects the general bias in American scholarship, in particular the scholar's conviction that a scholar should write only for other specialists, that any book which is widely read is almost a useless book, that we should all come to know more and more about less and less, and that the scholar has no obligation to his field of interest or to society in general. Since scholars tend to reproduce themselves, new generations of scholars have fundamentally the same attitude as the old ones. We all believe that the high standards of American scholarship must be maintained and improved, but we must also recognize the growing need for teacher-scholars. We must recognize the need for writing and publishing books useful for the average college student and for the informed and interested American citizen. American scholarship on this area and American policy in general will never be on solid foundations so long as our scholarship is so picayune and so deadly in its specialization.

We need a broad base; we need to train teachers who will interest students in this area so that there will be an increasing flow from the undergraduate colleges to the graduate schools and to the learned institutions. In other words, we need a new type of person in the field, a combination of teacher and scholar with a broad knowledge of the area, sound professional training, a genuine interest in scholarship, and ability and enthusiasm in teaching.

I would also suggest that those now teaching and now engaged in scholarship seek graduate fellowships for a year or two, so that they cease to be experts on Poland or Yugoslavia or the economic problems of the area, but become genuine area specialists knowing all or most of the languages, having some knowledge of all of the countries, and, above all, understanding the methods and techniques of other disciplines than their own.

A third point in this general category involves the production and publication of teaching tools. East Central European studies are a neglected field in part because so little attention is devoted to the area in American education, especially on the undergraduate level. This will remain the case so long as there are so few teaching materials available for use in the colleges. In other words, the scholars in the field must prepare teaching materials, such as general histories of the area, histories of those countries where there are not excellent histories now available, bibliographies and guides to the literature, translations of the best books written in other languages, collections of documents not available in English, and translations of memoirs, which constitute one of the most stimulating ways to interest students in a foreign country or area. I would even suggest that the scholars in this area urge one university press, or several university presses, to establish a series, something like the Cambridge Modern History, with some dignity and style and including several varieties of books for use by informed citizens and undergraduates as introductions into the area. Some scholars for the next five or ten years thus might relax their pursuit of specialized scholarly knowledge and instead concentrate upon the production of materials which can be used in teaching.

As I said earlier, the scholar today has a responsibility for the collection and maintenance of materials on this area. Those universities which have libraries interested in the collection of materials on East Central Europe should coordinate their purchasing programs to insure that no great gaps develop and to reduce to sensible levels the amount of duplication. They should create a well-organized system for collecting materials, and should agree to some degree of specialization for each library concerned. The university libraries should make arrangements for the purchase of all important newspapers, books, journals, tracts and pamphlets, documents, government publications, and United Nations publications. They should also complete arrangements with those organizations which are now destroying material, in order to see that it be preserved and distributed in an equitable and useful way.

With regard to the general ignorance concerning some collections, I suggest that a review be made of the important collections of materials, and that a descriptive analysis be published. Each important library should publish articles or small books describing its materials and informing scholars of what is available.

In addition, those scholars working in this field should raise their heads and recognize the connection between scholarship on East Central Europe and other basic fields, interests, and problems. All scholars in this field must recognize that work on this area will never be on solid foundations in the American academic community until considerable progress has been made in foreign language instruction. Fundamentally, so long as most men and women graduate from American colleges and universities with no knowledge or little knowledge of foreign languages, few will be able to do research in this area. It is the obligation of scholars to advocate increased language instruction in American colleges and universities, and, indeed, in American high schools. There will not be a flow of graduate students so long as this language problem has not been faced and resolved.

Analysis of scholarship in this area also reveals that the flowering of the last decade reflects in large part the increased interest in the Soviet Union and in Russian control over East Central Europe. In other words, interest in this area is to a large degree a by-product of our concern about the Soviet Union. This is an unhealthy situation and provides an unsound foundation for study and teaching. Interest in East Central Europe must reflect concern with the area itself and concern with the larger European geographical and cultural unit of which it is a part. Thus, scholars interested in East Central Europe must support research in European studies in general. They must also support study of those countries or areas which throughout history have been closely bound to East Central Europe, but which are now relatively weak in American scholarship and education. In particular, scholars interested in East Central Europe should work within their own institutions for the promotion of German studies, because the study of Germany or of Central Europe and that of East Central Europe are closely bound together. A boom in German studies would produce the same kind of spilling-over process we have witnessed in the last twelve years with regard to Russia. To some degree, the same point applies with regard to Italy, which is also strangely neglected by American scholars, and to Turkey and the Middle East. Thus, the revival of Turkic studies in this country would almost certainly lead to a better appreciation of the history of the Balkans, where the Turk impact in general has been ignored.

Scholars working in this area ought also cease to be isolationists with regard to general education and to other kinds of programs. East Central Europe, after all, is a part of Europe, and no one can acquire a good knowledge of Europe in any kind of program, Russian or West European, unless he also understands East Central Europe. Those interested in this area ought to promote the injection of knowledge of this area into all American education.

I strongly urge that those scholars interested in East Central Europe press for increased conferences, bringing together the isolated scholars, who will thereby learn what their colleagues are doing and who will derive ideas and inspiration from their fellows. Effective conferences increase cooperative organization, break down barriers, and create new connections among individuals and among universities.

The scholars working in this area should also work for increased funds for travel. One of the real shortcomings of American scholarship on East Central Europe has been due to the closing of this area, fundamentally, in the last twenty years to outsiders. In the long run, scholarship which is not based on some understanding reflecting residence in the area is likely to be shallow. There are indications now that doors are beginning to open in East Central Europe. Scholars interested in this area should press in an organized fashion for the establishment of additional travel grants, so that in this present opportunity, which may be brief, those interested in the area may visit the peoples and the countries in which they are interested.

Finally, there should be closer cooperation between scholars living in the United States and their colleagues, not only in Western Europe, but also in Eastern Europe and the Soviet Union as well. We are, after all, members of an international community. We believe in the universality of knowledge, we recognize that every scholar in every country has the capacity and ability to make a unique contribution to our general understanding. We must act upon our faith and our convictions.

I. EAST-CENTRAL EUROPE

BIBLIOGRAPHY

1. Anon., "Bibliography of Father Francis Dvornik." HSS, II, 385-390.

2. _____. "A Bibliography of the Publications of Roman Jakobson." Morris Halle, et al., comp., For Roman Jakobson, pp. 1-12.

3. Avakumovic, Ivan, "Bibliographical Note—Literature on the First Serbian Insurrection (1804-1813)." JCEA, XIII, 257-260.

4. _____, "Literature on the Marxist Movement in Yugoslavia." JCEA, XV, 66-70.

5. Bako, Elemer, "Hungarica." QJCA, XIII, 200-205, XIV, 140-145.

6. Bobula, Ida Miriam. The Hungarian Material in the Library of Congress. Washington, D.C.: Mid-European Studies Center, 1953.

7. Conover, Helen Field. Current National Bibliographies. Washington, D.C.: Library of Congress, General Reference and Bibliography Division, 1955.

8. _____. A Guide to Bibliographic Tools for Research in Foreign Affairs. Washington, D.C.: Library of Congress, 1956, 145 pp.

9. Djaparidze, David. Mediaeval Slavic Manuscripts. A Bibliography of Printed Catalogues. Cambridge, Massachusetts: Mediaeval Academy of America, 1957, 134 pp.

10. Dorosh, John T., "Slavica." QJCA, VIII, iii, 51-55.

11. Fischer, George, "The Russian Archive in Prague." ASEER, VIII, 289-295.

12. Free Europe Committee. Mid-European Studies Center. Current Research on Central and Eastern Europe. Ed. by Dagmar Horna, assisted by Lily Feiler and others. Publication No. 28. New York: Free Europe Committee, 1956, 25 pp.

13. _____. Mid-European Studies Center. Index to Unpublished Studies Prepared for Mid-European Studies Center, Studies 1-164. New York: Free Europe Committee, 1953.

14. Free Europe Press Research Staff. Critical Bibliography of Communist Purges and Trials in the Soviet Union and in the "People's Democracies." New York: Free Europe Press, 1953.

15. Fryde, Matthew M. Selected Works on Polish Agrarian History and Agriculture: A Bibliographical Survey. New York: Mid-European Studies Center, 1952.

16. Gsovski, Vladimir, ed. Bibliography of Legal Sources in Eastern Europe. 7 Vols. (Publications in Russian History No. 18-24, a Research Study of Mid-European Law Project at the Library of Congress.) New York: Praeger, 1957.

17. Haiman, Miecislaus, "Polish Scholarship in the United States 1939-1947." Polish American Studies, IV, 65-87.

18. Harkins, William Edward. Bibliography of Slavic Folk Literature. (Columbia University Department of Slavic Languages. Columbia Slavic Studies.) New York: King's Crown Press, 1953, 28 pp.

19. _____. Bibliography of Slavic Philology. (Columbia University Slavic Studies). New York: King's Crown Press, 1951, 32 pp.

20. Horecky, Paul L., "Archives of Yugoslavia, Czechoslovakia, and Bulgaria." AA, XX, 195-199.

21. _____, "Slavica and Hungarica: Non-USSR Slavica." QJCA, XII, 80-97.

22. _____, "Slavica and Hungarica: Other Slavic Countries." QJCA, X, 114-122; XI, 108-120; XIII, 258-275.

23. _____, "Slavica: Other Slavic Countries." QJCA, XIV, 166-179.

24. Jelavich, Charles, "Bulgarian 'Incunabula.'" LQ, XIV, 77-94.

25. Kardos, Bela T., "Slavica and Hungarica: Hungary." QJCA, X, 123-125; XI, 121-125; XII, 97-101.

26. Milojevic, Borivoje Z. Geography of Yugoslavia — A Selective Bibliography. Washington: United States Library of Congress, Reference Department, Slavic and East European Division, 1955, 79 pp.

27. New York Public Library. Slavonic Division. A Bibliography of Slavonic Bibliography in English. New York: New York Public Library, 1947, 11 pp.

28. Polisensky, J. V., "The Present State of Czechoslovak Archives." AA, XI, 223-226.

29. Polish Roman Catholic Union of America. Archives and Museum. Polonica in English. Annotated catalogue by Alphonse S. Wolanin. Chicago: Polish Roman Catholic Union of America, 1945, 186 pp.

30. Rand Corporation. Index of Publications. Santa Monica, California: Rand Corporation, 1955—. [Annual.]

31. Roberts, Henry L., ed. Foreign Affairs Bibliography, 1942-1952. New York: Council on Foreign Relations, 1955.

32. Roucek, Joseph S. Recent Literature on Central-Eastern Europe. Hofstra College, Hempstead, New York: The Author, 1945, 16 pp.

33. Shaw, Joseph T., et al., eds. The 1956 American Bibliography of Slavic and East European Studies in Language, Literature, Folklore, and Pedagogy. (Slavic and East European Series, IX.) Bloomington: Indiana University Publications, 1957.

34. Skendi, Stavro, "Studies on Balkan Slavic Languages, Literatures and History in the Soviet Union During the Last Decade." ASEER, XVI, 524-533.

35. Stolz, George. Forced Labor in the Soviet Orbit: A Selective Bibliography. (Mimeo Series No. 20.) New York: Mid-European Studies Center, 1954, 13 pp.

36. _____. Satellite Economy and Labor: A Tentative Bibliography. [n.p.]: [n. pub.], 1952.

37. Sworakowski, Witold S., and H. Sworakowski, eds. List of Archive Material Dealing with Federation Plans for Central and Eastern Europe Developed During the Second World War. (Mimeo.) Stanford: Stanford University, 1954.

38. Sztachova, Jirina. Mid-Europe: A Selective Bibliography. (Publication of the Mid-European Studies Center, No. 19.) New York: Mid-European Studies Center, 1953.

39. Tihany, Leslie C., "Bibliography of Post-Armistice Hungarian Historiography." ASEER, VI, xvi-xvii, 158-178.

40. Tobias, Henry J., "The Archives of the Jewish Bund: New Materials on the Revolutionary Movement." ASEER, XVII, 81-85.

41. United States. Department of State. Division of Library and Reference Services. Rumanian Imprints, 1945-1952; A Bibliography of Selected Economic and Social Publications. Washington, D.C.: United States Government Printing Office, 1952.

42. _____. Department of State. Division of Library and Reference Services. The Tito Defection. (Bibliographic List BL/16.) Washington, D.C.: United States Government Printing Office, 1949.

43. _____. Department of State. Intelligence Research Office. External Research: Eastern Europe. (Series 7, External Research Lists.) Washington, D.C.: Department of State, 1952—. [Twice per year since 1954; April on research in progress, October on completed research studies.]

44. _____. Library of Congress. The Balkans. Washington: United States Library of Congress, General Reference and Bibliography Division, 1943, 1945. [A bibliography in five parts, on the Balkans in general and on Albania, Bulgaria, Romania, and Yugoslavia.]

45. _____. Library of Congress. East European Accessions Index. Washington, D.C.: United States Government Printing Office, 1951—. [Monthly.]

46. _____. Library of Congress. European Affairs Division. Political, Economic and Social Writings in Postwar Finland. A Bibliographic Survey prepared as a working paper by Kirsti Jaanlila. Washington, D.C.: United States Government Printing Office, 1952, 41 pp.

47. Wepsiec, Jan. Polish Newspapers in 1953. A Union List. New York: Mid-European Studies Center, 1955.

48. Ziffer, Bernard. Poland: History and Historians. Three Bibliographical Essays. (Publication of the Mid-European Studies Center, No. 9.) New York: Mid-European Studies Center, 1952.

AREA STUDIES

49. Black, Cyril E., "Contributions of the Joint Committee on Slavic Studies to the Advancement of Research in Its Field." SSRC, IX, 40-42.

50. _____. "The Development of Slavic and East European Studies in the United States." Royden James Dangerfield, Ed.,

Area Studies Programs: The Soviet Union and Eastern Europe, pp. 15-34. (Mid-European Studies Center and University of Illinois).

51. California, University of. Asiatic and Slavic Studies on the Berkeley Campus, 1896-1947. Berkeley: University of California, Mailing Division, 1947, 44 pp.

52. Clarke, James F. "Some Problems in East European Area Studies." Royden James Dangerfield, Ed., Area Studies Programs: The Soviet Union and Eastern Europe, pp. 34-63. (Mid-European Studies Center and University of Illinois).

53. Coleman, Arthur Prudden, "American Area and Language Courses in Slavic and East European Studies, 1946-1947." ASEER, V, xiv-xv, 162-192.

54. _____, "Area and Language Courses in Slavic and East European Studies." ASEER, IV, viii-ix, 185-208.

55. _____. Report on the Status of Russian and other Slavic and East European Languages in the Educational Institutions of the United States, its Territories, Possessions and Mandates. Columbia University, New York: American Association of Teachers of Slavic and East European Languages, 1948.

56. Cowan, Laing Gray. History of the Russian Institute, Columbia University, 1946-1953. New York: Columbia Press, 1954, 65 pp.

57. Dangerfield, Royden James, ed. Area Study Programs: The Soviet Union and Eastern Europe. (Sponsored by the Mid-European Studies Center of the National Committee for a Free Europe and the University of Illinois.) Champaign: University of Illinois, Institute of Government and Public Affairs, 1955. [Papers read at the conference on the Soviet Union and Eastern Europe at the University of Illinois, Jan. 9-10, 1954.]

58. Fenton, William N. Area Studies in American Universities. Washington, D.C.: American Council on Education, 1947.

59. Fizer, John, "In Defence of American Slavic Studies." AATSEEL, XIV, 106-111.

60. Georgetown University. School of Foreign Service, Institute of Languages and Linguistics. Monograph Series on Area Studies. No. 1. Washington, D.C.: Georgetown University, 1952.

61. Hall, Robert B. Area Studies. New York: Social Science Research Council, 1947.

62. Harvard University. Russian Research Center. Five Year Report and Current Projects. Cambridge, Mass.: Harvard University, 1953.

63. _____. Russian Research Center. Ten-Year Report and Current Projects, 1948-1958. Cambridge, Mass.: Harvard University, 1958.

64. Lednicki, Waclaw, "The State of Slavic Studies in America." ASEER, XIII, 100-116.

65. Manning, Clarence A. History of Slavic Studies in the United States. (Marquette Slavic Studies, Vol. III.) Milwaukee, Wisconsin: Marquette University Press, 1957, 117 pp.

66. Mehnert, Klaus, "Survey of Slavic and East European Studies in Germany since 1945." ASEER, IX, 191-206.

67. Ornstein, Jacob, "A Brief Preliminary Survey of Activities and Research in the East European Area (Exclusive of Russia) in America." AATSEEL, XII, 18-25.

68. _____, "The Development and Status of Slavic and East European Studies in America since World War II." ASEER, XVI, 369-388.

69. _____, "Facilities and Activities of the Library of Congress in the Slavic and East European Field." ASEER, XII, 549-554.

70. _____. Slavic and East European Studies: Their Development and Status in the Western Hemisphere. (Department of State, External Research Paper No. 129). Washington, D.C.: United States Government Printing Office, 1957.

71. Rose, W. J. Cradle Days of Slavic Studies: Some Reflections. (Slavistica, XXIII.) Winnipeg: 1955.

72. Senn, Alfred, "Obstacles in the Way of Slavic Studies." ATTSEEL, VI, 59-62.

73. Staar, Richard F., "Conference on East-Central Europe at Columbia University." CEF, V, ii, 19-22.

74. Steward, Julian Haynes. Area Research: Theory and Practice. New York: Social Science Research Council, 1950, 164 pp.

75. Strakhovsky, Leonid I. "A General Approach to Slavic Studies." Leonid I. Strakhovsky, Ed., Handbook of Slavic Studies, pp. ix-xxi.

76. United States. Department of State. Office of Intelligence

Research. Area Study Programs in American Universities. Washington, 1956, 58 pp.

77. Wagley, Charles. Area Research and Training: A Conference Report. New York: Social Science Research Council, 1948.

78. Wandycz, Piotr S., "Historical Studies of East-Central Europe in the United States." CEF, IV, ii, 4-7.

79. _____, "The Treatment of East-Central Europe in History Textbooks." ASEER, XVI, 515-523.

GENERAL

80. Aizsienieks, Arnold P. Cooperation Behind the Iron Curtain. Tr. Eric V. Youngquist. Ed. Henry H. Bakken. Madison, Wisconsin: Mimir, 1952, 49 pp.

81. Anon., "Amnesties and Releases." NBIC, V, v, 3-15.

82. _____, "As They See Themselves." NBIC, IV, viii, 25-37.

83. _____, "As They See Us." EE, VI, vi, 3-5; 8-11, 14-25.

84. _____, "As They See Us." NBIC, IV, viii, 4-24.

85. _____, "Before the Olympics; A Review of Sports in the Satellites." NBIC, V, xi, 11-18.

86. _____, "Behind the Iron Curtain: A Year-End Review." DSB, XXVI, 84-86.

87. _____, "The Critics Cornered." NBIC, III, vi, 27-36.

88. _____, "Critiques and Celebrations." NBIC, II, vi, 3-19.

89. _____, "The Full Circle." NBIC, II, ii, 3-15.

90. _____, "The Gloved Fist." NBIC, II, vii, 3-16.

91. _____, "Go Away Closer." NBIC, II, ix, 3-18.

92. _____, "Gods, Graves and Hollers." NBIC, II, iv, 3-14.

93. _____, "Hollow Laughter." NBIC, II, i, 32-37.

94. _____, "The Iron Tower." NBIC, II, xi, 24-31.

95. _____, "Labyrinthine Ways." NBIC, II, v, 3-17.

96. _____, "The 'New Course.'" NBIC, II, xi, 34-43.

97. _____, "The Partisan Reviewer." NBIC, III, vii, 39-45.

98. _____, "Passive Resistance." NBIC, III, viii, 25-32.

99. _____, "The Politics of Conciliation." NBIC, II, x, 3-12.

100. _____, "Rigid Pattern." NBIC, II, iii, 3-17.

101. _____, "The Sound and the Fury." NBIC, III, ii, 3-12.

102. _____, "The State Militant." NBIC, I, x, 1-17.

103. _____, "The State of Vigilance." NBIC, I, ix, 1-14.

104. _____, "The Stratagem of Abuse." NBIC, I, vii, 1-15.

105. _____, "The Unfinished Revolution." UQ, XIII, 5-14.

106. _____, "Vacation with the Big Brother." NBIC, II, viii, 27-37.

107. Bartlett, Vernon. East of the Iron Curtain. New York: Medill McBride, 1950, 212 pp.

108. Basch, Antonin. A Price for Peace. New York: Columbia University Press, 1945, 209 pp.

109. Beamish, Tufton Victor Hamilton. Must Night Fall? New York: British Book Centre, 1951, 292 pp.

110. Bemelmans, Ludwig. Blue Danube. New York: The Viking Press, 1945, 153 pp.

111. Black, Cyril E., ed. Challenge in Eastern Europe. Prepared under the auspices of the Mid-European Studies Center of the National Committee for a Free Europe. New Brunswick, New Jersey: Rutgers University Press, 1954, 276 pp.

112. _____. Readings on Contemporary Eastern Europe. (Publication of the Mid-European Studies Center, No. 11.) New York: Mid-European Studies Center, 1953, 346 pp.

113. Boray, Alexander, "Resistance Behind the Iron Curtain Now?" Rept, VII, viii, 17-19.

114. Buber, Margarete. Under Two Dictators. Tr. by Edward Fitzgerald. New York: Dodd, Mead, 1949, 331 pp.

115. Burnham, James, "The East European Strategy." UQ, VIII, 307-319.

116. Byrnes, Robert F., ed. East Central Europe Under the

Communists. 7 vols. (Publications in Russian History, No. 46-52. New York: Praeger, 1957.

117. _____, "East Europe in Crisis." CH, XXXII, 71-76.

118. Chudoba, Bohdan, "And What of the Satellites?" Thought, XXV, 611-629.

119. Clippinger, Frances. Satellite. New York: Random House, 1951, 240 pp.

120. Cohesive Forces, Tensions, and Instabilities in the European Satellites. Cambridge, Massachusetts: Center for International Studies, Massachusetts Institute of Technology, 1952.

121. Cornell, Charles. Where Sleeps the Jagged Sword. Toronto: Ryerson Press, 1956.

122. Cox, Henry B., "Red Youth in Blue Shirts." DSB, XXV, 483-485.

123. Craemer, Alice R., "Re-aligning Europe." CH, XIV, 84-89.

124. Cramer, Frederick H., "Masters of Europe: Germans or Slavs?" CH, XVIII, 211-216; 273-278.

125. Dean, Vera Micheles, "Political Trends in Europe Reflect East-West Split." FPB, XXVII, iv, 1-2.

126. Edelman, Irwin. Myth of the Iron Curtain. Los Angeles: The Author, n.d., 31 pp.

127. Fodor, M. W., "Along the Danube." YR, XXXVII, 449-468.

128. Free Europe Committee. Europe: Nine Panel Studies by Experts from Central and Eastern Europe. New York: Free Europe Committee, 1954, 146 pp.

129. _____. Statistical Handbook of the Soviet Block. New York: Free Europe Press, 1954.

130. Free Europe Press Research Staff. Analytic Survey of Major Trends in the Soviet Sphere—July 1953-July 1954. New York: Free Europe Press, 1954.

131. _____. New Policies in the Soviet Sphere. New York: Free Europe Press, 1953.

132. Gross, Feliks. "Recent Developments in Eastern Europe." Royden James Dangerfield, Ed., <u>Area</u> <u>Study</u> <u>Programs:</u>

The Soviet Union and Eastern Europe, pp. 63-79. (Mid-European Studies Center and University of Illinois).

133. Gunther, John. Behind the Curtain. New York: Harper, 1949, 363 pp.

134. Gurian, Waldemar, ed. The Soviet Union: Background, Ideology, Reality. Notre Dame, Indiana: University of Notre Dame Press, 1951.

135. Harsch, Joseph C. Curtain Isn't Iron. New York: Doubleday, 1950, 192 pp.

136. Higgins, Marguerite, "The Barbed-Wire Curtain." Rept, II, iii, 8-11.

137. Hoptner, J. B. The Soviet Orbit. (Mid-European Studies Center, Mimeo. Series, No. 3.) New York: Mid-European Studies Center, 1953.

138. Horm, Arvo, "300 Million Forgotten Allies of the West." BR, II, ii, 3-8.

139. Jaszi, Oscar. Danubia: Old and New. Philadelphia: American Philosophical Society, 1949, 31 pp.

140. Kaasik, N., "Europe Indivisible." BR, II, iii, 3-8.

141. Karasz, Arthur, "Resistance in the Iron Curtain Countries." AAPSS, CCLXXI, 145-156.

142. Kerr, Walter. Behind the "Iron Curtain." New York: 1947.

143. Kirkconnel, Watson, "The Future of European Freedom." UQ, II, 210-226.

144. Klausner, Leopold C., "Danger Zones in Europe." WAI, XV, 122-135.

145. Kohn, Hans, "Eastern Europe, 1948." CH, XVI, 72-78; 193-198.

146. _____, "The Permanent Mission." RPol, X, 267-289.

147. Kolarz, Walter. Myths and Realities in Eastern Europe. Forest Hills, New York: Transatlantic Arts, 1946.

148. Kulski, W. W., "Central Europe in Transition." JCEA, VIII, 345-365.

149. Leading Personalities in Eastern Europe: Bulgaria, Czechoslovakia, Hungary, Poland, Romania. West New York, New Jersey: Intercontinental Press Service, 1957.

150. Lehrman, Hal, and Gilbert Burck, "In Russia's Europe." Fortune, XXXV, ii, 79-83, 188-202.

151. Lehrman, Harold Arthur. Russia's Europe. New York: Appleton-Century Co., 1947, 341 pp.

152. Lengyel, Emil. Eastern Europe Today. With Joseph C. Harsch. American Policy in Eastern Europe. (Foreign Policy Association. Headline Series No. 77.) New York: Foreign Policy Association, 1949.

153. Lowenthal, Richard, "Revolution over Eastern Europe." PoC, V, vi, 4-9.

154. Lucas, William O. (William Van Narvig, pseud.). East of the Iron Curtain. By William Van Narvig. New York: Ziff-Davis, 1946, 361 pp.

155. Lutz, Ralph Haswell, "The Changing Role of Iron Curtain Countries." AAAPSS, CCLXXI, 20-31.

156. Mieczkowski, B., "Looking Backward or Forward." CEF, IV, i, 15-30.

157. Moennich, Martha L. Europe Behind the Iron Curtain. Ottawa: Zondervan, 1948, 153 pp.

158. Moorad, George. Behind the Iron Curtain. Introd. W. L. White. Philadelphia: Fireside Press, Inc., 1946, 309 pp.

159. Morawski, Brigitte (pseud.). Godless: A True Story of Escape From Behind the Iron Curtain. New York: The Exposition Press, 1955, 182 pp.

160. Morin, F. Alfred. The Serpent and the Satellite. New York: Philosophical Library, 1953, 467 pp.

161. Mosely, Philip E., "Czechoslovakia, Poland, Yugoslavia: Observations and Reflections." PSQ, LXIII, 1-15.

162. Mowrer, Edgar Ansel, "Plight; 'Behind the Curtain' by John Gunther." SatR, XXXII, xxvii, 10-12.

163. Namier, Lewis Bernstein. Facing East. New York: Harper, 1948, 124 pp.

164. Norwid, T., "The Struggle Behind the Iron Curtain." BR, II, iii, 28-31.

165. Nyaradi, Nicholas, "Six Satellites and an Octopus." Rept, II, iii, 5-8.

166. Odlozilik, Otakar, "Storm Over The Danube." JCEA, VIII, 129-138.

167. Ogilvie, Alan Grant. Europe and Its Borderlands. Edinburgh and New York: T. Nelson, 1957.

168. Pollack, Stephen Walter. Strange Land Behind Me. (Falcon Press Book.) New York: British Book Centre, 1952, 337 pp.

169. Poulos, Constantine, "Upheaval in East Europe: The People and the Communists." Nation, CLXIV, 734.

170. Raymond, Jack. New Era in Eastern Europe. (Headline Series, Foreign Policy Association.) New York: Foreign Policy Association, 1957.

171. _____, "New Trends in Eastern Europe." FPB, XXXV, xviii, 141-144.

172. Rezac, Vaclav, et al., "Satellite Bookshelf." NBIC, III, iii, 27-31.

173. Roberts, Chalmers M., "The Widening Chinks in the Iron Curtain." Rept, XV, v, 11-14.

174. Roberts, Henry L., "The Crisis in the Soviet Empire." FA, XXXV, 191-200.

175. _____, " The Future of Eastern Europe." JIA, XI, i, 72-77.

176. Roucek, Joseph S. Central-Eastern Europe: Crucible of World Wars. New York: Prentice-Hall, Incorporated, 1946, 679 pp.

177. _____, ed. Slavonic Encyclopedia. New York: Philosophical Library, 1949, 1445 pp.

178. Scheynius, Ignas J., "Why Can't They Exist as Free Countries?" BR, I, 65-71.

179. Schuman, Frederick L., "East Europe and Two Worlds." CH, XI, 357-364.

180. Sedillot, Rene, "Europe After Stalin." YR, XLIII, 24-36.

181. Seton-Watson, Hugh, "Eastern Europe Since Stalin." PoC, III, ii, 10-17.

182. _____, "Eruption in East Europe; A Myth Destroyed and a Revolution Betrayed." Com, XXII, 518-524.

183. _____. From Lenin to Malenkov: The History of World Communism. New York: Praeger, 1953, 377 pp.

184. Sharp, Samuel L. Political and Economic Aspects of the Eastern European Communist Bloc. n.p., n.d. [1952], 121 pp.

185. Shipkov, Mikhail. Breakdown. [New York]: Free Europe Committee, [1950].

186. de Somogyi, Joseph, "Central Europe and the Middle East." JCEA, XIII, 1-12.

187. Straight, Michael, "There Are Great Fears." NR, CXVIII (22 March), 6-7.

188. Strakhovsky, Leonid I. "Comparative Chronology." Leonid I. Strakhovsky, Ed., Handbook of Slavic Studies, pp. 675-722. [Table of events in East Central Europe, 811- A.D. 1946].

189. _____, ed. A Handbook of Slavic Studies. Cambridge, Massachusetts: Harvard University Press, 1949, 753 pp.

190. Sulzberger, Cyrus Leo. Big Thaw: A Personal Exploration of the New Russia and the Orbit Countries. New York: Harper, 1956, 275 pp.

191. United States. Department of State. Moscow's European Satellites. (Publication No. 5914.) Washington, D.C.: United States Government Printing Office, 1955.

192. _____. Library of Congress. Legislative Reference Service. Tensions within the Soviet Captive Countries. Prepared at the Request of the Committee on Foreign Relations. (83rd Congress, 1st session, Senate Document No. 70). Washington: United States Government Printing Office, 1954.

193. Vlahovic, Vlaho S. Two Hundred 50 Million and One Slavs: An Outline of Slav History with Maps and Annotation. Introd. Joseph S. Roucek. New York: Slav Publications, 1945, 110 pp.

194. Vosnjak, Bogumil, "Slav and Balkan Freedom." CH, XVIII, 342-345.

195. Vucinich, Wayne S., "Russia's Satellites." CH, XXXII, 146-154.

196. Waskovich, George, "The Ideological Shadow of the U.S.S.R." AAPSS, CCLXXI, 43-54.

197. Wilmot, Chester. The Struggle for Europe. New York: Harper, 1952.

198. Zulawski, M., et al., "Satellite Bookshelf." NBIC, III, ii, 21-31.

GEOGRAPHY AND POPULATION

199. Anon., "Satellite Demography." NBIC, IV, ii, 27-36; v, 25-32.

200. Dolnytsky, Myron A., "A Geographer Looks at East Europe." UQ, VII, 34-41.

201. Dombrovsky A., "The Struggle With The East—European Space." UQ, VIII, 73-79.

202. Drahomanov, Mykhaylo, "A Geographic and Historical Survey of Eastern Europe." AUA, II, i, 141-152.

203. Frumkin, Gregory. Population Changes in Europe Since 1939: A Study of Population Changes in Europe During and Since World War II as Shown by the Balance Sheets of 24 European Countries. New York: Kelley, 1951, 191 pp.

204. Guri, Dita, "The 'Red' Danube—A History Making River." WAI, XXIV, 87-96.

205. Hainsworth, Reginald G., "Agricultural Geography of Europe and The Near East." FAgr, XIII, 3-7.

206. Hoffman, George W., "Boundary Problems in Europe." AAGA, XLIV, 102-105.

207. _____, ed. A Geography of Europe. New York: The Ronald Press, 1953.

208. Kirk, Dudley. Europe's Population in the Interwar Years. New York: Columbia University Press, 1946.

209. Kulischer, Eugene M. Europe on the Move—War and Population Changes, 1917-1947. New York: Columbia University Press, 1948.

210. _____, "Population Changes Behind the Iron Curtain." AAPSS, CCLXXI, 100-111.

211. Kulski, W. W., "The Problem of the Heartland of Europe." JCEA, VII, 253-261.

212. Meyer, Henry Cord, "Mitteleuropa in German Political Geography." AAAG, XXXVI, 178-194.

213. Moore, Wilbert Ellis. Economic Demography of

Eastern and Southern Europe. (League of Nations Publication, 1945. II. A.9.) New York: Columbia University Press; London: Allen and Unwin, 1946.

214. Newbigin, Marion Isabel. Southern Europe: A Regional and Economic Geography of the Mediterranean Lands. 3rd rev. ed. Under the editorship of R. J. Harrison Church. New York: E. P. Dutton,[1949], 404 pp.

215. Nuttonson, Michael Y. Barley-Climate Relationships and the Use of Phenology in Ascertaining the Thermal and Photo-thermal Requirements of Barley: Based on Data of North America and of Some Thermally Analagous Areas of North America in the Soviet Union, Finland, Poland, and Czechoslovakia. Sponsored by the United States Weather Bureau. Washington, D.C.: American Institute of Crop Ecology, 1957, 280 pp.

216. _____. Rye-Climate Relationships and the Use of Phenology in Ascertaining the Thermal and Photo-thermal Requirements of Rye: Based on Data of North America and of Some Thermally Analagous Areas of North America in the Soviet Union, Finland, Poland, and Czechoslovakia. Sponsored by the United States Weather Bureau. Washington, D.C.: American Institute of Crop Ecology, 1957, 219 pp.

217. Roucek, Joseph S., "Geopolitical Aspects of the Satellites." UQ, XII, 220-230.

218. _____, "Geopolitical Trends in Central-Eastern Europe." AAAPSS, CCLXXI, 11-19.

219. _____, "The Geopolitics of Danubia." WAI, XVII, 316-322.

220. Teleki, Geza. "East Central Europe." George W. Hoffman, Ed., A Geography of Europe, pp. 509-583.

HISTORY

221. Andrusiak, N., "Genesis and Development of East Slavic Nations." EEProb, I, i, 5-21.

222. Black, Cyril E. "Eastern Europe in Historical Perspective." Cyril E. Black, Ed., Challenge in Eastern Europe, pp. 3-27. (Mid-European Studies Center).

223. Blum, Jerome, "The Rise of Serfdom in Eastern Europe." AHR, LXII, 807-836.

224. Cross, Samuel Hazzard. "Primitive Slavic Culture." Leonid I. Strakhovsky, Ed., Handbook of Slavic Studies, pp. 24-43.

225. _____. Slavic Civilization Through the Ages. Ed. and Introd. Leonid Strakhovsky. Cambridge: Harvard University Press, 1948, 195 pp.

226. _____. "Slavic Origins and Migrations." Leonid I. Strakhovsky, Ed., Handbook of Slavic Studies, pp. 1-23.

227. Dvornik, Francis, "The Mediaeval Cultural Heritage of the Mid-European Area." RPol, XVIII, 487-507.

228. _____. The Slavs: Their Early History and Civilization. (Survey of Slavic Civilization, Vol. II.) Boston: American Academy of Arts and Sciences, 1956.

229. _____, "Western and Eastern Traditions of Central Europe." RPol, IX, 463-481.

230. _____. Photian Schism: History and Legend. New York: Macmillan, 1948, 504 pp.

231. Erickson, John, "Recent Soviet and Marxist Writings: 1848 in Central and Eastern Europe." JCEA, XVII, 119-126.

232. Gimbutas, Marija (Alseikaite). Prehistory of Eastern Europe. Hugh Hencken, Ed., (Harvard University. American School of Prehistoric Research Bulletin.) Cambridge, Massachusetts: Peabody Museum, Harvard University, 1957. [Part 1, Mesolithic, neolithic and copper age cultures in Russia and the Baltic area], 241 pp.

233. Grbic, Miodrag, "Preclassical Pottery in the Central Balkans: Connections and Parallels with the Aegean, the Central Danube Area and Anatolia." AJA, LXI, 137-149.

234. Halecki, Oscar. Borderlands of Western Civilization: A History of East Central Europe. New York: The Ronald Press, 1952, 503 pp.

235. _____. The Limits and Divisions of European History. New York: Sheed and Ward, 1950, 242 pp.

236. Harsanyi, Andrew. A Christian Victory: 500th Anniversary of Western Resistance at Nandorfejervar-Belgrade. Toronto: Hungarian Helicon, 1956.

237. Horthy de Nagybanya, Nicholas V. Memoirs. Introd. Nicholas Roosevelt. New York: Robert Speller and Sons, 1957, 268 pp.

238. Jakobson, Roman, "The Beginnings of National Self-Determination in Europe." RPol, VII, 29-42.

239. Jelavich, Barbara, "The British Traveller in the Slavonic Provinces." SEER, XXXIII, 396-413.

240. Kann, Robert A. Habsburg Empire: A Study in Integration and Disintegration. (Princeton University Center for Research on World Political Institutions Publications.) New York: Praeger, 1957, 227 pp.

241. _____. The Multinational Empire. Nationalism and National Reform in the Hapsburg Monarchy, 1848-1918. 2 vols. New York: Columbia University Press, 1950.

242. Kot, Stanislaw, "Old International Insults and Praises: I. The Medieval Period." HSS, II, 181-210.

243. Lewis, Archibald R., "Was Eastern Europe European in the High Middle Ages?" PolR, II, i, 18-26.

244. May, Arthur J. The Hapsburg Monarchy, 1867-1914. Cambridge, Massachusetts: Harvard University Press, 1951, 532 pp.

245. Odlozilik, Otakar, "The Contest for East Central Europe in the Eleventh Century." PolR, II, i, 3-17.

246. Ohloblyn, Oleksander, "The Pereyaslav Treaty and Eastern Europe." UQ, X, 41-50.

247. Okinshevich, Leo, "History of Civilization of Eastern Europe in the Work of Arnold Toynbee." AUA, II, ii, 305-315.

248. Pundeff, Marin, "World War II in Eastern Europe." WAI, XXVII, 72-82.

249. Purre, Arnold, "The Resistance Movement from a Military Point of View." BR, II, iii, 31-33.

250. Seton-Watson, Hugh. East European Revolution. 2nd ed. New York: Praeger, 1952, 406 pp.

251. _____. Eastern Europe Between the Wars 1918-1941. New York: Praeger, 1945, 406 pp.

252. de Somogyi, Joseph, "The Historical Development of the Danubian Problem to the Present." JCEA, VIII, 45-57.

253. Squier, Robert J., "The Problem of Race in the Mesolithic of Europe." KASP, No. 13, pp. 55-104.

254. Sydoruk, John P., "Herder and the Slavs." AATSEEL, XIII, 71-75.

255. _____, "Herder and the Slavs (On the 150th Anniversary of Herder's Death, 1803-1953)." UQ, XII, 58-62.

256. Taylor, A. J. P. The Habsburg Monarchy, 1809-1918. New York: Macmillan, 1949. [New ed.]

257. Tuleja, Thaddeus V., "Eugenius IV and the Crusade of Narna." CHR, XXXV, 257-275.

258. Vasiliev, A. A. History of the Byzantine Empire. Madison, Wisconsin: University of Wisconsin Press, 1953.

259. Vettes, William George, "The German Social-Democrats and the Eastern Question, 1848-1900." ASEER, XVII, 86-100.

260. Weinberg, Saul S., "Vladimir Milojcic: 'Chronologie der juengeren Steinzeit Mittel- und Suedosteuropa.'" (Chronology of the pre Stone Age of Central and Southeast Europe). AJA, LV, 404-409.

GOVERNMENT AND POLITICS

261. Anon., "The Bureaucracy Wavers; An Analysis of Managerial and Party Morale under the New Course." NBIC, III, i, 25-36.

262. _____, "Collective Leadership." NBIC, III, vii, 21-33.

263. _____, "Communism on Display." NBIC, I, ix, 35-43.

264. _____, "The Communist Road to Utopia." NBIC, I, xi, 1-17.

265. _____, "Conscience and Communism." NBIC, I, viii, 34-41.

266. _____, "The Debasement of Sovereignty." NBIC, I, iii, 1-15.

267. _____, "Doctrinal Rhetoric: Exhort, Denounce, Repeat." NBIC, I, viii, 1-16.

268. _____, "Election Masquerade." NBIC, I, x, 40-50.

269. _____, "Ideological Weapons." NBIC, I, v, 29-35.

270. _____, "Levers of Party Pressure." NBIC, I, v, 1-15.

271. _____, "Non-Communists' Political Organizations." EE, VI, x, 3-13.

272. _____, "Terrorists, Spies, Diversionists..." NBIC, I, ii, 1-3; 6-16.

273. Black, Cyril E. "Communist Europe." Reprint from Taylor Cole, Ed., European Political Systems. (Special ed. for the Mid-European Studies Center. Publication No. 12.) New York: Alfred A. Knopf, 1955.

274. _____. "Constitutional Trends in Eastern Europe." RPol, XI, 196-207.

275. _____. "The People's Democracies of Eastern Europe." Taylor Cole, Ed., European Political Systems, pp. 188-269.

276. Borkenau, Franz. European Communism. New York: Harpers Brothers, 1953, 564 pp.

277. Brzezinski, Zbigniew, "Communist Ideology and Power: From Unity to Diversity." JPol, XIX, 549-590.

278. _____, "Ideology and Power: Crisis in the Soviet Bloc." PoC, VI, i, 12-17.

279. _____, "Shifts in the Satellites." NR, CXXXII, 37-41.

280. Cole, Taylor, ed. European Political Systems. New York: Alfred A. Knopf, 1953.

281. Dean, Vera Micheles, "International Communism Hits Nationalist Snags." FPB, XXVII, xxxix, 2-3.

282. Deutscher, Isaac, "The Great Flight from Stalinism." Rept, XII, xii, 23-24.

283. Dimitrov, George M., and Victor Zenzinor. "Agrarianism." Feliks Gross, Ed., European Ideologies, pp. 391-452.

284. Ebon, Martin. World Communism Today. (Whittlesey House Publication.) New York: McGraw-Hill Book Company, 1948.

285. Gross, Feliks, ed. European Ideologies. New York: Philosophical Library, 1948.

286. Guins, George C. Communism on the Decline. New York: Philosophical Library, 1956, 287 pp.

287. _____, "Constitutions of the Soviet Satellites." AAAPSS, CCLXXI, 64-67.

288. Gulick, Charles A., et al., "After Hungary: Review and Prospects of Democratic Socialism in Europe." WPQ, X, 802-816.

289. Gyorgy, Andrew. "Constitutional Developments in the Danube Area." James Kerr Pollock, Ed., Change and Crisis in European Government, pp. 17-28.

290. _____. Governments of Danubian Europe. New York: Rinehart, 1949.

291. _____, "Political Trends in Eastern Europe." FPR, XXIV, 146-155.

292. Hadsel, Winifred N., "Big-Three Competition Reflected in European Elections." FPB, XXV (7 June), 1-2.

293. _____, "Political Currents in Liberated Europe." FPR, XXI, 66-78.

294. Hook, Sidney, "The Import of Ideological Diversity." PoC, VI, vi, 11-18.

295. Kecskemeti, Paul. "How Totalitarians Gain Absolute Power." Elliot Cohen, Ed., New Red Anti-Semitism: A Symposium, pp. 49-58.

296. Matossian, Mary, "Two Marxist Approaches to Nationalism." ASEER, XVI, 489-500.

297. Mikolajczyk, Stanislaw. "'People's Democracy' in Theory and Practice." Cyril E. Black, Ed., Challenge in Eastern Europe, pp. 65-90. (Mid-European Studies Center).

298. Neumann, Robert G., "Constitutional Documents of East-Central Europe." JPol, XII, 622-636.

299. _____. "Constitutional Documents of East Central Europe." Arnold J. Zurcher, Ed., Constitutions and Constitutional Trends Since World War II, pp. 175-191.

300. Peaslee, Amos J. Constitutions of Nations. Concord, New Hampshire: Ramford Press, 1950. [Contains the texts of all the new constitutions of the People's Democracies, except those of Hungary and Poland.]

301. Pollock, James Kerr, ed. Change and Crisis in European Government. New York: Rinehart and Co., 1947, 253 pp.

302. Pool, Ithiel de Sola, et al. Satellite Generals: A

Study of Military Elites in the Soviet Sphere. (Stanford University. Hoover Institute and Library on War, Revolution, and Peace. Studies, Series B: Elites, No. 5.) Stanford, California: Stanford University Press, 1955, 165 pp.

303. Possony, Stefan Thomas. Century of Conflict: Communist Techniques and World Revolution. Chicago: Regnery, 1953, 439 pp.

304. Revai, Jozsef, "The Character of a 'People's Democracy.'" FA, XXVIII, 143-153.

305. Ripka, Hubert. "The Liberal Tradition." C. E. Black, Ed., Challenge in Eastern Europe, pp. 27-46. (Mid-European Studies Center).

306. Rosa, Ruth Amende, "The Soviet Theory of People's Democracies." WP, I, 489-510.

307. Rudzinski, Alexander W. The Myth of Satellite Sovereignity. (Mimeo. Series No. 26.) New York: Mid-European Studies Center, 1954.

308. Schlesinger, Rudolf. Central European Democracy and its Background; Economic and Political Group Organization. (International Library of Sociology and Social Reconstruction.) New York: Grove Press, 1953, 402 pp.

309. Sharp, Samuel L., "Communist Regimes in Eastern Europe." FPR, XXVI, 178-186.

310. _____. New Constitutions in the Soviet Sphere. Washington, D.C.: Foundation for Foreign Affairs, 1950, 114 pp.

311. _____, "People's Democracy: Evolution of a Concept." FPR, XXVI, 186-198.

312. _____. Recent Trends in the New Democracies. Washington, D.C.: Foundation for Foreign Affairs, 1949, 502 pp.

313. Steanu, P. B., "Constitutionalism in the Satellite States." JCEA, XII, 56-69.

314. Sweezy, Paul M. Socialism. New York: McGraw-Hill Book Co., 1949.

315. Taborsky, Edward, "Government in the 'People's Democracies.'" AAAPSS, CCLXXI, 55-63.

316. Tellman, David, ed. Post-war Governments of Europe. Gainesville, Florida: Kallman Publishing Co., 1946.

317. Tomasic, Dinko. National Communism and Soviet Strategy. With the assistance of Joseph Strmecki. Introd. Elmer Louis Kayser. Washington, D.C.: Public Affairs Press, 1957, 222 pp.

318. Ulam, Adam B., "The Cominform and the People's Democracies." WP, III, 200-217.

319. Willen, Paul, "Communist Experiments with the Ballot." PoC, VI, ii, 33-37.

320. Young, Commander Edgar, R. N., "Socialist Revolution by Consent." JCEA, VIII, 79-85.

321. Zinner, Paul, ed. National Communism and Popular Revolt in Eastern Europe: A Selection of Documents on Events in Poland and Hungary, February-November, 1956. New York: Columbia University Press, 1956, 563 pp.

322. _____, "Politics in East Central Europe." JIA, XI, i, 9-19.

323. Zurcher, Arnold J. "Authoritarian Forms of Government Between the Wars." Cyril E. Black, Ed., Challenge in Eastern Europe, pp. 47-64. (Mid-European Studies Center).

324. _____, ed. Constitutions and Constitutional Trends Since World War II. New York: New York University Press, 1951.

325. _____, "The Outlook for Democratic Institutions." PolR, II, ii-iii, 3-16.

PROPAGANDA

326. Anon., "The Anti-Balloon Campaign." NBIC, V, iv, 25-27.

327. _____, "The Anti-Federation Campaign." NBIC, II, xii, 38-41.

328. _____, "The Ideology of Agitation." NBIC, III, viii, 3-24.

329. _____, "The Pied Piper of the Kremlin." NBIC, IV, ii, 37-47.

330. _____, "The Red Network." NBIC, II, viii, 56-69.

331. _____, "Soviet Foreign Policy Propaganda." EE, VI, v, 3-16.

332. _____, "Soviet Propaganda Policy." NBIC, III, xi, 17-27.

333. _____, "The Word is also a Weapon." NBIC, I, xi, 47-50.

334. Benton, William, "Why Soviet Propaganda Misfired." NR, CXXXIV, 11-12.

335. Evans, T. Bowen, ed. Worldwide Communist Propaganda Activities. New York: Macmillan, 1955, 222 pp.

336. Kirkpatrick, Evron M., ed. Year of Crisis: Communist Propaganda Activities in 1956. New York: Macmillan, 1957, 414 pp.

337. Kracauer, Siegfried, and Paul L. Berkman. Satellite Mentality: Politcal Attitudes and Propaganda Susceptibilities of Noncommunists in Hungary, Poland, and Czechoslovakia. Foreword by Henry L. Roberts. New York: Praeger, 1956, 194 pp.

LAW

338. Anon., "Annual Reports: Law." QJCA, XI, 229-238; XII, 195-206.

339. _____, "Law." QJCA, XIV, 208-217; 219-222; 223-228.

340. Drobnig, Ulrich, "Conflict of Laws in Recent East-European Treaties." AJCL, V, 487-497.

341. Dwyer, Francis X., et al., "Annual Reports: Law." QJCA, V, iv, 36-37; VI, iv, 58-59.

342. Grzybowski, Kazimierz, "Continuity of Law in Eastern Europe." AJCL, VI, 44-78.

343. _____, and Pundeff, Marin, "The Soviet Bloc Peace Defense Laws." AJIL, XLVI, 537-542.

344. Gsovski, V., ed. High Lights of Current Legislation and Activities in Mid-Europe. Washington, D.C.: Mid-European Law Project, 1953—1957. [Monthly]

345. _____, ed. Nationality Legislation in Eastern Europe. New York: Praeger, 1957.

346. Keitt, W. Lawrence, et al., "Law; Other Slavic Countries." QJCA, VII, iv, 53-57.

347. Peselj, Branko M., "Legal Trends in 'People's Democracies.'" GWLR, XX, 513-553.

348. _____. Legal Trends in the People's Democracies. New York: Mid European Studies Center of the Free Europe Committee, n.d. [1954.]

349. Pundeff, Marin, "Soviet Bloc Peace Defense Laws." AJIL, XLVI, 537-542.

PEACE TREATIES AND INTERNATIONAL AFFAIRS

350. Black, Cyril E., "The Axis Satellites and the Great Powers." FPR, XXII, 38-50.

351. _____. "Eastern Europe and the Postwar Balance of Power." Cyril E. Black, Ed., Challenge in Eastern Europe, pp. 245-266. (Mid-European Studies Center).

352. Bolles, Blair, "U.S. and Russia Contend for Influence in Danubian Basin." FPB, XXV, xxxiii, 4.

353. Cahnman, Werner J., "Frontiers Between East and West in Europe." GR, XXXIX, 605-624.

354. Campbell, John C., "Diplomacy on the Danube." FA, XXVII, 315-328.

355. _____, "The European Territorial Settlement." FA, XXVI, 196-218.

356. Carlston, Kenneth S., "Interpretation of Peace Treaties with Bulgaria, Hungary, and Rumania." AJIL, XLIV, 728-736.

357. Dean, Vera Micheles, "East-West Tension Weighs on Central Europe." FPB, XXVII, xL, 3.

358. Graham, Malbone W., "The Draft Treaties of Peace." AJIL, XL, 781-784.

359. Gsovski, Vladimir, ed. Economic Treaties and Agreements of the Soviet Block in Eastern Europe. 2nd ed. (Publication of the Mid-European Studies Center, Mid-European Law Project, Library of Congress, No. 4.) New York: Mid—European Studies Center, 1952.

360. Hadsel, Winifred N., "The Five Axis Satellite Peace Treaties." FPR, XXIII, 22-31.

361. International Court of Justice. Interpretation of Peace Treaties with Bulgaria, Hungary, and Romania. Advisory

Opinions of March 30th and July 18th 1950. New York: Columbia University Press (distributors), n.d., 455 pp.

362. Kertesz, Stephen D. "Human Rights in the Peace Treaties." Law and Contemporary Problems, XIV, 627-646.

363. _____, "The Plight of Satellite Diplomacy." RPol, XI, 26-62.

364. Koehl, Robert Lewis, "A Prelude to Hitler's Greater Germany." AHR, LIX, 43-65.

365. Kunz, Josef L., "The Danube Regime and the Belgrade Conference." AJIL, XLIII, 104-113.

366. Lang, Reginald, "Central Europe and European Unity." JCEA, VI, 21-29.

367. Lukacs, John A. The Great Powers and Eastern Europe. New York: American Book, 1952, 878 pp.

368. McClellan, Grant S., "Anglo-Russian Security Zones May Be Defined at Moscow Parley." FPB, XXIV, i, 2-3.

369. Opie, Redvers, et al. The Search for Peace Settlements. Washington, D.C.: Brookings Institution, 1951. [Contains a chapter on the peace settlement in Eastern Europe.]

370. Prigrada, Anthony. International Agreements Concerning the Danube. (Mimeo. Series No. 6.) New York: Mid-European Studies Center, 1953, 26 pp.

371. Radius, Walter A., "The Issues at Belgrade Were Clearly Drawn." DSB, XIX, 384-385.

372. Rasmussen, Charlotte B., "Freedom of the Danube." CH, XII, 27-31.

373. Roberts, Henry L., "Eastern Europe and the Balance of Power." IUGSSEES, IV, 1-11.

374. _____. "International Relations Between the Wars." Cyril E. Black, Ed., Challenge in Eastern Europe, pp. 179-195. (Mid-European Studies Center).

375. Schuman, Frederick L., "The Nazi Road to Power." CH, XXIV, 22-25; 209-213.

376. _____, "The Soviet Union: Cordon Sanitaire." CH, XI, 459-468.

377. Sontag, Raymond J., "The Last Months of Peace, 1939." FA, XXXV, 507-524.

378. Sturzo, Luigi, "The Vatican's Position in Europe." FA, XXIII, 211-222.

379. United States. Department of State. Documents on German Foreign Policy 1919-1945. Series D (1937-1945), Vol. V: Poland; the Balkans; Latin America; the Smaller Powers, June 1937-March 1939. Washington, D.C.: United States Government Printing Office, 1953, 977 pp.

380. _____. Department of State. Treaties of Peace with Italy, Bulgaria, Hungary, Roumania, and Finland. (Publication No. 2743, European Series, 21.) Washington, D.C.: United States Government Printing Office, 1947.

381. Werth, Alexander, "The Danube Conference." Nation, CLXVII, 200.

SOVIET RULE

382. Andriyevsky, Dmytro, "The Soviet Colonial Empire." UQ, XIII, 15-22.

383. Anon., "The Molotov Plan: Economics of Soviet Imperialism." NBIC, I, ix, 28-34.

384. _____, "Russia's Reverse ERP." Rept, I, iii, 14-15.

385. _____, "Soviet-Bound Economy." NBIC, I, v, 16-28.

386. _____, "Soviet Policies and Accusations." NBIC, I, iv, 1-15.

387. _____, "Stalin the Omniscient." NBIC II, iii, 35-38.

388. _____, "Stalinist Sophistry." NBIC, II, i, 3-17.

389. Black, Cyril E., "Soviet Policy in Eastern Europe." AAAPSS, CCLXIII, 152-164.

390. Bouscaren, Anthony T. Soviet Expansion and the West. San Francisco: Pacific States Printing Co., 1949.

391. Brannen, P. B., "Conquest by Chicanery: Introduction to Soviet Technique." USNIP, LXXVII, 791-797.

392. Dallin, Alexander, "Soviet Policy Toward Eastern Europe." JIA, XI, i, 48-59.

393. Dallin, David J. The New Soviet Empire. New Haven, Connecticut: Yale University Press, 1951, 216 pp.

394. _____, "Russia's New Empire." YR, XL, 6-26.

395. Dean, Vera Micheles, "Comprehension of Eastern Europe Strengthens Russia's Policy." FPB, XXIV, xv, 2-3. 2-3.

396. _____, "Will Strains in Eastern Europe Affect Soviet Policy?" FPB, XXX, xxiii, 2-3.

397. Deutscher, Isaac, "The New Soviet Policy Toward the Satellites." Rept, XI, x, 17-20.

398. Dexter, Byron, "Clausewitz and Soviet Strategy." FA, XXIX, 41-56.

399. d'Or, Romain, "The Inclined Plane; Some Observations on Russian Expansion." BR, II, ii, 48-51.

400. East, W. Gordon, "The New Frontiers of the Soviet Union." FA, XXIX, 591-608.

401. Fay, Sidney B., "The Cominform." CH, XIV, 1-5.

402. Fisher, Raymond H., "Agreements and Treaties Concluded by the USSR in 1945." DSB, XV, 391-398.

403. Florinsky, Michael T., "Soviet Expansion." CH, XXVI, 321-326.

404. Gluckstein, Ygael. Stalin's Satellites in Europe. Boston: Beacon Press, 1952, 333 pp.

405. Grzybowski, Kazimierz, "The Soviet Doctrine of Mare Clausum and Policies in Black and Baltic Seas." JCEA, XIV, 339-353.

406. Gurian, Waldemar, ed. Soviet Imperialism: Its Origins and Tactics. A Symposium. Notre Dame, Indiana: University of Notre Dame Press, 1953.

407. Hadsel, Winifred N., "Russia Consolidates Control of Danube at Belgrade." FPB, XXVII, xxxix, 2.

408. Halecki, Oscar, "Imperialism in Slavic and East European History." ASEER, XI, 1-26.

409. Herling, Albert Konrad. Soviet Slave Empire. New York: Wilfred Funk Inc., 1951, 230 pp.

410. Herman, Louis Jay, "The Communist Squeeze on Austria." SAQ, XLVIII, 192-203.

411. Hoptner, Jacob B. "The Structure of the Soviet Orbit." Cyril E. Black, Ed., <u>Challenge in Eastern Europe</u>, pp. 196-218. (Mid-European Studies Center).

412. de Huszar, George B., "Use of Satellite Outposts by the U.S.S.R." AAAPSS, CCLXXI, 157-164.

413. Jaszi, Oscar, "Central Europe and Russia." JCEA, V, 1-17.

414. Kertesz, Stephen D. "The Method of Soviet Penetration in Eastern Europe." Waldemar Gurian, Ed., The Soviet Union: Background, Ideology, Reality.

415. Kliewer, Don, "Why Do Soviets Want to Pull Out of Satellite Oil Firms?" WO, CXLI, vii, 229-230.

416. Kulski, W. W., "The Soviet System of Collective Security, Compared With The Western System." AJIL, XLIV, 453-476.

417. Lukacs, John A., "Political Expediency and Soviet Russian Military Operations." JCEA, VIII, 390-411.

418. Morris, Bernard S., "The Cominform: A Five-Year Perspective." WP, V, 368-376.

419. Nano, F. C., "The First Soviet Double Cross." JCEA, XII, 236-258.

420. Ozanne, Henry, "Russia's Oil Grab in Austria, Hungary, and Roumania." WO, CXXVII, xii, 248.

421. Polyzoides, A. Th., "The Russian Factor and The Peace." WAI, XVII, 91-98.

422. Ponikiewski, Jerzy G. Soviet Military Preparation in Central Europe. (Research Document, No. 28.) Washington, D.C.: Mid-European Studies Center, 1953.

423. Raditsa, Bogdan, "The Sovietization of the Satellites." AAAPSS, CCLXXI, 122-134.

424. Riasanovsky, Nicholas V., "Old Russia, The Soviet Union and Eastern Europe." ASEER, XI, 171-188.

425. Rothfels, Hans, "Russia and Central Europe." SoR, XII, 304-327.

426. Schwarz, Solomon M., "Revising the History of Russian Colonialism." FA, XXX, 488-494.

427. Shepherd, Gordon. Russia's Danubian Empire. New York: Praeger, 1955, 262 pp.

428. The Soviet Take-over in Eastern Europe. Communist Take-over and "Economic Reshaping" of Eastern Europe.

Cambridge, Mass.: Center of International Studies, Massachusetts Institute of Technology, 1954. [variable pagination]

429. Spulber, Nicolas, "Soviet Undertakings and Soviet Mixed Companies In East Europe." JCEA, XIV, 154-173.

430. Stowe, Leland. Conquest by Terror. The Story of Satellite Europe. New York: Random House, 1952.

431. Tomasic, Dinko, "The Structure of Soviet Power and Expansion." AAAPSS, CCLXXI, 32-42.

432. Towster, Julian, "Russia: Persistent Strategic Demands." CH, XXI, 2-7.

433. _____, "The Soviet Federation." CH, XVI, 131-135.

434. United States. Congress House. Committee on Foreign Affairs. The Strategy and Tactics of World Communism. Washington, D.C.: United States Government Printing Office, 1948.

435. _____. Congress (80th, 2nd. Sess.) House. Five Hundred Leading Communists. House Document 707. Supplement IV to Report: the Strategy and Tactics of World Communism. Washington, D.C.: United States Government Printing Office, 1948.

436. Vent, Herbert, "European Satellites of the U.S.S.R." JG, LVI, 26-35.

437. Walsh, Edmund A. Total Empire: The Roots and Progress of World Communism. (Science and Culture Series.) Milwaukee, Wisconsin: Bruce Publishing Co., 1951, 293 pp.

438. Wandycz, Piotr S., "The Soviet System of Alliances in East Central Europe." JCEA, XVI, 177-184.

439. Yakobson, Sergius, "The Soviet Concept of Satellite States." RPol, XI, 184-195.

440. Zinner, Paul E., "Soviet Policies in Eastern Europe." AAAPSS, CCCIII, 152-165.

AMERICAN POLICY

441. Anon., "Radio Free Europe." NBIC, II, vi, 37-43.

442. Bentley, Alvin M. "Post-Liberation Problems." Stephen D. Kertesz, Ed., The Fate of East Central Europe, pp. 425-447.

443. Brzezinski, Zbigniew, "U.S. Foreign Policy in East Central Europe—A Study in Contradiction." JIA, XI, i, 60-71.

444. Byrnes, Robert F. "Containment? Liberation? Coexistence? American Policy Toward East Central Europe, 1947-1955." Stephen D. Kertesz, Ed., The Fate of East Central Europe, pp. 75-99.

445. Chudoba, Bohdan, "Is Our Psychological Warfare Realistic?" America, LXXXVII, 351-353.

446. Ciechanowski, Jan, "Woodrow Wilson in the Spotlight of Versailles." PolR, I, ii-iii, 12-21.

447. Clucas, Lowell M., "Piercing the Iron Curtain." YR, XXXIX, 603-619.

448. Cowherd, Raymond G., "Waging the Cold War." CH, XV, 334-337.

449. Dennett, Raymond, and Joseph E. Johnson, eds. Negotiating with the Russians. Boston: World Peace Foundation, 1951.

450. Dobriansky, Lev E., "America's Eastern European Policy." UQ, IV, 253-262.

451. Ferrell, Robert H. "The United States and East Central Europe Before 1941." Stephen D. Kertesz, Ed., The Fate of East Central Europe, pp. 21-50.

452. Galantiere, Lewis. "America's Stake in Eastern Europe." Royden James Dangerfield, Ed., Area Study Programs: The Soviet Union and Eastern Europe, pp. 1-15. (Mid-European Studies Center and University of Illinois).

453. Hadsel, Winifred N., "U.S. Weighs Course Toward New Governments in Eastern Europe." FPB, XXVI, viii, 4.

454. Harsch, Joseph C. American Policy in Eastern Europe. With Emil Lengyel. Eastern Europe Today. (Foreign Policy Association. Headline Series No. 77.) New York: Foreign Policy Association, 1949.

455. Henderson, Loy W., "Political and Strategic Interests in the Middle East and Southeastern Europe." DSB, XVII, 996-1000.

456. Hess, Mary Anthoneta. American Tobacco and Central European Policy: Early Nineteenth Century. Washington, D.C.: Catholic University of America, 1948, 199 pp.

457. Kertesz, Stephen D. The Fate of East Central Europe. Hopes and Failures of American Foreign Policy. Notre Dame, Indiana: University of Notre Dame Press, 1956.

458. _____, "Peacemaking at Paris: Success, Failure or Farce." FA, XXV, 190-202.

459. Kostanick, Huey Louis, "American Aid in East-Central Europe." CH, XXXIII, 1-6.

460. Linehan, John, "Radio Free Europe—Behind the Beam of Truth." Rept, VII, vi, 13-16.

461. Lukas, Jan, "Cold War by Printed Word." CEF, III, i, 17-20.

462. Mamatey, Victor S. The United States and East Central Europe, 1914-1918: A Study in Wilsonian Diplomacy and Propaganda. Princeton, New Jersey: Princeton University Press, 1957.

463. Mitchell, Donald W., "The Risk of Cold War." CH, XIX, 5-9.

464. Mosely, Philip E., "Across the Green Table From Stalin." CH, XV, 129-133.

465. _____, "Hopes and Failures: American Policy Toward East Central Europe, 1941-1947." RPol, XVII, 461-485.

466. _____. "Hopes and Failures: American Policy Toward East Central Europe, 1941-1947." Stephen D. Kertesz, Ed., The Fate of East Central Europe, pp. 51-74.

467. Neumann, Robert G., "U.S. Foreign Policy and the Soviet Satellites." RPol, XI, 220-236.

468. Roucek, Joseph S., "American Misconceptions About Central-Eastern Europe." UQ, I, 342-350.

469. _____, "One World Versus An Iron Curtain World." AAAPSS, CCLVIII, 59-65.

470. Shayon, Robert Lewis, "Europe and the Voice of America." SatR, XXXIV, v, 7-8; 44-47.

471. Stone, Isaac A., "American Support of Free Elections in Eastern Europe." DSB, XVII, 311-323; 407-413.

472. Thompson, Carol L., "The United States and Communist Europe." CH, XXVI, 367-371.

473. Van Dyke, Vernon. American Support of Free Institutions in Eastern Europe. (Memorandum No. 28.) New

Haven, Connecticut: Yale Institute of International Studies, 1948.

474. Vucinich, Wayne S., "U.S. Policy Toward Russia's Satellites." CH, XXXII, 146-154.

FEDERATION PLANS

475. Birnbaum, Immanuel, "Warsaw and the Communist Bloc." PoC, VI, iii, 30-35.

476. Brzorad, V., et al., "The Case For a Regional East-Central European Federation." CEF, II, iii-iv, 15-18.

477. Busek, Vratislav, "Federation and Neutrality." CEF, IV, ii, 8-10.

478. Deutsch, Karl W. "Problems and Prospects of Federation." Cyril E. Black, Ed., Challenge in Eastern Europe, pp. 219-244. (Mid-European Studies Center).

479. Duchacek, Ivo, "Bonapartist Unity of Eastern Europe." AAAPSS, CCLXXI, 165-174.

480. Florinsky, Michael T. Integrated Europe? New York: Macmillan, 1955.

481. Gacki, Stefan K., "Federalism—Communist Style." CEF, III, ii-iii, 9-11.

482. Gilbert, Felix, "Mitteleuropa: The Final Stage." JCEA, VII, 58-67.

483. Goure, Leon, "The Eastern European Bloc and the United Nations Charter." JIA, III, ii, 36-46.

484. Gross, Feliks. Crossroads of Two Continents. A Democratic Federation of East-Central Europe. New York: Columbia University Press, 1945, 162 pp.

485. Grosser, Alfred, "Suez, Hungary, and European Integration." IO, XI, 470-480.

486. Halecki, Oscar, "Federalism As An Answer." AAAPSS, CCLVIII, 66-69.

487. Ignotus, Paul, et al., "Problems of Middle Europe." NR, CXII, iii, 81-82.

488. Kapustyansky, Mykola, "Thoughts on Solution of the East European Problem." UQ, XIII, 228-233.

489. May, Arthur J., "H. A. Miller and the Mid-European Union of 1918." ASEER, XVI, 473-488.

490. Mitrany, David, "Evolution of the Middle Zone." AAAPSS, CCLXXI, 1-10.

491. Raczynski, Edward, "The London Agreements and European Integration." CEF, III, i, 7-11.

492. Ripka, Hubert. A Federation of Central Europe. (Mimeo.) New York: The Author, 1953, 88 pp.

493. Roucek, Joseph S. Sociological Weaknesses of Federation Plans for Central-Eastern Europe. New York: Philosophical Library, n.d., 116 pp.

494. Schlesinger, Rudolf. Federalism in Central and Eastern Europe. New York: Oxford University Press, 1947; London: Routledge, 1945, 533 pp.

495. Silberman, David. A United Europe—or Else. New York: Richard R. Smith, 1946, 116 pp.

496. Valkenier, Elizabeth, "Eastern European Federation: A Study in the Conflicting Aims and Plans of the Exile Groups." JCEA, XIV, 354-370.

497. Wandycz, Piotr S., "Regionalism and European Integration." WAQ, XXVIII, 229-259.

THE ECONOMY

498. Allen, Robert Loring, "United Nations Technical Assistance: Soviet and East European Participation." IO, XI, 615-634.

499. American Federation of Labor, International Labor Relations Committee. What Happened to Trade Unions Behind the Iron Curtain. New York: Free Trade Union Committee, A.F. of L., 1948.

500. Ames, Edward, "Soviet Bloc Currency Conversions." AER, XLIV, 339-353.

501. Anon., "The Big Fall Sales Campaign." NBIC, II, xi, 3-11.

502. _____, "Black Bottleneck." NBIC, III, iii, 3-7.

503. _____, "Building Industry." EE, VI, vi, 26-36; viii, 23-33.

504. _____, "Central Europe Faces Petroleum Decline." WO, CXXXI, 220.

505. _____, "Coal, Harvest and Production Surveys." NBIC, III, ix, 42-51.

506. _____, "Coal Survey." NBIC, V, vii, 25-36.

507. _____, "The Cost of Living." NBIC, I, vii, 22-34.

508. _____, "Dead Reckoning." NBIC, I, ix, 15-27.

509. _____, "Economic Report: Agriculture." NBIC, III, ii, 13-20; iii, 8-20; iv, 23-35.

510. _____, "Economic Restlessness." NBIC, I, iii, 16-28.

511. _____, "Electric Power." NBIC, V, ix, 13-25.

512. _____, "Exploitation by Integration." NBIC, I, viii, 17-29.

513. _____, "The Facts of Life." NBIC, I, xii, 23-33.

514. _____, "The Financial Fix." NBIC, II, vi, 20-33.

515. _____, "From Discipline to Diversion." NBIC, II, iii, 39-48.

516. _____, "Heavy Chemicals." EE, VI, iii, 13-21.

517. _____, "In Second Gear." NBIC, II, ii, 39-49.

518. _____, "Iron and Steel." NBIC, V, x, 27-36.

519. _____, "Labor Productivity in the Captive Nations." NBIC, V, v, 19-28.

520. _____, "The Law of Demand." NBIC, II, vii, 25-34.

521. _____, "Men at Work." NBIC, II, i, 18-31.

522. _____, "Men, Money and Machines." NBIC, I, ii, 17-33.

523. _____, "Miners' Lives." NBIC, IV, iii, 39-51.

524. _____, "Miracles of the Market." NBIC, V, v, 60-61.

525. _____, "New Towns; A Survey of Industrial Communities under Construction in the Soviet Bloc." EE, VI, ii, 25-38.

526. _____, "October's Aftermath; The Effects of Satellite Unrest upon the Economic Integration of the Soviet Bloc, and the Resulting Shift in Policy." EE, VI, iv, 3-8.

527. _____, "Patterns and Currents in Economy of Europe." UNR, I, xi, 10-16.

East-Central Europe: The Economy   35

528. _____, "Payment by Results in the Building Industry in Eastern Europe." ILR, LXVIII, 524-541.

529. _____, "Progress on Paper." NBIC, I, iv, 16-30.

530. _____, "Satellite Drugs." NBIC, II, viii, 38-48.

531. _____, "Schweiks and Shockworkers." NBIC, II, v, 33-36.

532. _____, "Slanted Economy." NBIC, I, x, 18-31.

533. _____, "Socialist Competition." NBIC, IV, vi, 3-10.

534. _____, "Spectre of the Norm." NBIC, III, ii, 32-38.

535. _____, "The Summing-Up." NBIC, II, iii, 20-34.

536. _____, "Tourism in the Soviet Bloc." NBIC, V, i, 3-8.

537. _____, "Trade Unions in the Satellites." NBIC, III, xii, 28-34.

538. _____, "Ways to Means." NBIC, I, xi, 18-31.

539. _____, "Working for the State." NBIC, II, iv, 15-25.

540. Cannon, Cavendish W., "Conference to Consider Free Navigation of the Danube." DSB, XIX, 197-199; 283-292.

541. Cowherd, Raymond G., "Soviet Economic Progress." CH, XXI, 70-75.

542. Dean, Vera Micheles, "Economic Questions Paramount at Peace Conference." FPB, XXV, xLii, 1-2.

543. _____, "Economic Trends in Eastern Europe." FPR, XXIV, 14-28, 30-39.

544. _____. Economic Trends in Eastern Europe. 2 pts. (Foreign Policy Report, Vol. XXIV, Nos. 2-3.) New York: Foreign Policy Association, 1948, 15, 40 pp.

545. Doman, Nicholas R., "Postwar Nationalization of Foreign Property in Europe." CLR, XLVIII, 1125-1161.

546. Economic Research Group. Economic Development in S. E. Europe: Including Poland, Czechoslovakia, Austria, Hungary, Roumania, Yugoslavia, Bulgaria and Greece. Introd. David Mitrany. New York: Oxford University Press, 1945, 165 pp.

547. Foa, Bruno, "Economic Trends in Liberated Europe." FPR, XXI, 82-94.

548. Grzybowski, Kazimierz, "Foreign Investment and Political Control in Eastern Europe." JCEA, XIII, 13-27.

549. Haberler, Gottfried. "Economic Consequences of a Divided World." Stephen D. Kertesz, Ed., The Fate of East Central Europe, pp. 377-395.

550. Halasz, Andrew, "Labor's Status in Iron Curtain Countries." AAAPSS, CCLXXI, 78-99.

551. Harris, Seymour E. Economic Planning: The Plans of Fourteen Countries with Analysis of the Plans. New York: Alfred A. Knopf, 1949, 577 pp.

552. Hertz, Frederick. The Economic Problem of the Danubian States: A Study in Economic Nationalism. London: Victor Gollancz; Forest Hills, New York: Transatlantic Arts, 1947, 1948.

553. Joint Committee on the Economic Report. Trends in Economic Growth—A Comparison of the Western Powers and the Soviet Bloc. Washington, D.C.: 1955.

554. Kemeny, George, "Eastern Europe: Development in Social and Economic Structure." WP, VI, 67-83.

555. Kish, George, "TVA on the Danube?" GR, XXXVII, 274-302.

556. Lengyel, Emil, "Industrial Changes in Eastern Europe." AAAPSS, CCLXXI, 68-77.

557. Lisinski, Michael J., and Patrick C. Nieburg. Outline of the Economy of Eastern Europe. New York: Research and Publications Service of the National Committee for a Free Europe, n.d. [1952].

558. Margold, Stella K., "Economic Life in Russia's Orbit." HBR, XXVIII, v, 65-78, 86-113.

559. May, A. J., "Trans-Balkan Railway Schemes." JMH, XXIV, 353-367.

560. Mitrany, David. Economic Development of Southeast Europe. New York: 1946.

561. Nyaradi, Nicholas, "Notes on the Soviet Economy." Fortune, XLII, ix, 98-99, 142—143.

562. Oxenfeldt, Alfred Richard. Economic Systems in Action; the United States, the Soviet Union, with a Section on China and Eastern Europe [and] the United Kingdom. Rev. ed. New York: Rinehart and Co., 1957, 207 pp.

563. Paulat, V. J., "Investment Policy and the Standard of Living in East-Mid-European Countries." JCEA, XIV, 38-64.

564. Polach, Jaroslav G., "The Beginnings of Trade Unionism among the Slavs of the Austrian Empire." ASEER, XIV, 239-259.

565. Poulos, Constantine, "Revolution in Eastern Europe: A Regional Planned Economy." Nation, CLXV, 11-13.

566. Pounds, Norman J. G., and Nicolas Spulber. Resources and Planning in Eastern Europe. (Slavic and East European Series, Vol. IV.) Bloomington: Indiana University Publications, 1957.

567. Prigrada, Anthony. Danube Waterways. (Mimeo. Series No. 5.) New York: Mid-European Studies Center, 1953.

568. Rosu, G. G., "Austrian Oil a Victim of Tensions." WO, CXXXVI, i, 242-246.

569. Rudzki, Adam. East-Central European Transportation. Washington, D.C.: 1955.

570. _____. Organization of Transportation in Captive Europe. (Mimeo. Series No. 10.) New York: Mid-European Studies Center, 1954.

571. _____. Roads, Waterways, and Seaports of Captive Europe. (Mimeo. Series No. 15.) New York: Mid-European Studies Center, 1954.

572. _____. Railroad Systems in Captive Europe. (Mimeo. Series No. 13.) New York: Mid-European Studies Center, 1954.

573. Sharp, Samuel L. Nationalization of Key Industries in Eastern Europe: With an Appendix Containing the Nationalization Decrees of the Czechoslovak Republic and Poland. (Pamphlet No. 1.) Washington, D.C.: Foundation for Foreign Affairs, 1946, 80 pp.

574. Shimkin, Dmitri B. Minerals, A Key to Soviet Power. Cambridge, Massachusetts: Harvard University Press, 1953.

575. Southard, Frank A. The Finances of European Liberation. New York: King's Crown Press for the Carnegie Endowment for International Peace, 1946, 206 pp.

576. Spulber, Nicolas, "Eastern Europe: The Changes in Agriculture from Land Reforms to Collectivization." ASEER, XIII, 389-401.

577. _____, "Economic Thinking and its Application and Methodology in Eastern Europe Outside of Soviet Russia." AER, XLVI, 367-379.

578. _____ . The Economics of Communist Eastern Europe. New York: Technology Press of Massachusetts Institute of Technology and John Wiley and Sons, 1957, 525 pp.

579. _____ , "Planning and Development." IUGSSEES, IV, 87-114.

580. Sturmthal, Adolf, "The New Five Year Plan." CH, X, 424-428.

581. Suranyi-Unger, Theo, "The Eastern European Economic Cycle." WAI, XXVI, 275-301.

582. Taborsky, Edward, "The 'Old' and the 'New' Course in Satellite Economy." JCEA, XVII, 378-403.

583. Teleki, Geza. "Industrial and Social Policies Between the Wars." Cyril E. Black, Ed., Challenge in Eastern Europe, pp. 132-149. (Mid-European Studies Center).

584. United Nations Relief and Rehabilitation Agency. Twelfth Report to Congress on Operations of UNRRA. Washington, D.C.: United States Government Printing Office, 1948.

585. United States. Library of Congress. Legislative Reference Service. Trends in Economic Growth: A Comparison of the Western Powers and the Soviet Block. Washington, D.C.: United States Government Printing Office, 1955.

586. J. W., "A Selected List of Sources on Economic Problems of Central European Countries." CEF, III, ii-iii, 15-20.

587. Wandycz, Damian S., "Oil Resources of East-Central Europe." CEF, III, i, 21-25.

588. Whitnack, Doris S., and David Handler, "Danubian Transportation Problems in Relation to Development of the Basin." DSB, XIV, 1108-1110.

589. Winston, Victor H., "Mineral Resources." IUGSSEES, IV, 36-86.

590. Women as Workers in Captive Europe. Material from Mid-European Law Project of the Library of Congress and News from Behind the Iron Curtain, compiled and written under the supervision of the Mid-European Studies Center. (Mimeo. Series No. 28.) New York: Mid-European Studies Center, 1954, 22 pp.

591. Wszelaki, Jan H. Fuel and Power in Captive Middle Europe. New York: Mid-European Studies Center, 1952.

592. _____ . "Industrial and Social Policies of the

Communist Regimes." Cyril E. Black, Ed., Challenge in Eastern Europe, pp. 150-176. (Mid-European Studies Center).

593. _____, "Petroleum for Power in Red Europe." WO, CXXXIV, v, 252-256.

594. _____, "The Rise of Industrial Middle Europe." FA, XXX, 123-135.

595. _____, "Some Social and Political Implications of Planning." IUGSSEES, IV, 154-170.

Agriculture
596. Anon., "Animal Farm: The Livestock Crisis." NBIC, IV, v, 15-23.

597. _____, "Food, Fodder and Farmers." NBIC, II, x, 13-26.

598. _____, "Household Plots." NBIC, IV, ix, 3-9.

599. _____, "Machine Tractor Stations." NBIC, III, vi, 3-14.

600. _____, "Satellite Harvest Prospects." NBIC, II, ix, 19-25.

601. _____, "State Farms." NBIC, III, xi, 3-16.

602. Bass, Robert H. Force Versus Food: A Short History of Agriculture in the Soviet Sphere. New York: Free Europe Press, 1957, 72 pp.

603. Brandt, Karl, "The Reconstruction of European Agriculture." FA, XXIII, 284-295.

604. Brunner, E. S. Farmers of the World. New York: Columbia University Press, 1945.

605. Deacon, Kenneth J. Land Tenure and Nationalism in Eastern Europe, 1919-1929. New York: New York University, 1951, 10 pp.

606. Ekbaum, Arthur. Destruction of Independent Farming in East Europe. Stockholm and New York: Estonian Information Center, 1949. [Digest of a forthcoming book with the same title], 59 pp.

607. Feierabend, Ladislav. "Land Reform and Agricultural Improvement." Cyril E. Black, Ed., Challenge in Eastern Europe, pp. 93-108. (Mid-European Studies Center).

608. Free Europe Press Research Staff. Satellite Agriculture in Crisis; A Study of Land Policy in the Soviet Sphere;

Prepared by the Research Staff of Free Europe Press, A Division of the Committee. (Praeger Publications in Russian History and World Communism.) New York: Praeger, 1954, 130 pp.

609. Gunda, Bela, "Plant Gathering in The Economic Life of Eurasia." SJA, V, 369-378.

610. Jasny, Naum, "Unirrigated Cotton in Southern Russia and the Danubian Countries." FAgr, XI, 2-13.

611. Kish, George, "Rural Problems of Central and Southeastern Europe: A Review." GR, XXXV, 286-290.

612. Moodie, Arthur E., "Agricultural Resources." IUGSSEES, IV, 12-35.

613. Peselj, Branko M. The Industrialization of Peasant Europe. (Publication of the Mid-European Studies Center, No. 13.) New York: Mid-European Studies Center, 1953, 88 pp.

614. Rosdolsky, Roman, "On the Nature of Peasant Serfdom in Central and Eastern Europe." JCEA, XII, 128-139.

615. Sanders, Irwin T., "Changing Status of the Peasant in Eastern Europe." AAAPSS, CCLXXI, 78-93.

616. Schweng, L. D., "Recent Agricultural Developments in Eastern Europe." JFE, XXXIII, 40-54.

617. Sharp, Samuel L., "Cooperatives and Collectives in Eastern Europe." FPR, XXVI, 14-16.

618. _____, et al., "Industry and Agriculture in Eastern Europe." FPR, XXVI, 2-8, 10-14.

619. Zagorov, Slavcho Dimitroff, et al. Agricultural Economy of the Danubian Countries, 1935-1945. (Stanford University Food Research Institute. Food, Agriculture, and World War II.) Stanford, California: Stanford University Press, 1955, 478 pp.

Trade

620. Allen, Robert Loring, "The Soviet and East European Foreign Credit Program." ASEER, XVI, 433-449.

621. Anon., "Economic Report: Foreign Trade." NBIC, III, i, 15-22.

622. _____, "Farms and Foreign Trade." NBIC, II, v, 18-32.

623. _____, "The Soviet Bloc's Penetration of Africa and Asia." NBIC, V, ix, 3-12.

624. _____, "Soviet Trade Offensive: Balkans and Near East." NBIC, IV, ix, 10-23.

625. _____, "Soviet Trade Offensive: Far East." NBIC, IV, x, 14-28.

626. _____, "Soviet Trade Offensive: West Europe." NBIC, IV, vi, 11-22.

627. Bacon, Lois, "Europe's East-West Trade in Food." FAgr, XVIII, 130-132.

628. _____, "Europe's East-West Trade in Food—A Statistical Note." FAgr, XV, 78-82.

629. _____, "Europe's East-West Trade in Food, 1950 and 1951." FAgr, XVI, 216-219.

630. Dewar, Margaret. Soviet Trade With Eastern Europe, 1945-1949. New York: Royal Institute of International Affairs, 1951, 123 pp.

631. Granick, David, "Economic Relations with the USSR." IUGSSEES, IV, 129-148.

632. _____, "The Pattern of Foreign Trade in Eastern Europe and its Relation to Economic Development Policy." QJE, LXVIII, 377-400.

633. Grzybowski, Kazimierz, "Foreign Trade Policy of the Soviet Bloc." PolR, I, ii-iii, 97-117.

634. Hadsel, Fred L., "Freedom of Navigation on the Danube." DSB, XVIII, 787-793.

635. Hansen, Kenneth R., "The Facts of Life About East-West Trade." DSB, XXIX, 271-274.

636. Hoffman, Michael L., "Problems of East-West Trade." IC, No. 511, pp. 259-308.

637. Hutcheson, Harold H., "Eastern Europe Anxious to Increase East-West Trade." FPB, XXVII, xxx, 2.

638. _____, "Pre-War Trade of Eastern Europe." FPR, XXIV, 40.

639. Josephson, Eric., "East Europe's New Trade Potential." Nation, CLXXIV, 363-365.

640. Marx, Daniel, Jr., "Economic and Political Factors Affecting Trade Between Eastern and Western Europe." PSQ, LXVI, 161-190.

641. Matecki, Bronislaw. Foreign Trade in the People's Democracies of Central and Eastern Europe. New York: 1952.

642. Meyer, Henry Cord, "German Economic Relations with Southeastern Europe, 1870-1914." AHR, LVII, 77-90.

643. Spulber, Nicolas, "Factors in Eastern Europe's Intratrade and Cooperation." JIA, XI, i, 20-30.

644. _____. "Problems of East-West Trade and Economic Trends in the European Satellites of Soviet Russia." Stephen D. Kertesz, Ed., The Fate of East Central Europe, pp. 396-421.

645. United States. Department of Commerce. Annual Exports and Imports of the Free World to and from the Soviet Bloc. Washington, D.C.: United States Government Printing Office, 1953.

646. 'Veritas.' "What Do Mounting Soviet Exports Mean?" WO, CXXXIX, x, 260-264.

647. Viner, Jacob. The Customs Union Issue. New York: Carnegie Endowment for International Peace, 1950, 210 pp.

648. Wright, Herman W., Jr., "Trade with East Europe." CH, XXVII, 179-184.

Forced Labor

649. Baldwin, Roger N., ed. A New Slavery, Forced Labor: The Communist Betrayal of Human Rights. New York: Oceana Publications, 1953, 158 pp.

650. Carlton, Richard K. The Economic Role of Forced Labor in Eastern Europe. (Mid-European Studies Center, Mimeo. Series, No. 35.) New York: Mid-European Studies Center, 1954.

651. _____, ed. Forced Labor in the "People's Democracies." Reprint of the Supplement to the Statement on Forced Labor by the International League for the Rights of Man to the Secretary-General of the United Nations under Economic and Social Council Resolution 524 (XVII) of April 27, 1954. Prepared for the International League for the Rights of Man. New York: Mid-European Studies Center, 1955, 56 pp.

652. Dallin, David J. The Economics of Slave Labor. Chicago: Regnery, 1949, 35 pp.

653. Forced Labor and Confinement Without Trial in Bulgaria. Washington, D.C.: Mid-European Law Project, Library of Congress, 1952, 30 pp. Mimeographed.

654. Forced Labor and Confinement Without Trial in Czechoslovakia. Washington, D.C.: Mid-European Law Project, Library of Congress, 1951, 9 pp.

655. Forced Labor and Confinement Without Trial in Hungary. Washington, D.C.: Mid-European Law Project, Library of Congress, 1951, 9 pp.

656. Forced Labor and Confinement Without Trial in Poland. Washington, D.C.: Mid-European Law Project, Library of Congress, 1951, 8 pp.

657. Forced Labor and Confinement Without Trial in Rumania. Washington, D.C.: Mid-European Law Project, Library of Congress, 1951, 8 pp.

658. Forced Labor and Confinement Without Trial in Yugoslavia. Washington, D.C.: Mid-European Law Project, Library of Congress, 1952, 16 pp.

659. Free Europe Committee. Slave Labor and Slave Labor Camps in Poland. New York: Free Europe Committee, 1951.

660. Free Europe Press, Hungarian Desk. The Legal Aspects of Forced Labor in Hungary. Ed. Laszlo Varga. New York: Free Europe Committee, [1954?].

661. Gliksman, Jerzy. Tell the West: An Account of His Experiences as a Slave Laborer in the Union of Soviet Socialist Republics. New York: Gresham, 1948, 358 pp.

662. Gsovski, Vladimir, ed. Forced Labor and Confinement Without Trial. Study in six parts: Bulgaria, Czechoslovakia, Hungary, Poland, Rumania, Yugoslavia. With Supplement: Forced Labor in the Satellite Countries as of January 7, 1955. Washington: Mid-European Law Project, Library of Congress, 1952, 1955.

663. Hungarian National Council. Memorandum on Forced Labor and Forced Labor Camps in Hungary. To the Ad Hoc Committee on forced labor of the U.N. Social and Economic Council. n.p., n.d.

664. Kotschnig, Walter, "Forced Labor Conditions in Communist-Dominated Countries." DSB, XXIII, 510-513.

665. Lithuanian Consultative Panel. Statement on Forced Labor and Forced Labor Camps in Lithuania and the Soviet Union. New York: Lithuanian Consultative Panel, 1952. [Presented to the Ad Hoc Committee on Forced Labor of the U.N. Social and Economic Council by the Lithuanian Consultative Panel.] n.p., n.d.

666. Nenoff, Dragomir. Forced Labor Camps and Prisons in Bulgaria. New York: Free Europe Committee, 1951, 24 pp.

667. Orr, Charles A. Stalin's Slave Camps: An Indictment of Modern Slavery. Boston: Beacon Press, 1952, 105 pp.

668. Radescu, Nicolae. Forced Labor in Roumania. New York: Commission on Inquiry into Forced Labor, 1949.

669. Szumski, Romuald. Labor and the Soviet System. New York: Free Europe Committee, 1951, 30 pp.

670. United States. Library of Congress. Law Library. Yugoslavia: Confinement Without Trial (Forced Labor). Washington, D.C.: Library of Congress, 1951.

LANGUAGES

671. Caro, James, et al. Conversational Guide Book in English, German, Russian, Polish, Latvian, and French. Assisted by Tatyana Boreyscha and others. Philadelphia: The Peter Reilly Co., 1951, 203 pp.

672. De Bray, Reginald George Arthur. Guide to the Slavonic Languages. New York: E. P. Dutton, 1951.

673. Entwistle, William James, and W. A. Morison. Russian and the Slavonic Languages. (Great Languages Series.) New York: Macmillan, 1949.

674. Halle, Morris, "The Old Church Slavonic Conjugation." Word, VII, 155-167.

675. Jakobson, Roman, "On Slavic Diphthongs Ending in a Liquid." Word, VIII, 306-310.

676. _____. Slavic Languages. 2nd ed. (Columbia University Slavic Philology Series.) New York: King's Crown Press 1955, pp. 26.

677. _____, "Vestiges of the Earliest Russian Vernacular." Word, VIII, 350-355.

678. Jofen, Jean Blech, "The Dialectological Makeup of East European Yiddish: Phonological and Lexicological Criteria." DA, XIV, 703.

679. Lunt, Horace G., "On Old Church Slavonic Phonemes: The 'Codex Zographensis.'" Word, VIII, 311-328.

680. _____. "On the Origins of Phonemic Palatalization

in Slavic." Morris Halle, et al., comp., For Roman Jakobson, pp. 306-315.

681. Martinet, Andre, "Concerning some Slavic and Aryan Reflexes of IE's." Word, VII, 91-95.

682. Menges, Karl H., "The Altaic Languages." AATSEEL, III, 74-76.

683. _____, "Indo-European Influences on Ural-Altaic Languages." Word, I, 188-193.

684. Merzbach, Herbert, "The Phonological Theory of the School of Prague: An Exposition and Revision." DA, XIV, 530-531.

685. Mikofsky, Bernard S., "The Origins of Slavic sobota." ISS, I, 209-224.

686. Rusic, Branislav, "The Mute Language in the Tradition and Oral Literature of the South Slavs." JAF, LXIX, 299-309.

687. Schmalstieg, William R., "Criteria for the Determination of Slavic Borrowings in Lithuanian." DA, XV, 1680.

688. _____, "The Phoneme /V/ in Slavic Verbal Suffixes." Word, XII, 255-259.

689. Sebeok, Thomas A., "Finno-Ugric and the Languages of India." JAOS, LXV, 59-62.

690. _____, "The Meaning of Ural-Altaic." Lingua, II, 124-139.

691. Senn, Alfred. "Slavic Linguistics." Leonid I. Strakhovsky, Ed., Handbook of Slavic Studies, pp. 44-61.

692. Serech, Jury, "A New Comparative Grammar of Slavic Languages." AUA, I, 157-163. (review article).

693. _____, "On Slavic Linguistic Interrelations." AUA, III, ii, 696-730.

694. Spitzer, Leo. "Figl." Morris Halle, et al., comp., For Roman Jakobson, pp. 503.

695. Stang, Chr. S. "Slavonic sŭ with the Accusative in Expressions of Measure." Morris Halle, et al., comp., For Roman Jakobson, pp. 514-517.

696. Tedesco, P., "Slavic ne Presents from Older je Presents." Language, XXIV, 346-387.

697. van Schooneveld, C. H. "The Aspect System of the Old Church Slavonic and Old Russian Verbum finitum 'byti.'" Word, VII, 96-103.

698. Weinreich, Max. "Yiddish, Knaanic, Slavic: The Basic Relationships." Morris Halle, et al., comp., <u>For Roman Jakobson</u>, pp. 622-632.

699. Weinreich, Uriel, "Yiddish Blends with a Slavic Element." Word, XI, 603-610.

THE ARTS

700. Anon., "The Architecture of Empire." NBIC, III, ix, 30-41.

701. _____, "Art for Politics' Sake." NBIC, III, i, 40-45.

702. _____, "Art under the New Course." NBIC, IV, i, 18-30.

703. _____, "Artists' Lives: A Study in Privilege." NBIC, V, viii, 28-37.

704. _____, "Command Performance." NBIC, III, v, 25-36.

705. _____, "Marx in the Muse." NBIC, II, ii, 50-57.

706. _____, "Movies for the Masses." NBIC, IV, vii, 29-41.

707. _____, "Music for the Masses." NBIC, II, i, 38-49.

708. _____, "The New Architecture." NBIC, II, vi, 44-54.

709. _____, "The New Jazz Line." NBIC, V, vi, 27-32.

710. _____, "The Recall of the Intelligentsia." NBIC, IV, v, 33-40.

711. _____, "The 'Revolt' of the Intellectuals." NBIC, V, vi, 3-5, 8-17; vii, 3-14.

712. _____, "The Satellite Arabesque." NBIC, II, v, 37-46.

713. _____, "Stage and Screen." NBIC, I, xi, 32-46.

714. _____, "Taming of the Muse." NBIC, II, iv, 37-47.

715. _____, "Words and Music by Decree." NBIC, I, iii, 29-43.

716. Hertz, Alexander, "The Case of An Eastern European Intelligentsia." JCEA, XI, 10-26.

717. Lengyel, Emil, "Europe's Intellectual Starvation Diet." SatR, XXX, xx, 7-8; 29-30.

718. Taborsky, Edward, "The Revolt of the Communist Intellectuals." RPol, XIX, 308-329.

719. Wagner, Francis S. Cultural Revolution in East Europe. Washington, D.C.: The Author, 1955.

720. Weisser, Albert. The Modern Renaissance of Jewish Music, Events and Figures. Eastern Europe and America. New York: Bloch Publishing Company, 1954, 175 pp.

721. Werner, Alfred. Religious Art of Eastern Europe. (Little Art Series.) New York: A. A. Wyn, 1949, 10 pp.

LITERATURE AND FOLKLORE

722. Anon., "Folklore in the Communist State." NBIC, V, iii, 23-31.

723. Chyzhevskyi, Dmytro. Outline of Comparative Slavic Literatures. (Survey of Slavic Civilization, I.) Boston: American Academy of Arts and Sciences, 1952, 143 pp.

724. Harkins, William E., "Slavic Formalist Theories in Literary Scholarship." Word, VII, 177-185.

725. Jakobson, Roman, "The Kernel of Comparative Slavic Literature." HSS, I, 1-71.

726. Kramoris, Ivan Joseph, ed. and tr. Anthology of Slavic Poetry: A Selection of Lyric and Narrative Poems and Folk Ballads in Slovak and English. Scranton, Pennsylvania: Obrana Press, 1947, 146 pp.

727. Kurath, Gertrude Prokosch, "Dance Relatives of Mid-Europe and Middle America: A Venture in Comparative Choreology." JAF, LXIX, 286-298.

728. Lord, Albert Bates, ed. Slavic Folklore: A Symposium. Philadelphia: American Folklore Society, 1956. [Vol. LXIX, No. 273 of Journal of American Folklore.]

729. Mann, Kathleen. Peasant Costume in Europe. New York: Macmillan, 1950, 191 pp.

730. Remenyi, Joseph, "Literature of Small Nations." JAAC, XII, 119-125.

731. _____, et al. World Literatures: Arabic, Chinese, Czechoslovak, French, German, Greek, Hungarian, Italian, Lithuanian, Norwegian, Polish, Romanian, Russian, Scottish, Swedish, Yugoslav. Sponsored by the committees for the nationality rooms in the Cathedral of Learning and presented by the University of Pittsburg. Pittsburg, Pennsylvania: University of Pittsburg Press, 1956.

732. Schimmerling, Hanns Aldo. Folk Dance Music of the Slavic Nations. New York: Associated Music Publishers, 1951, 167 pp.

733. Senn, Alfred, "Folklore in Slavic Studies." AATSEEL, X, 3-4.

734. Smith, Horatio, ed. Columbia Dictionary of Modern European Literature. New York: Columbia University Press, 1947.

735. Vincenz, Stanislaw. On the High Uplands: Sagas, Songs, Tales and Legends of the Carpathians. Tr. H. C. Stevens. New York: Roy Publishers, 1956.

EDUCATION

736. Anon., "The Big Red Schoolhouse." NBIC, II, x, 34-45.

737. _____, "Books and Buildings." NBIC, I, xii, 40-46.

738. _____, "Infant Communists." NBIC, III, v, 37-40.

739. _____, "'Patriotic' Re-education." NBIC, I, iv, 31-40.

740. _____, "Pragmatic Approach to Culture." NBIC, I, ii, 34-41.

741. Buhler, Neal, and Stanley Zukowski. Discrimination in Education in the People's Democracies: Bulgaria, Czechoslovakia, Hungary, Poland and Romania. New York: Mid-European Studies Center, Free Europe Committee, 1955, 61 pp.

742. Infeld, Leopold, "For the Dignity of Science." EE, VI, iv, 23-26.

743. Reshetar, John S., "The Educational Weapon." AAAPSS, CCLXXI, 135-144.

PHILOSOPHY AND RELIGION

744. Anon., "The Cross and the Party; A Two-Year Review of Church-State Relations." EE, VI, xii, 3-11.

745. _____, "The Mitre and the Sword." NBIC, II, xi, 12-16.

746. _____, "The Red and the Black." NBIC, II, ii, 16-38.

747. _____, "Religion in the Captive Nations." NBIC, IV, xii, 3-13.

748. Barron, J.B., and H. M. Waddams. Communism and the Churches. New York: Morehouse-Gorham, 1951, 102 pp.

749. Bolles, Blair, "Clash With Vatican Sharpened in Eastern Europe." FPB, XXVIII, xLii, 2-3.

750. The Church under Communism. Second Report of the Commission on Communism. General Assembly of the Church of Scotland. New York: Philosophical Library, 1953, 79 pp.

751. Cockburn, J. Hutchinson. Religious Freedom in Eastern Europe. Richmond, Virginia: Presbyterian Committee, 1953, 140 pp.

752. Cowherd, Raymond G., "The War on the Church." CH, XVIII, 148-153.

753. de Korostovetz, Vladimir, "Religion and Nationality as Political Factors in Eastern Europe." UQ, VII, 127-133.

754. Free Europe Committee. The Red and the Black. The Church in the Communist State. New York: America Press, 1953, 75 pp.

755. French, Reginald Michael. The Eastern Orthodox Church. (Hutchinson's Univ. Library: Christian Religious Series.) New York: Longmans, Green and Co., 1951, 186 pp.

756. Graham, Robert A., "Church's Dilemma under Red Tyrants." America, XCIII, 261-263.

757. Gsovski, Vladimir, ed. Church and State Behind the Iron Curtain: Czechoslovakia, Hungary, Poland, Romania, with an Introduction on the Soviet Union. (Mid-European Studies Center of the Free Europe Committee.) New York: Praeger, 1955.

758. Juhasz, William. Persecution of Churches Behind the Iron Curtain. New York: Free Europe Committee, 1952.

759. Kiviranna, Rudolf, "Christian Reconstruction in Europe." BR, I, 359-362.

760. Manning, Clarence A., "Religion Within the Iron Curtain." AAAPSS, CCLXXI, 112-121.

761. Markham, Reuben Henry, ed. Communists Crush Churches in Eastern Europe. Boston: Meador, 1950, 143 pp.

762. Presviteros, "Religion Contra Power Politics." BR, I, 185-192.

763. Sadler, George W., et al. Europe—Whither Bound? A Symposium Telling of Southern Baptist Missionary Work in Italy, Spain, and the Balkan States—Hungary and Yugoslavia. Comp. by Nan F. Weeks. Nashville, Tennessee: The Broadman Press, 1951, 144 pp.

764. Shuster, George N. Religion Behind the Iron Curtain. New York: Macmillan, 1954, 281 pp.

765. Tobias, Robert. Communist-Christian Encounter in East Europe. Indianapolis: School of Religion Press, 1956, 567 pp.

766. Winner, Percy, "Alarm in the Vatican." NR, CXXXV, vi, 11-14.

SOCIOLOGY

767. Anon., "The Alcohol Problem in the Soviet Bloc." EE, VI, xii, 16-25.

768. _____, "Captive Communications." NBIC, I, vii, 35-42.

769. _____, "The Collective Life." NBIC, I, x, 32-40.

770. _____, "Crime Under Communism." NBIC, IV, ix, 24-34.

771. _____, "Crisis in the Youth Leagues." NBIC, IV, vi, 25-35; vii, 17-28.

772. _____, "The Family Circle." NBIC, IV, v, 41-43.

773. _____, "The Fettered Fourth Estate." NBIC, II, vii, 35-50.

774. _____, "Handmaidens of Communism; Women in a New Dimension." NBIC, II, iv, 26-36.

775. _____, "The House of Culture." NBIC, IV, vii, 42-49.

776. _____, "Marriage and Family under Communism." EE, VI, iii, 22-31.

777. _____, "The New Line on Love." NBIC, IV, iv, 28-37.

778. _____, "New Look in Fashions; A Review of Post-Stalinist Attitudes Toward Style, Good Taste and Diversity in Dress." EE, VI, iv, 11-19; 22.

779. _____, "The Party and the Peasant." EE, VI, x, 15-25; xi, 14-24.

780. Blair, Russel. "The Food Habits of the East Slavs." DA, XVI, 1425 (Pennsylvania).

781. Gross, Feliks, "Some Sociological Considerations on Underground Movements." PolR, II, ii-iii, 33-56.

782. Kracauer, Siegfried, and Berkman, Paul L., "Attitudes Toward Various Communist Types in Hungary, Poland and Czechoslovakia." SocP, III, 109-114.

783. Mitrany, David. Marx Against the Peasant: A Study in Social Dogmatism. Chapel Hill, North Carolina: University of North Carolina Press, 1951.

784. Peselj, Branko M. "Peasantism: Its Ideology and Achievements." Cyril E. Black, Ed., Challenge in Eastern Europe, pp. 109-131. (Mid-European Studies Center).

785. Psathas, George, "Ethnicity, Social Class, and Adolescent Independence from Parental Control." ASoR, XXII, 415-423.

786. Tomasic, Dinko, "Ideologies and the Structure of Eastern European Society." AJS, LIII, 367-375.

787. _____. Personality and Culture in Eastern European Politics. (Library of Political Sciences.) New York: George W. Stewart, 1948, 249 pp.

PAN-SLAVISM

788. Boucek, J. A., "The Pan-Slavic Ideal - Historical Sketch." CEF, III, i, 3-7; ii-iii, 12-14.

789. Bryner, Cyril, "Russia and the Slavs." CH, XXVIII, 74-79.

790. Drahomanov, Mykhaylo, "Panslav Federalism." AUA, II, i, 175-180.

791. Kerner, Robert J., "Visions of the East; Hans Kohn's 'Pan-Slavism: Its History and Ideology.'" SatR, XXXVI, xxxix, 21; 39.

792. Kohn, Hans, "Pan-Slavism and World War II." APSR, XLVI, 699-722.

793. _____. Pan-Slavism: Its History and Ideology. (Notre Dame. University Committee on International Relations. International Studies.) Notre Dame, Indiana: University of Notre Dame Press, 1953, 356 pp.

794. Lednicki, Waclaw. "Panslavism." Feliks Gross, Ed., European Ideologies, pp. 808-912.

795. Manning, Clarence A., "The Soviet Union and the Slavs." RusR, V, 3-9.

796. Mousset, Albert. The World of the Slavs. New York: Praeger, 1951, 204 pp. [Mostly ideological history of Panslavism].

797. Petrovich, Michael B., "Juraj Krizanic: A Precursor of Pan-Slavism." ASEER, VI, xviii-xix, 75-92.

798. _____. "L'udovit Stur and Russian Panslavism." JCEA, XII, 1-19.

799. Pundeff, Marin, "Pan-Slavism: From Japan to the Adriatic." Com, XVI, 278-280.

800. Riasanovsky, Nicholas V. Russia and the West in the Teaching of the Slavophiles. (Harvard University. Harvard Hist. Studies.) Cambridge: Harvard University Press, 1952, 244 pp.

801. Roucek, Joseph S., "Soviet Nationality Policy: Pan-Slavism as an Ideological Weapon." PoC, III, iv, 20-28.

802. Thomson, S. Harrison, "A Century of a Phantom Panslavism and the Western Slavs." JCEA, XI, 57-77.

MINORITIES

803. Carey, Jane Perry Clark, "Displaced Populations in Europe in 1944 with Particular Reference to Germany." DSB, XII, 491-500.

804. Celovsky, Boris, "The Transferred Sudeten-Germans and Their Political Activity." JCEA, XVII, 127-149.

805. Central and Eastern European Conferences. Human

Freedom is Being Crushed—The Story of Deportations Behind the Iron Curtain. Washington, D.C.: 1951.

806. Committee Against Mass Expulsion. Men Without Rights of Man: A Report on the Expulsion and Extermination of German Speaking Minority Groups in the Balkans and Prewar Poland. Preface signed by Roger Baldwin and others. New York: Committee Against Mass Expulsion, n.d., 32 pp.

807. de Azcarate y Florez, Pablo. League of Nations and National Minorities. Washington, D.C.: Carnegie Endowment for International Peace, 1945, 216 pp.

808. Fay, Sidney B., "Displaced Persons in Europe." CH, X, 199-205.

809. _____, "Europe's Expellees." CH, XII, 321-328.

810. Fetter, Joseph. Sudetens—A Moral Question. New York: The William-Frederick Press, Pamphlet Distributing Co., 1947, 59 pp.

811. Ginsburg, George, "The Soviet Union and the Problem of Refugees and Displaced Persons: 1917-1956." AJIL, LI, 325-361.

812. Halecki, Oscar, "Nationalism in East Central Europe." JIA, XI, i, 31-36.

813. Hungarian National Council. Genocide by Deportation. New York: Hungarian National Council, 1951, 131 pp.

814. Janowski, Oscar I. Nationalities and National Minorities: With Special Reference to East-Central Europe. Foreword by James T. Shotwell. New York: Macmillan, 1945.

815. Kertesz, Stephen, "The Expulsion of the Germans from Hungary; A Study in Postwar Diplomacy." RPol, XV, 179-208.

816. Kostanick, Huey Louis. Turkish Resettlement of Bulgarian Turks, 1950-1953. (California University Publications in Geography, Vol. VIII, No. 2.) Berkeley: University of California Press, 1957, 163 pp.

817. Mosely, Philip E. "Soviet Policy and Nationality Conflicts in East Central Europe." Waldemar Gurian, Ed., The Soviet Union: Background, Ideology, Reality, pp. 67-84.

818. Paikert, G. C., "Hungary's National Minority Policies, 1920-1945." ASEER, XII, 201-218.

819. Parker, Ralph, "Czechs and Sudetens." Nation, CLXI, 307-308.

820. Rothfels, Hans, "Frontiers and Mass Migrations in Eastern Central Europe." RPol, VIII, 37-67.

821. Roucek, Joseph S., "Yugoslavia's Minorities." WAI, XIX, 292-310.

822. Schechtman, Joseph B., "Compulsory Transfer of the Turkish Minority From Bulgaria." JCEA, XII, 154-169.

823. _____. European Population Transfers, 1939-1945. New York: Oxford University Press, 1946, 532 pp.

824. _____, "Postwar Population Transfers in Europe: A Survey." RPol, XV, 151-178.

825. Smal-Stocki, Roman. Slavs and Teutons: The Oldest Germanic-Slavic Relations. Pref. Alfred Senn. Milwaukee, Wisconsin: Bruce Publishing Co., 1950, 108 pp.

826. Taubert, Helen, and Margaret Brooke, trs. Documents of Humanity During the Mass Expulsions. New York: Harper, 1954. [Originally published as Dokumente der Menschlichkeit. Goettingen: Goettinger Arbeitskreis, 1950.]

827. Thomson, S. Harrison. "The Conflict of Slav and German." Leonid I. Strakhovsky, Ed., Handbook of Slavic Studies, pp. 140-176.

828. Wiskemann, Elizabeth. Germany's Eastern Neighbors: Problems Relating to the Oder-Neisse Line and the Czech Frontier Regions. New York: Oxford University Press, 1956, 309 pp.

REFUGEES

829. Anon., "The Bakers' Dozen." NBIC, V, i, 39-41.

830. _____, "The Baltic University; Three Nations in Quest of Spiritual Freedom." BR, II, iii, 34-38.

831. _____, "Emigre Go Home." NBIC, IV, x, 3-13.

832. _____, "Flight to Freedom; Five Escaped Fishermen Tell of Life in Soviet Latvia." NBIC, I, viii, 30-33.

833. Assembly of Captive European Nations. Official Report of Debates, Second Session, 26th—29th meetings of the Plenary Assembly, December 13-December 14, 1955. Held at Carnegie Endowment International Center, United Nations

Plaza, New York City. New York: The Assembly, 1955, 134 pp.

834. _____. Organization, Resolutions, Reports, Second Session, September 1955–November 1956. (Publication No. 16.) New York: The Assembly, 1957, 221 pp.

835. Chalupa, V. Possibilities of Dissolving the Soviet Sphere of Power. (Czechoslovak Foreign Institute in Exile. Studies.) Chicago: The Author, 1956, 22 pp.

836. Gross, Feliks, "Political Emigration from Iron Curtain Countries." AAPSS, CCLXXI, 175-184.

837. Kaasik, N., "The Baltic Refugees in Sweden; A Successful Experiment." BR, II, i, 55-61.

838. _____, "The Legal Status of Baltic Refugees." BR, I, 21-26.

839. Kolaja, Jiri, "A Sociological Note on the Czechoslovak Anti-Communist Refugee." AJS, LVIII, 289-291.

840. Lingis, Juozas, "The Lithuanian Emigrant Press." BR, I, 299-303.

841. Nagorski, Zygmunt, Jr., "Liberation Movements in Exile." JCEA, X, 129-144.

842. Pirinsky, George. Slavic Americans in the Fight for Victory and Peace. New York: American Slav Congress, 1946, 61 pp.

843. Proudfoot, Malcolm Jarvis. European Refugees: 1939-52. A Study in Forced Population Movement. (Northwestern University Studies: Social Science Series, No. 10.) Evanston, Illinois: Northwestern University Press, 1956, 542 pp.

844. Radio Free Europe. Information and Reference Department. The Experience of a Polish Youth in Communist Prisons. (Special Report, No. 29.) New York: Free Europe Committee, 1952, 6 pp.

845. Sheldon, R. C., and Dutkowski, J., "Are Soviet Satellite Refugee Interviews Projectable?" POQ, XVI, 579-594.

846. Sturm, Rudolf, "Operation Return." CEF, IV, i, 8-14.

847. Valkenier, Elizabeth, "Eastern European Refugees and Exiles." JIA, XI, i, 37-47.

848. Veedam, Voldemar, and Carl B. Wall. Sailing to Freedom. New York: The Thomas Y. Crowell Co., 1952.

849. Vernant, Jacques. The Refugee in the Postwar World. New Haven: Yale University Press, 1953, 827 pp.

850. Wittlin, Joseph, "Sorrow and Grandeur of Exile." PolR, II, ii-iii, 99-111.

851. Zubrzycki, Jerzy. Polish Immigrants in Britain: A Study of Adjustment. Prefaces by Rene Clemens and Florian Znaniecki. (Studies in Social Life, 3.) New York: Heinman, 1956, 220 pp.

THE JEWS AND ANTI-SEMITISM

852. Alexander, Mark, "Israel's Left Reels to the Shock of 'Prague.'" Com, XV, 379-389.

853. Berg, Mary. Warsaw Ghetto: A Diary. Tr. Norbert Gutermann and Sylvia Glass. Ed. S. L. Schneiderman. New York: L. B. Fischer, 1945, 253 pp.

854. Bienenstok, Theodore, "Anti-authoritarian Attitudes in the Eastern European 'Shtetel' Community." AJS, LVII, 150-158.

855. _____. "Social Life and Authority in the East European Jewish Shtetel Community." SJA, VI, 238-254.

856. Blit, Lucjan, "Poland and the Jewish Remnant; End of a Long History?" Com, XXIII, 215-221.

857. Borkenau, Franz, "Was Malenkov Behind the Anti-Semitic Plot?" Com, XV, 438-446.

858. Cahnman, Werner J., "Socio-Economic Causes of Anti-semitism." SocP, V, 21-29.

859. Cohen, Elliot E., ed. New Red Anti-Semitism; A Symposium. Boston: Beacon Press, 1953, 58 pp. [A Beacon-Commentary study.]

860. Czechoslovak Jewish Representative Committee. Czechoslovakia and the Czechoslovak Jews: Addresses Delivered at the Meeting of the [Committee] Affiliated with the World Jewish Congress, Nov. 18, 1944, at the Community Center, New York. New York: Czechoslovak Jewish Representative Committee, 1945, 32 pp.

861. Diamond, Stanley, "Kibbutz and Shtetel: The History of an Idea." SocP, V, 71-99.

862. Duker, Abraham Gordon, "The Polish 'Great Emigration' and the Jew: Studies in Political and Cultural History." DA, XVI, 740.

863. Fabian, Bela. "Hungary's Jewry Faces Liquidation." Elliot Cohen, Ed., New Red Anti-Semitism: A Symposium, pp. 32-37.

864. Friedman, Philip, Aleksander Hertz, and Joseph L. Lichten, eds. Jacob Shatsky in Memoriam. New York: Club of Polish Jews, 1957, pp. 71, 56, ports.

865. _____. Martyrs and Fighters: The Epic of the Warsaw Ghetto. (Instituted and sponsored by the Club of Polish Jews, New York.) New York: Praeger, 1954, 325 pp.

866. _____. Polish Jewish Historiography between the Two Wars (1918-1939). New York: Conference of Jewish Relations, 1949.

867. Hannover, Nathan Nata. Abyss of Despair (Yeven Melzulah): The Famous 17th Century Chronicle Depicting Jewish Life in Russia and Poland During the Chmielnicki Massacres of 1648-1649. Tr. from the Hebrew by Abrahm Mesch. Introd. biographical sketch of the author and explanatory notes by the translator. Pref. by Soloman Grayzel. New York: Bloch Publishing Co., 1950, 128 pp.

868. Jewish Labor Committee. Jews Behind the Iron Curtain: A Survey of the Condition of Jews in Countries Behind the Iron Curtain According to Latest Information. Issued in connection with its [Jewish Labor Committee] national convention in Atlantic City, New Jersey, Feb. 24-27, 1949. Prepared by Emmanuel Patt. New York: Jewish Labor Committee, 1949, 56 pp.

869. Kann, Robert A. German-Speaking Jewry during Austria-Hungary's Constitutional Era (1867-1918). New York: Conference on Jewish Relations, 1948, 256 pp.

870. Kutas, E. R., "Judaism, Zionism, and Anti-Semitism in Hungary." JCEA, VIII, 377-389.

871. Landes, Ruth, and Mark Zborowski, "Hypotheses Concerning the Eastern European Jewish Family." Psychiatry, XIII, 447-464.

872. Laqueur, W. Z., "The Kastner Case; Aftermath of the Catastrophe." Com, XX, 500-511.

873. Lestchinsky, Jacob. Economic Struggle of the Jews in Independent Lithuania. New York: Conference on Jewish Relations, 1946.

874. Meyer, Peter, "The Jewish Purge in the Satellite Countries." Com, XIV, 212-218.

875. _____. "The Jewish Purge in the Satellite Countries." Elliot Cohen, Ed., New Red Anti-Semitism: A Symposium, pp. 25-31.

876. _____. "Soviet-Anti-Semitism in High Gear." Elliot Cohen, Ed., New Red Anti-Semitism: A Symposium, pp. 19-24.

877. _____, "Stalin Follows in Hitler's Footsteps." Com, XV, 1-18.

878. _____. "Stalin Follows in Hitler's Footsteps." Elliot Cohen, Ed., New Red Anti-Semitism: A Symposium, pp. 1-18.

879. _____, Bernard D. Weinryb, Eugene Dushinsky, and Nicolas Sylvain. The Jews in the Soviet Satellites. Syracuse, New York: Syracuse University Press, 1953.

880. Milosz, Czeslaw, "Anti-Semitism in Poland." PoC, VI, iii, 35-40.

881. Niemira, Piotr, "The Situation of the Jews in Poland." JCEA, XI, 172-183.

882. Pat, Jacob. Ashes and Fire. Tr. by Leo Steinberg. New York: International Universities Press, 1948.

883. Reich, Nathan, "Jewish Life in the Russian Satellites." Com, VII, 328-334.

884. Rosenthal, Celia Stopnicka, "Deviation and Social Change in the Jewish Community of a Small Polish Town." AJS, LX, 177-181.

885. _____, "How the Polish Jew Saw His World: A Study of a Small-Town Community Before 1939." Com, XVIII, 70-75.

886. _____, "Social Stratification of the Jewish Community in a Small Polish Town." AJS, LIX, 1-10.

887. Schneiderman, Samuel Leob. Between Fear and Hope. Tr. Norbert Guterman. New York: Arco Publishing Co., 1948, 316 pp.

888. Schuster, Zachariah, "Between the Millstones in Poland: The Story Behind the Mass Flight of Polish Jewry." Com, II, 107-115.

889. Schwarz, Solomon M. "The New Anti-Semitism of the Soviet Union." Elliot Cohen, Ed., New Red Anti-Semitism: A Symposium, pp. 38-48.

890. Sterling, Claire, "Anti-Semitism in the Satellites: The Wave of Fear Advances." Rept, VIII, viii, 17-20.

891. Tenenbaum, Joseph Leib. In Search of a Lost People—The Old and the New Poland. New York: Beechhurst Press, 1948, 312 pp. [Jews and W. W. II]

892. _____. Underground: The Story of a People. New York: Philosophical Library, 1952, 532 pp. [Polish Jewry]

893. Vishniac, Roman. Polish Jews: A Pictoral Record. Introd. essay by Abraham Joshua Heschel. New York: Schocken Books Inc., 1947.

894. Weinryb, Bernar D., "Jews in Central Europe." JCEA, VI, 43-77.

895. Zborowski, Mark, and Elizabeth Herzog. Life Is With People: The Jewish Little Town of Eastern Europe. New York: International Universities Press, 1952, 456 pp.

II. THE BALKANS

GENERAL

896. Anon., "Bulgaria, Hungary, and Rumania Accused of Violating Fundamental Freedoms." DSB, XX, 450-453.

897. _____, "The Balkan Observers: A Mission Completed." UNR, I, ii, 17-25.

898. Bishop, Robert, and E. S. Crayfield. Russia Astride the Balkans. New York: Medill McBride Co., 1948.

899. Cohen, Benjamin V., "Violations of Human Rights in the Balkans." DSB, XXIII, 666-670.

900. _____, and Charles Fahy, "The Balkan and Korean Problems." DSB, XXI, 691-695.

901. del Vayo, J. Alvarez, "Balkan Triangle." Nation, CLXXV, 224.

902. Ehrenburg, Ilya G. European Crossroad. New York: Alfred A. Knopf, 1947.

903. Hadsel, Winifred N., "Will Security Council Act on Report of Balkan Commission." FPB, XXVI, xxxiii, 3-4.

904. Kendrick, Alexander, "Soviet 'Sweet Talk' in the Balkans." NR, CXXXI, ix, 12-14.

905. King, Francis, "Balkan Backwater." Rept, V, i, 17-20.

906. King, William B., and Frank O'Brien. The Balkans: Frontier of Two Worlds. New York: Alfred A. Knopf, 1947, 278 pp.

907. Lee, Dwight E. "The Liberation of the Balkan Slavs." Leonid I. Strakhovsky, Ed., Handbook of Slavic Studies, pp. 271-292.

908. Newman, Bernard. Balkan Background. New York: Macmillan, 1945, 354 pp.

909. Poulos, Constantine, "Cold War: No One is Neutral in The Balkans." NR, CXVII, xi, 14-15.

910. Radovich, Eugene. Land of Destiny: A Tale from the Balkans. New York: Philosophical Library, 1951, 108 pp.

911. Roucek, Joseph S., "Rumania, Albania, and Bulgaria, At the End of the Beginning." WAI, XV, 88-101.

912. Royal Institute of International Affairs. Information Department. Balkans, Together with Hungary. Rev. ed. New York: Royal Institute of International Affairs, 1945.

913. United Nations. General Assembly. Interim Report of the U.N. Special Committee on the Balkans, December 31, 1947. U.N. Doc. A/521, January 9, 1948.

914. _____. General Assembly. Report of the Special Committee on the Balkans. U.N. Doc. A/574, June 1948 (printed as Supplement 8, General Assembly Official Records, Third Session); and Supplementary Report for the Period 17 June to 10 September 1948. U.N. Doc. A/644, September 16, 1948 (printed as Supplement 8A, General Assembly Official Records, Third Session).

915. _____. General Assembly (4th Session). Report of the U.N. Special Committee on the Balkans. U.N. Doc. A/935, August 1949 (printed as Supplement 8, General Assembly Official Records, Fourth Session).

916. Vucinich, Wayne S., "Sovietization in the Balkans." CH, XXVI, 339-346.

917. Werth, Alexander, "The Cominform's Plans for the Balkans." Nation, CLXXVIII, 101-102, 127-128.

GEOGRAPHY

918. Roucek, Joseph S. Geopolitics of the Balkans. Hofstra College, Hempstead, New York: The Author, 1947.

919. _____, "The Geopolitics of the Balkans." WAI, XV, 419-440.

HISTORY

920. Black, Cyril E. "The Balkan Slavs in the Middle Ages." Leonid I. Strakhovsky, Ed., Handbook of Slavic Studies, pp. 180-198.

921. Fisher, Sydney N., "Ottoman Feudalism and Its Influence Upon the Balkans." Hist, XV, i, 3-22.

922. Marcovitch, Lazare, "Lord Curzon and Pashitch—

Light on Jugoslavia, Turkey and Greece in 1922." JCEA, XIII, 329-337.

923. Mylonas, George E. The Balkan States: An Introduction to Their History. 2nd ed. Washington, D.C.: American Council on Foreign Affairs, 1947, 239 pp.

924. _____, "An Introduction to the History of the Southern Balkan States." Athene, VI, ii, 21-29, iv, 25-31.

925. Shotwell, James T. A Balkan Mission. New York: Columbia University Press, 1949, 180 pp.

926. Stavrianos, L. S., "Antecedents to the Balkan Revolutions of the Nineteenth Century." JMH, XXIX, 335-348.

927. Wolff, Robert Lee. The Balkans in Our Time. Cambridge, Massachusetts: Harvard University Press, 1956, 618 pp.

928. Wren, Melvin C., "Pobedonostsev and Russian Influence in the Balkans, 1881-1888." JMH, XIX, 130-141.

GOVERNMENT AND POLITICS

929. Lukacs, John A., "Communist Tactics in Balkan Government." Thought, XXII, 219-244.

930. Roucek, Joseph S. Balkan Politics. Stanford: Stanford University Press, 1948, 298 pp.

INTERNATIONAL AFFAIRS

931. Braun, Charlotte E., "The Balkan States at London." CH, IX, 447-451.

932. Ethridge, M., and Cyril E. Black. "Negotiating on the Balkans, 1945-47." Raymond Dennett and Joseph E. Johnson, Eds., Negotiating With the Russians, pp. 171-206.

933. Pundeff, Marin, "The Balkan Entente Treaties." AJIL, XLVIII, 630-635.

934. Roucek, Joseph S., "The Bulgarian, Roumanian and Hungarian Peace Treaties." AAAPSS, CCLVII, 97-105.

935. Xydis, Stephen G., "The Secret Anglo-Soviet Agreement on the Balkans of October 8, 1944." JCEA, XV, 248-271.

THE ECONOMY

936. Stoianovich, Traian, "Land Tenure and Related Sectors of the Balkan Economy, 1600-1800." JEH, XIII, 398-411.

937. United States. War Department. Coal Mining Industries of the Balkan States. (Pamphlet No. 31-207.) Washington, D.C.: United States Government Printing Office, 1945.

LITERATURE

938. Manning, Clarence A. "The Literature of the Balkan Slavs." Leonid I. Strakhovsky, Ed., Handbook of Slavic Studies, pp. 512-531.

PHILOSOPHY AND RELIGION

939. Obolensky, Dmitri. The Bogomils: A Study in Balkan Neo-Manichaeism. New York: Cambridge University Press, 1948, 317 pp.

SOCIOLOGY

940. Mosely, Philip E. The Distribution of the Zadruga Within South-Eastern Europe. Reprint from the Joshua Starr Memorial Volume. (Jewish Social Studies, Publications, Vol. V.) New York: Conference on Jewish Relations, 1953, pp. 219-230.

941. Peselj, Branko M., "Peasant Movements in Southeastern Europe." (Doctoral Dissertation, Georgetown University, 1950.)

942. Sanders, Irwin Taylor. Balkan Village. Lexington: University of Kentucky Press, 1949, 291 pp. [Sociological analysis of life in a Bulgarian Village]

943. Thurner, Majda, "A Survey of Balkan Houses and Farm Buildings." KASP, No. 14, pp. 19-92.

944. Tomasic, Dinko, "The Family in the Balkans." MFL, XVI, 301-307.

945. _____, "Personality Development of the Dinaric Warriors." Psychiatry, VIII, 449-493.

946. _____, "The Structure of Balkan Society." AJS, LII, i, 132-140.

III. THE BALTIC STATES

GENERAL

947. Augustinas, V. Our Country Lithuania. New York: Išleido Jungtinese Amerikos Valstybese Leidykla Vaga, 1951, 114 pp.

948. Baltramoitis, Casimer V., ed. Lithuanian Affairs: An Index to the N.Y. Times on Subjects Pertaining to Lithuania and Lithuanians. (Mimeographed.) Elizabeth, New Jersey: The Author, 1945, 136 pp.

949. Bilmanis, Alfred. Baltic Essays. Washington, D.C.: Latvian Legation, 1945, 268 pp.

950. _____, ed. Dictionary of Events in Latvia. Washington, D.C.: The Latvian Legation, 1946, 47 pp.

951. _____. Latvia As An Independent State. Washington, D.C.: Latvian Legation, 1947, 405 pp. [Revised edition of a handbook on Latvia]

952. _____, "The Legend of the Baltic Barrier States." JCEA, VI, 126-146.

953. Dauzvardis, Josephine J., ed. Popular Lithuanian Recipes. Chicago: Lithuanian Catholic Press Society, 1955, 120 pp.

954. Jackson, John Hampden. Estonia. New York: Macmillan, 1949. [2nd ed. with a postscript on the years 1940-1947.]

955. Kaelas, A., "What Did Estonian Social Policy Achieve in Twenty Odd Years?" BR, I, 94-99.

956. Manning, Clarence A. The Forgotten Republics. New York: Philosophical Library, 1952.

957. Purre, Arnold, "Why the Baltic Soldiers Fought the Soviets." BR, II, ii, 23-30.

958. Rank, Gustav, "The Baltic Cultural Area." BR, I, 161-170.

959. Raud, Villibald. Estonia: A Reference Book. New York: Nordic Press, 1953, 158 pp.

960. Schwabe, Arvid. "Baltic States." Stephen D. Kertesz, Ed., The Fate of East Central Europe, pp. 103-128.

961. Swettenham, John Alexander. Tragedy of the Baltic States: A Report Compiled from Official Documents and Eyewitnesses Reports. New York: Praeger, 1955, 216 pp.

GEOGRAPHY AND POPULATION

962. Andersons, Edgars. Cross Road Country: Latvia. Waverly, Iowa: Latvju Gramata, 1953, 386 pp. [Articles on the geography, people, culture, and history of Latvia]

963. Balodis, Francis, "Latvia and the Latvians." JCEA, VI, 241-282.

964. Parts, Anton, "Baltic States: Brief Survey of Their Landscape, Economy, Population, and Settlement." JG, LVI, 305-314.

965. Salys, A. Gazetteer to the Map of Lithuania. South Boston, Massachusetts: Lithuanian Encyclopedia, 1956.

966. Straubergs, K., "The Latvian People." BR, I, 14-17.

967. Van Cleef, Eugene, "East Baltic Ports and Boundaries: With Special Reference to Konigsberg." GR, XXXV, 257-272.

HISTORY

968. Backus, Oswald Prentiss. Motives of West Russian Nobles in Deserting Lithuania for Moscow, 1377-1514. Lawrence: University of Kansas Press, 1957, 174 pp.

969. Bilmanis, Alfred. A History of Latvia. Princeton, New Jersey: Princeton University Press, 1951, 441 pp.

970. _____, "Latvia's Contribution to Historical Science." ASEER, IV, 163-173.

971. _____, "The Problem of the Baltic in Historical Perspective." BR, II, ii, 14-22.

972. _____, "The Struggle for the Domination of the Baltic." JCEA, V, 119-143.

973. Chase, Thomas G. The Story of Lithuania. Foreword by William H. Chamberlin. New York: Stratford House, 1946, 392 pp.

974. Harrison, Ernst John. Lithuania's Fight for Freedom. New York: Lithuanian American Information Center, 1945, 95 pp.

975. Jurgela, Constantine Rudyard. History of the Lithuanian Nation. Introd. Clarence Augustus Manning. New York: Lithuanian American Information Center, 1948, 544 pp.

976. _____, Kazyz Gecys, and Simas Suziedelis. Lithuania in a Twin Teutonic Clutch: A Historical Review of German-Lithuanian Relations. New York: Lithuanian American Information Center, 1945, 112 pp.

977. Kirchner, Walther. The Rise of the Baltic Question. (Delaware. University Monograph Series, No. 3.) Newark: University of Delaware Press, 1954, 283 pp.

978. Klimas, Petras. Ghillebert de Lannoy in Medieval Lithuania. New York: The Lithuanian American Information Center, 1945.

979. Maciuika, Benedict V. Lithuania in the Last 30 Years. New Haven: Human Relations Area Files, 1955, 411 pp.

980. Matthews, W. K., "Medieval Baltic Tribes." ASEER, VIII, 126-136.

981. Nodel, Emanual, "Rise and Development of Estonian National Consciousness, 1700-1905." DA, XVI, 2144.

982. Okinshevych, Lev. The Law of the Grand Duchy of Lithuania: Background and Bibliography. (East Europe Fund, Mineograph Series No. 32.) New York: Research Program on the U.S.S.R., 1953, 53 pp.

983. Page, Stanley W., "Social and National Currents in Latvia, 1860-1917." ASEER, VIII, 25-36.

984. Pick, F. W., "1939: The Evidence Re-Examined." BR, I, 154-160.

985. Survel, Jaak, "Misconceptions in the History of the Baltic Peoples." BR, I, 56-64.

GOVERNMENT AND POLITICS

986. Venster, Steven, "Bolshevik Elections in Lithuania." BR, II, ii, 52-60.

LAW

987. Bilmanis, Alfred. Law and Courts in Latvia. Washington, D.C.: Latvian Legation, 1946, 82 pp.

988. Prunskis, Joseph. Comparative Law, Ecclesiastical and Civil, in Lithuanian Concordat. (Canon Law Studies, No. 222.) Washington: Catholic University of America, 1945, 161 pp.

INTERNATIONAL AFFAIRS

989. Bilmanis, Alfred. Baltic States and World Security Organization. Washington, D.C.: The Latvian Legation, 1945, 67 pp.

990. _____, "Collective Security and the Baltic States." BR, I, 51-55.

991. Chevrier, Bruno, "The International Status of the Baltic States." BR, I, 270-276.

992. Graham, Malbone W., "What Does Non-Recognition Mean?" BR, I, 171-174.

993. Horm, Avro, "Lessons of Two Dictatorships." BR, I, 363-375.

994. Manning, Clarence A., "The Baltic States as the Tragedy of Western Ignorance." BR, I, 267-269.

995. Pick, F. W., "Baltic Question and Moral Condition of Peace." BR, I, 27-31.

996. _____, "Britain and the Baltic." BR, II, i, 12-17.

997. Sidzikauskas, Vaclovas, "Baltic States and The European Federation." CEF, II, xii, 3-4.

998. Wuorinen, John H., "Russia, Scandinavia and the Baltic States." CH, XXVIII, 70-74.

SOVIET RULE

999. Berzinsh, Alfreds. I Saw Vishinsky Bolshevize Latvia. Washington, D.C.: The Latvian Legation, 1946, 47 pp.

1000. Bilmanis, Alfred. Latvia Between the Anvil and the Hammer. Washington, D.C.: Latvian Legation, 1945, 64 pp.

1001. _____, "Relations Between Latvia and Soviet-Russia in the Light of International Law." BR, I, 277-281.

1002. Cakste, Mintauts, "Latvia and the Soviet Union." JCEA, IX, 32-60, 173-211.

1003. _____, "Soviet Aggression and Its Historical and Ideological Background." BR, II, iii, 9-17.

1004. _____, "Two Aggressions Compared: The Russo-German Deal of 1939." BR, II, ii, 31-39.

1005. Garbuny, Siegfried, "Russia's Claim to East Prussia." CH, XII, 339-344.

1006. Hessler, William H., "The Baltic: Russian Bottle with a Swedish Cork." Rept, VII, iv, 21-24.

1007. Kaasik, N., "The Soviet Ultimatum to Estonia." BR, I, 211-213.

1008. Kajeckas, J., "The Lithuanian Annexation." BR, I, 214-216.

1009. Kalme, Albert. Total Terror: An Expose of Genocide in the Baltics. New York: Appleton-Century-Crofts, 1951, 310 pp.

1010. Matusevicius, K., "Russia's Westward Drive; The Destruction of Lithuania Minor." BR, II, i, 46-54.

1011. Oras, Ants, "Deportations in Estonia." BR, II, i, 18-25.

1012. _____, "Soviet Policy in Estonia." JCEA, VIII, 366-376.

1013. Page, Stanley W., "Lenin, The National Question and the Baltic States, 1917-1919." ASEER, VII, 15-31.

1014. Vitols, Hugo, "Annexation of Latvia by the Soviet Union and the International Law." BR, I, 211-212.

THE ECONOMY

1015. Anon., "Economic Report: The Baltics." NBIC, III, x, 3-15; xi, 31-45.

1016. Ceichners, Alfred, "Latvian and Soviet Russian State Economy." JCEA, VII, 374-393.

1017. Ginters, Valdis, "Baltic Amber." BR, I, 72-76.

1018. Jaska, E., "The Results of Collectivization of Estonian Agriculture." LE, XXVIII, 212-217.

1019. Krumin, Peter O. Review of the Estonian Oil Shale Industry, with a Brief Account of Oil Shale Development in the United States. (Ohio State University Studies, Engineering Series, Vol. XVIII, No. 6, November, 1949. Engineering Experiment Station Circular No. 50.) Columbus: Ohio State University, 1949, 126 pp.

1020. Raud, Villibald. Collectivisation of Agriculture in Estonia: A Pattern for Central Europe and Other Communist-Dominated Countries. (Lecture and Debate at the Meeting of the Association of Central European Economists on the 15th Feb., 1951.) Reprinted from the Eastern Quarterly, Vol. IV, No. 2, April, 1951.

1021. Ronimois, H., "The Baltic Trade of the Soviet Union." ASEER, IV, x-xi, 174-178.

1022. _____, "Soviet Baltic Trade: Expectations and Probabilities." BR, I, 77-81.

1023. Zilinskas, Vl., "Independent Lithuania's Economic Progress." BR, I, 175-178.

LANGUAGES AND LITERATURES

1024. Judas, Elizabeth. "Estonian Literature." Horatio Smith, Ed., <u>Columbia Dictionary of Modern European Literature</u>, pp. 252-253.

1025. Matthews, William K., ed. Anthology of Modern Estonian Poetry. Gainesville: University of Florida Press, 1953, 161 pp.

1026. _____, "Nationality and Language in the East Baltic Area." ASEER, VI, xvi-xvii, 62-78.

1027. Maurina, Zenta, et al., "Literatures of the Baltic Peoples." BA, XXIX, 134-148.

1028. Oinas, Felix J., "Russian Calques in the Balto-Finnic Languages." ISS, I, 225-240.

1029. Oras, Ants, "A Note on Estonian Poetry." BR, II, -ii, 40-47.

1030. Pranspill, Andres, ed. and tr. Estonian Anthology: Intimate Stories of Life, Love, Labor and War of the Estonian

People. With some of the editor's own writings. Ms. ed. by Milton Millhauser. Milford, Connecticut: A. Pranspill, 1956.

1031. Roditi, Edouard, "Esthonian Letters Today." BA, XXVI, 141-143.

1032. Saagpakk, Paul F. An Estonian-English Dictionary. Introd. Johannes Aavik. New York: Nordic Press, 1955.

1033. Schmalstieg, William R., "Criteria for the Determination of Slavic Borrowings in Lithuanian." DA, XV, 1680. (Pennsylvania).

1034. Senn, Alfred, "Christmas Eve in Lithuania." ASEER, V, xiv-xv, 132-134.

1035. _____. "Lettish Literature." Horatio Smith, Ed., Columbia Dictionary of Modern European Literature, pp. 479-480.

1036. _____. "Lithuanian Literature." Horatio Smith, Ed., Columbia Dictionary of Modern European Literature, pp. 485-488.

1037. _____, "Lithuanian Surnames." ASEER, IV, viii-ix, 127-137.

1038. _____. "Vincent Kreve and Lithuanian Folklore." Morris Halle, et al., comp., For Roman Jakobson, pp. 444-448.

1039. Turkina, E. Lettish-English Dictionary. New York: Hafner Publishing Co., 1948, 392 pp.

1040. Ziverts, Martin, "Tragedy of the Latvian Theatre." BR, I, 82-86.

THE ARTS

1041. Laid, Ferik, "The Origin and Age of the Estonian Culture." BR, I, 18-20.

1042. Veiler, Rein, "The Cultural Standard of the Baltic States." BR, I, 282-287.

EDUCATION

1043. Martinoff, G., "The Fate of the University of Tartu." BR, I, 90-93.

1044. Pick, F. W., "Tartu, the History of an Estonian University." ASEER, V, xiv-xv, 150-161.

1045. Tallgren, A., "The University of Tartu—Centre of National Education." BR, I, 87-89.

PHILOSOPHY AND RELIGION

1046. Bilmanis, Alfred. The Church in Latvia. New York: Drauga Vests, 1945, 35 pp.

1047. Bourgeois, Charles. Priest in Russia and the Baltic. Introd. Sir David Kelly. Tr. from the French by the Earl of Wicklow. Fresno, California: Academy Library Guild, 1954, 146 pp.

1048. Free Europe Committee. Research and Publications Service. Lithuanian, Latvian and Estonian Sections. Religious Persecution in the Baltic Countries, 1940-1952. New York: National Committee for a Free Europe, 1952, 26 pp.

1049. Sirvaitis, Casimir Peter. Religious Folkways in Lithuania and Their Conservation among the Lithuanian Immigrants in the United States. Washington: Catholic University of America Press, 1952, 56 pp. [An abstract of a thesis]

SOCIOLOGY

1050. Lingis, Juozas, "The National Character of Lithuanian People." BR, I, 3-13.

IV. SOME DISPUTED AREAS

BUKOVINA

1051. Fedynskyj, Jurij, "Sovietization of an Occupied Area through the Medium of the Courts (Northern Bukovina)." ASEER, XII, 44-56.

1052. Free Europe Committee. Romanian Section. Research and Publications Service. Historical Background of the Bessarabian Question with an Appendix on the Legal Status of Bessarabia and Northern Bukovina. New York: Free Europe Committee, 1951, 9 pp.

1053. Valeanu, Adrian, "The Question of Bukovina—Then and Now." JCEA, IV, 372-394.

CARPATHO-UKRAINE

1054. Manning Clarence A., "The Linguistic Question in Carpatho-Ukraine." UQ, X, 247-251.

1055. Markus, Vasyl, "Carpatho-Ukraine Under Hungarian Occupation (1939-1944)." UQ, X, 252-256.

1056. Nemec, Frantisek, and Vladimir Moudry. Soviet Seizure of Subcarpathian Ruthenia. Toronto: W. B. Anderson, 1955, 375 pp.

1057. Neuman, Dov, "Five Hucul Healing Incantations." ISS, I, 191-207.

1058. Perenyi, Eleanor (Stone), baroness. More Was Lost. Boston: Little, Brown and Co., 1946, 278 pp. [Social life and customs in Ruthenia]

1059. Revay, Julian, "The March to Liberation of Carpatho-Ukraine." UQ, X, 227-234.

1060. Roucek, Joseph S., "Ruthenia: Football of International Politics." WAI, XIX, 65-75.

1061. Shandor, Vincent, "Carpatho-Ukraine in the International Bargaining of 1918-1939." UQ, X, 235-246.

1062. Stefan, Augustin, "Myths About Carpatho-Ukraine." UQ, X, 219-226.

MACEDONIA

1063. Anastasoff, Christ, ed. Case for an Autonomous Macedonia: A Symposium. (Published by the Central Committee of the Macedonian Political Organization of the United States and Canada.) St. Louis: The Editor, 1945, 206 pp.

1064. Barker, Elizabeth. Macedonia: Its Place in Balkan Power Politics. New York: Royal Institute of International Affairs, 1950, 129 pp.

1065. Butler, Allan C., "Journey in Macedonia." Rept, V, ii, 24-26.

1066. Caruthers, Osgood, "Macedonia." Rept, II, iii, 17-19.

1067. The Cyprus Problem and Macedonia: An Expose of Greece's Oppression of her Ethnic Minorities. Indianapolis: Central Committee of Macedonian Political Organization, n.d., 14 pp.

1068. Drohan, Leonard. Come With Me to Macedonia. New York: Alfred A. Knopf, 1957.

1069. Ivic, Pavle, "On the Present State of the Study of Standard Macedonian." Word, IX, 325-338.

1070. Keramopoulos, Antonios D. Origin of the Macedonians. Detroit: Pan-Macedonian Hellenic Association, 1946, 36 pp.

1071. Kostanick, Huey Louis, "Political Geography of Macedonia." AAGA, XLII, 107-108.

1072. Lunt, Horace, "A Survey of Macedonian Literature." HSS, I, 363-395.

1073. Mikhailov, Ivan (Macedonicus, pseud.). Macedonia: A Switzerland of the Balkans. Tr. by Christ Anastasoff. Introd. John Bakeless. St. Louis: Pearlstone Publishing Co., 1950.

1074. _____. Stalin and the Macedonian Question. Tr. and ed. Christ Anastasoff. St. Louis: Pearlstone Publishing Co., 1948, 92 pp.

1075. Roucek, Joseph S., "The Geopolitical Implications of the Eternal Macedonian Problem." WAI, XXI, 95-107.

1076. Tozis, John, "Greece Begins at Macedonia." Athene, IX, iv, 22-24; 42.

NORTHERN EPIRUS

1077. Philon, Philon Alexander. The Question of Northern Epirus, Its Historical and Diplomatic Background. Washington, D.C.: Greek Government Office of Information, 1945, 33 pp.

1078. Shepis, P. G., "The Persecution of the Greek Population of Northern Epirus." Athene, VI, ii, 50-51.

1079. Skendi, Stavro, "The Northern Epirus Question Reconsidered." JCEA, XIV, 143-153.

TRIESTE

1080. Haines, Charles G., "Trieste—A Storm Center of Europe." FPR, XXII, 14-23.

1081. Jessup, Philip C., "U.S. Position on the Free Territory of Trieste." DSB, XIX, 225-233.

1082. Kish, George, "Italian Boundary Problems." GR, XXXVII, 137-141.

1083. Kunz, Josef L., "The Free Territory of Trieste." WPQ, I, 99-112.

1084. Mangone, Gerard J., "Renewed Struggle for Trieste." FPB, XXXIII, iii, 3, 8.

1085. _____, "What Can Be Done About Trieste." FPB, XXXIII, vii, 4, 6.

1086. Mosely, Philip E., "Trieste Apple of Discord." FPB, XXXII, vi, 3, 8.

1087. Salvemini, Gaetano, "The Italo-Jugoslav Frontier." FA, XXIV, 341-347.

1088. Schwelb, Egon, "The Trieste Settlement and Human Rights." AJIL, XLIX, 240-247.

1089. Smyth, Howard McGaw, "Trieste." AFSJ, XXV, vi, 7-9.

1090. Sterling, Claire, "The Mess in Trieste." Rept, IX, viii, 8-10.

1091. Stone, I. F., "Trieste and San Francisco." Nation, CLX, 589-590.

1092. Sullam, Victor B., "Food and Agriculture in the Trieste Region of Italy." FAgr, IX, 190-192.

1093. Unger, Leonard, "The Economy of the Free Territory of Trieste." GR, XXXVII, 583-608.

1094. Werth, Alexander, "The Trieste Boomerang." Nation, CLXXIV, 361-362.

1095. Zauertnik, Richard J., "A Yugoslav on Trieste." NR, CXIII, i, 24.

V. ALBANIA

GENERAL

1096. Anon. "Public Health." Stavro Skendi, Ed., <u>Albania</u>, pp. 255-268. (East-Central Europe under the Communists).

1097. Marker, Michael. The Red Pioneer. New York: Comet Press, 1955, 68 pp. [Albania]

1098. Norman, Daniel, "Albania: A Communist Colony." PoC, V, iii, 34-41.

1099. Skendi, Stavro, ed., Albania. (East-Central Europe Under the Communists: Mid-European Studies Center Series.) New York: Frederick A. Praeger for the Mid-European Studies Center of the Free Europe Committee, 1956.

1100. _____ . "Albania." Stephen D. Kertesz, Ed., <u>The Fate of East Central Europe</u>, pp. 297-318.

GEOGRAPHY AND POPULATION

1101. Anon. "The Land." Stavro Skendi, Ed., <u>Albania</u>, pp. 31-48. (East-Central Europe under the Communists).

1102. _____ . "The People." Stavro Skendi, Ed., <u>Albania</u>, pp. 48-59. (East-Central Europe under the Communists).

1103. Nuttonson, Michael Y. Ecological Plant Geography of Albania: Its Agricultural Crops and Some North American Climatic Anologues. Washington, D.C.: American Institute of Crop Ecology, 1947, 16 pp.

1104. Roucek, Joseph S., "The Geopolitics of Albania." WAI, XXIII, 320-334.

1105. United States. Office of Geography. Albania. Official Standard Names Approved by the United States Board on Geographic Names. Washington, D.C.: United States Government Printing Office, 1955, 156 pp.

HISTORY

1106. Amery, Julian. Sons of the Eagle: A Study in Guerrilla War. New York: Macmillan, 1949.

1107. Anon. "Historical Background." Stavro Skendi, Ed., Albania, pp. 1-30. (East-Central Europe under the Communists).

1108. _____, "History of the Albanian Communist Party." NBIC, IV, xi, 3-10; V, I, 22-30.

1109. Coon, Carleton S. The Mountains of Giants: A Racial and Cultural Study of the North Albanian Mountain Ghegs. (Papers of the Peabody Museum of American Archaeology and Ethnology, Harvard University, XXIII, No. 3.) Cambridge, Massachusetts: Peabody Museum, 1950.

1110. Free Europe Press. A Chronology of Events in Albania 1942-52. New York: Free Europe Committee, 1955.

1111. Hasluck, Margaret Masson (Hardie). The Unwritten Law in Albania. J. H. Hutton, Ed. New York: Cambridge University Press, 1954, 285 pp.

1112. Noli, Bishop Fan S. George Castriati Scanderbeg. New York: International Universities Press, 1947, 240 pp.

1113. Skendi, Stavro, "Beginnings of Albanian Nationalist and Autonomous Trends: The Albanian League, 1878-1881." ASEER, XII, 219-232.

1114. _____. The Political Evolution of Albania, 1912-1944. (Mimeo. Series No. 19.) New York: Mid-European Studies Center, 1954.

1115. Story, Someville, ed. Memoirs of Ismail Kemal Bey. New York: E. P. Dutton, n.d.

GOVERNMENT AND POLITICS

1116. Anon. "The Constitutional System." Stavro Skendi, Ed., Albania, pp. 60-72. (East-Central Europe under the Communists).

1117. _____. "The Government." Stavro Skendi, Ed., Albania, pp. 92-108. (East-Central Europe under the Communists).

1118. _____. "National Security." Stavro Skendi, Ed.,

Albania, pp. 109-124. (East-Central Europe under the Communists).

    1119. _____. "Politics and Political Organizations." Stavro Skendi, Ed., Albania, pp. 73-91. (East-Central Europe under the Communists).

    1120. _____. "Propaganda." Stavro Skendi, Ed., Albania, pp. 125-137. (East-Central Europe under the Communists).

    1121. Constitution of 1946 of the People's Republic of Albania. Gazeta Zyrtare (Official Gazette) (Tirana), March 19, 1946, No. 19. Tr. by Bishop Fan Noli. Boston: Committee for the Defense of Albania, n.d. [1946.]

    1122. McLain, Glenn A. Albanian Expose: Communism versus Liberation for Albania. Quincy, Massachusetts: Premier Press, 1952, 99 pp.

    1123. Radio Free Europe. Information and Reference Department. Political Attitudes in Albania. New York: Free Europe Committee, 1952.

    1124. Skendi, Stavro, "Albania within the Slav Orbit: Advent to Power of the Communist Party." PSQ, LXIII, 257-274.

    1125. United States. Congress. House of Representatives. Select Committee on Communist Aggression. Communist Takeover and Occupation of Albania. (83rd. Congress, 1st Sess., Special report No. 13.) Washington, D.C.: United States Government Printing Office, 1954.

    1126. _____. Library of Congress. Legislative Reference Service. Tensions Within the Soviet Captive Countries. Albania, Pt. 6, pp. 149-171. Prepared at the request of the Committee on Foreign Relations. Washington, D.C.: United States Government Printing Office, 1954.

    1127. Vucinich, Wayne S., "Communism Gains in Albania." CH, XXI, 212-219; 345-352.

INTERNATIONAL AFFAIRS

    1128. Anthem, Thomas, "Albania and Greece." Athene, VI, i, 5-7.

    1129. Dedijer, Vladimir, "Albania, Soviet Pawn." FA, XXX, 103-112.

1130. Holmes, Olive, "Great Power Rivalry Mounts in Greco-Albanian Dispute." FPB, XXV, xlvii, 2-3.

1131. Kadragic, Catherine Schaffer, "International Delimitation of Albania, 1921-1925: A Study of Cooperation Between The League of Nations and the Conference of Ambassadors in Paris." DA, XVII, 1111-1112.

1132. United Nations. Security Council. Subcommittee on Incidents in the Corfu Channel. Report. New York: Lake Success, 1947, 40 pp.

THE ECONOMY

1133. Anon. "Agriculture." Stavro Skendi, Ed., Albania, pp. 148-172. (East-Central Europe under the Communists).

1134. _____. "Domestic Trade and Finance." Stavro Skendi, Ed., Albania, pp. 205-223. (East-Central Europe under the Communists).

1135. _____. "Economic Report: Albania." NBIC, III, v, 12-22.

1136. _____. "Foreign Trade." Stavro Skendi, Ed., Albania, pp. 224-238. (East-Central Europe under the Communists).

1137. _____. "Industry." Stavro Skendi, Ed., Albania, pp. 190-204. (East-Central Europe under the Communists).

1138. _____. "Labor." Stavro Skendi, Ed., Albania, pp. 138-147. (East-Central Europe under the Communists).

1139. _____. "Mining and Quarrying." Stavro Skendi, Ed., Albania, pp. 173-189. (East-Central Europe under the Communists).

1140. _____. "Transportation and Communications." Stavro Skendi, Ed., Albania, pp. 239-254. (East-Central Europe under the Communists).

LANGUAGE AND LITERATURE

1141. Anon. "Literature and the Arts." Stavro Skendi, Ed., Albania, pp. 300-322. (East-Central Europe under the Communists).

1142. Ascom, B. B., "Notes on the Development of the Scanderbeg Theme." CL, V, 16-29.

1143. Drizari, Nelo. Albanian-English and English-Albanian Dictionary. New York: Ungar, 1957, 320 pp. [2nd ed]

1144. _____. "Albanian Literature." Horatio Smith, Ed., Columbia Dictionary of Modern European Literature, pp. 10-12.

1145. _____. Basic Guide to the Albanian Language. Monterey: United States Army Language School, 1948.

1146. _____. Spoken and Written Albanian. New York: Hafner Publishing Co., 1947, 188 pp.

1147. Hamp, Eric P., "Two Notes on Albanian." Language, XXXIII, 530-532.

1148. Logoreci, Anton, "The Dialogue of Modern Albanian Writing." BA, XXX, 155-159.

1149. Mann, Stuart E. Historical Albanian-English Dictionary. Published for the British Council. New York: Longmans, Green and Co., 1948, 601 pp.

1150. Messing, Gordon M., "Modern Greek trík and Albanian triske." Language, XXXI, 232-235.

1151. Minshall, Robert, "Initial Voiced Laryngeal */y/ in Albanian." Language, XXXII, 627-630.

1152. Newmark, Leonard Dan. Spoken Albanian (Tosk). Mimeo. Bloomington, Indiana, 1954.

1153. _____. Structural Grammar of Albanian. (Indiana University Publications: Slavic and East European Series, No. 8.) Bloomington: Indiana University Graduate Division, 1957, 130 pp.

1154. Skendi, Stavro, "Albanian and South Slavic Oral Epic Poetry." DA, XII, 71-72.

1155. _____. Albanian and South Slavic Oral Epic Poetry. (Memoirs of the American Folklore Society, Vol. XLIV.) Philadelphia: American Folklore Society, 1954.

1156. _____, "The South Slavic Decasyllable in Albanian Oral Poetry." Word, IX, 339-348.

1157. United States. Army Language School, Monterey, California. Albanian Exercises in Grammar. Reference Material. Monterey: United States Army Language Training School, 1957, 61 pp.

1158. _____. Army Language School, Monterey, California. Albanian Pronunciation Guide, Oral Drill, and Reader. Books 1-3. Monterey: United States Army Language Training School, 1950.

1159. _____. Army Language School, Monterey, California. 12-Month Course in Albanian. United States Army Language Training School, 1955.

EDUCATION

1160. Anon. "Education." Stavro Skendi, Ed., Albania, pp. 269-284. (East-Central Europe under the Communists).

1161. Skendi, Stavro, "Beginnings of Albanian Nationalist Trends in Culture and Education (1878-1912)." JCEA, XII, 356-367.

PHILOSOPHY AND RELIGION

1162. Anon. "Religion." Stavro Skendi, Ed., Albania, pp. 285-299. (East-Central Europe under the Communists).

1163. Skendi, Stavro, "Religion in Albania during the Ottoman Rule." SOF, XV, 311-327.

VI. BULGARIA

GENERAL

1164. Anon., "Bulgarian Balance Sheet." NBIC, IV, ii, 3-12.

1165. _____., "The Bulgarian Course." NBIC, III, v, 3-11.

1166. Dellin, A. D., ed. Bulgaria. (East-Central Europe Under the Communists: Mid-European Studies Center Series.) New York: Frederick A. Praeger for the Mid-European Studies Center of the Free Europe Committee, 1957.

1167. Graham, Robert A., "Bulgaria: Dead End for the Free World?" America, LXXXVIII, 352-354.

1168. Poulos, Constantine, "Bulgaria from the Inside." Nation, CLX, 695-696.

1169. Pundeff, Marin, "Recent Development in Bulgaria." WAI, XXI, 139-154.

1170. Roucek, Joseph S. American Bulgarians. Hofstra College, Hempstead, New York: The Author, 1947, 15 pp.

1171. Stillman, E. O., and R. H. Bass, "Bulgaria: A Study in Satellite Non-Conformity." PoC, IV, vi, 26-33.

1172. United States. Congress. House Select Committee on Communist Aggression. Report on Bulgaria. Washington, D.C.: United States Government Printing Office, 1955.

1173. _____. Library of Congress. Legislative Reference Service. Tensions Within the Soviet Captive Countries. Bulgaria, Pt. 1, pp. 1-25. Prepared at the request of the Committee on Foreign Relations. Washington, D.C.: United States Government Printing Office, 1954.

1174. Wolff, Robert Lee. "Bulgaria." Stephen D. Kertesz, Ed., The Fate of East Central Europe, pp. 274-296.

GEOGRAPHY AND POPULATION

1175. Hubbard, George, "Turning of Tirnovo." EG, XXII, 109-115.

1176. Pisky, Fred S. "The People." L. A. D. Dellin, Ed., Bulgaria, pp. 59-82. (East-Central Europe under the Communists).

1177. Winston, Victor H. "The Land." L. A. D. Dellin, Ed., Bulgaria, pp. 28-58. (East-Central Europe under the Communists).

HISTORY

1178. Black, Cyril E. "Bulgaria in Historical Perspective." L. A. D. Dellin, Ed., Bulgaria, pp. 1-25. (East-Central Europe under the Communists).

1179. Clarke, James F., "Russia and Bulgaria." JCEA, V, 394-398.

1180. _____, "The Russian Bible Society and the Bulgarians." HSS, III, 67-104.

1181. Gimbutas, M., "Slavianske keramika v Bulgarija. (Slavic Pottery in Bulgaria and Its Importance for the Prehistory of the Slavs in the Balkans), by Krsto Miatev." AJA, LV, 120.

1182. Jelavich, Charles and Barbara, "The Occupation Fund Documents: Additional Evidence." ASEER, XIV, 390-401.

1183. _____, and Barbara, "The Occupation Fund Documents: A Diplomatic Forgery." ASEER, XII, 343-349.

1184. _____, "Russo-Bulgarian Relations, 1892-1896: With Particular Reference to the Problem of the Bulgarian Succession." JMH, XXIV, 341-351.

1185. Setton, Kenneth M., "The Bulgars in the Balkans and the Occupation of Corinth in the Seventh Century." Spec, XXV, 502-543.

1186. Weinberg, Saul S., "'The Neolithic Period in Bulgaria: Early Food-Producing Cultures in Eastern Europe,' by James Harvey Gaul." AJA, LIII, 404-406.

1187. Wolff, Robert Lee, "The 'Second Bulgarian Empire.' Its Origin and History to 1204." Spec, XXIV, 167-206.

GOVERNMENT AND POLITICS

1188. Anon., "The Chervenkov Bid." NBIC, II, xi, 44-45.

1189. _____. "The Constitutional System." L. A. D. Dellin, Ed., Bulgaria, pp. 84-101. (East-Central Europe under the Communists).

1190. _____. "Government Organizations." L. A. D. Dellin, Ed., Bulgaria, pp. 132-146. (East-Central Europe under the Communists).

1191. Dellin, L. A. D. "Politics and Political Organizations." L. A. D. Dellin, Ed., Bulgaria, pp. 102-131. (East-Central Europe under the Communists).

1192. Eulau, Heinz, "Democracy v. Tyranny in Bulgaria." NR, CXIII, x, 273-274.

1193. Free Europe Committee. The Bulgarian Communist Party. Dragomir Nenoff, Ed. New York: Free Europe Committee, 1951, 72 pp.

1194. _____. Communist Party Congresses in the Soviet Bloc, I. Bulgaria. New York: Free Europe Committee, 1954.

1195. National Committee for a Free Europe. Biographies of 16 Leading Bulgarian Communists. New York: National Committee for a Free Europe, 1954.

1196. Padev, Michael. "National Security." L. A. D. Dellin, Ed., Bulgaria, pp. 147-161. (East-Central Europe under the Communists).

1197. Popoff, Emil. "Information Media." L. A. D. Dellin, Ed., Bulgaria, pp. 162-180. (East-Central Europe under the Communists).

1198. Sipkov, Ivan. Administrative-territorial Division of Bulgaria (Past and Present: Changes). Washington, D.C.: Mid-European Law Project, Library of Congress, 1955, 14 pp.

1199. United States. Congress. House of Representatives. Communist Take-over and Occupation of Bulgaria. Special Report No. 7 of the Selective Committee on Communist Aggression. (83rd Congress, 2nd Sess.) Washington, D.C.: United States Government Printing Office, 1954, 18 pp.

1200. Vucinich, Wayne S., "Bulgaria: A Balkan Soviet." CH, XX, 129-135; 208-212.

1201. _____, "Bulgaria: I. Consolidation of the Fatherland Front." CH, XIII, 273-279; II. "Development of Slavic Solidarity." CH, XIII, 341-346.

LAW

1202. Anon., "Justice in 'Democratic' Bulgaria." ABAJ, XXXVI, 875.

1203. _____, "The Story of Michael Shipkov's Detention and Interrogation by The Bulgarian Militia." DSB, XXII, 387-396.

1204. Dellin, L. A. D., "Labor Law and Relations in Communist Bulgaria." LLR, V, 609-616.

1205. Ganeff, Venelin. "Abstract of Bulgarian Civil and Commercial Laws." The Lawyers Directory. Cincinnati, Ohio: Sharp and Alleman Co., 1949.

1206. Mileff, Milio. Inquiry into the Legality of Communist Rule in Bulgaria. New York: Union of Bulgarian Jurists, 1955, 68 pp.

1207. Nicoloff, Antonii M., "An 'Act for the Protection of Peace' in Bulgaria." AJIL, XLV, 353.

1208. Sipkov, Ivan. Laws on Nationalization in Bulgaria. Washington, D.C.: Mid-European Law Project, Library of Congress, 1955, 9 pp. Mimeographed.

1209. _____. Legal Sources and Bibliography of Bulgaria. Vladimir Gsovski, Ed., Legal Sources and Bibliography of Eastern Europe. New York: Praeger, for the Free Europe Committee, 1956, 199 pp.

INTERNATIONAL AFFAIRS

1210. Johnston, Mary., "Diplomatic Drama." AFSJ, XXVII, vii, 11-15. [Diplomatic relations with Bulgaria.]

1211. Lee, Dwight E. "Bulgaria and Yugoslavia." Leonid I. Strakhovsky, Ed., Handbook of Slavic Studies, pp. 604-627.

1212. Mamatey, Victor S., "The United States and Bulgaria in World War I." ASEER, XII, 233-257.

1213. Pundeff, Marin., "Bulgarian Decree on Territorial Waters." AJIL, XLVI, 330-333.

1214. _____, "Two Documents on Soviet-Bulgarian Relations in November, 1940." JCEA, XV, 367-379.

1215. United States. Department of State. Armistice Agreement with Bulgaria, Signed at Moscow, October 28, 1944.

(Executive Agreement Series 437.) Washington, D.C.: Department of State, 1945.

THE ECONOMY

1216. Anon. "Consumer Goods and Internal Trade in Bulgaria." NBIC, IV, ii, 13-26.

1217. Beltchev, Koitcho. Tobacco in Bulgaria. Durham, North Carolina: Duke University Press, 1952.

1218. Dellin, L. A. D. "Labor." L. A. D. Dellin, Ed., Bulgaria, pp. 228-250. (East-Central Europe under the Communists).

1219. _____. Trade Unions and Legislation in Bulgaria 1878-1953. (Mimeo. Series, No. 7.) New York: Mid-European Studies Center, 1953, 30 pp.

1220. Free Europe Committee. Bulgarian Economy. Ivanko Gabensky, Ed., New York: Free Europe Committee, 1952, 59 pp.

1221. Gabensky, Ivanko. "Trade." L. A. D. Dellin, Ed., Bulgaria, pp. 333-364. (East-Central Europe under the Communists).

1222. Jankoff, Dimiter A. Bulgarian Agricultural Producers' Cooperatives. (Mimeo. Series No. 21.) New York: Mid-European Studies Center, 1954, 19 pp.

1223. _____. Labor Cooperative Farms in Bulgaria. (Mimeo. Series, No. 1.) New York: Mid-European Studies Center, 1953, 17 pp.

1224. Jones, B. D., and Dimiter A. Jankoff. "Agriculture." L. A. D. Dellin, Ed., Bulgaria, pp. 287-312. (East-Central Europe under the Communists).

1225. Kliewer, Don, "Bulgaria Joins Ranks of Oil-Producing Nations." WO, CXL, 298-299.

1226. Quandt, Richard E., "Problems of Efficiency in the Post-War Bulgarian Economy." EEH, VIII, 131-147.

1227. Rangeloff, Grigor. "Transportation and Communications." L. A. D. Dellin, Ed., Bulgaria, pp. 365-384. (East Central Europe under the Communists).

1228. Spulber, Nicolas. "National Income and Product."

L. A. D. Dellin, Ed., Bulgaria, pp. 276-286. (East-Central Europe under the Communists).

1229. _____. "Planned Economy: 1947-1957." L. A. D. Dellin, Ed., Bulgaria, pp. 268-275. (East-Central Europe under the Communists).

1230. Todorov, V., and L. A. D. Dellin. "Public Health and Social Security." L. A. D. Dellin, Ed., Bulgaria, pp. 251-266. (East-Central Europe under the Communists).

1231. Vucinich, Wayne S., "Economic Development in Bulgaria." CH, XXXIII, 29-36.

1232. Wszelaki, Jan. "Industry." L. A. D. Dellin, Ed., Bulgaria, pp. 313-332. (East-Central Europe under the Communists).

1233. Zlatin, Ivan. Regulations of Foreign Exchange in Bulgaria. Washington: Mid-European Law Project, Library of Congress, 1954, 14 pp. [Mimeographed].

LANGUAGE, LITERATURE, AND FOLKLORE

1234. Christophorov, P., "Aspects of Modern Bulgarian Literature." BA, XXX, 27-30.

1235. Diver, William, "The Problem of Old Bulgarian 'st.'" Word, XI, 228-236.

1236. Ham, Edith M. "Literature and the Arts." L. A. D. Dellin, Ed., Bulgaria, pp. 210-227. (East-Central Europe under the Communists).

1237. Kremenliev, Boris A. Bulgarian-Macedonian Folk Music. Berkeley: University of California Press, 1952, 165 pp.

1238. _____, "Some Social Aspects of Bulgarian Folksongs." JAF, LXIX, 310-319.

1239. Manning, Clarence A. "Bulgarian Literature." Horatio Smith, Ed., Columbia Dictionary of Modern European Literature, pp. 125-127.

1240. Marinoff, Stefan, "Literary Ferment in Bulgaria." PoC, V, iii, 37-41.

1241. Petroff, Louis, "Magical Beliefs and Practices in Old Bulgaria." MF, VII, 214-220.

1242. Rusev, Rusi. Bulgarian-English Dictionary. 1947

ed. New York: Ungar, 1953, 235 pp. [Added title page in Bulgarian]

1243. _____. English-Bulgarian, Bulgarian-English Dictionary. 2 vols. New York: Heinman, 1946-1947, 374, 235 pp.

EDUCATION

1244. Anon. "Education." L. A. D. Dellin, Ed., Bulgaria, pp. 194-209. (East-Central Europe under the Communists).

1245. Sanders, Irwin T., "Communist-Dominated Education in Bulgaria: A Study in Social Relationships." ASEER, XV, 364-381.

PHILOSOPHY AND RELIGION

1246. Anon. "Religion." L. A. D. Dellin, Ed., Bulgaria, pp. 182-193. (East-Central Europe under the Communists).

1247. Antonoff, Nicholas, and Marin Pundeff. Churches and Religion in Bulgaria. Washington: Mid-European Law Project, Library of Congress, 1951, 51 pp.

1248. Bagranov, Tzvetko S. The American Mission's Share in the Regeneration and Defense of Bulgaria. Pittsburgh, Pennsylvania: 1947.

1249. Free Europe Committee. Religious Persecution in Bulgaria. New York: Free Europe Committee, n.d., 12 pp.

1250. United States. Library of Congress. Law Library. Bulgaria: Churches and Religion. Washington, D.C.: Library of Congress, 1951, 53 pp.

VII. CZECHOSLOVAKIA

GENERAL

1251. Andic, V. E., "The Contribution of American Slovaks to the National War Effort." ASEER, IV, x-xi, 179-185.

1252. Anon., "The Czechoslovak Course." NBIC, III, iv, 3-12.

1253. Beuer, Gustav. New Czechoslovakia and her Historic Background. Toronto: Progress Books, 1947.

1254. Busek, Vratislav, and Nicolas Spulber, eds. Czechoslovakia. (East-Central Europe Under the Communists: Mid-European Studies Center Series.) New York: Frederick A. Praeger for the Mid-European Studies Center of the Free Europe Committee, 1957.

1255. David, Vaclav, "Czechoslovakia." UNR, II, v, 53-54.

1256. Duchacek, Ivo. "Czechoslovakia." Stephen D. Kertesz, Ed., The Fate of East Central Europe, pp. 179-218.

1257. _____, "Czechoslovakia: New Course or No Course?" PoC, IV, i, 12-19.

1258. Eisner, Karel. The "Unknown" Little Democracy. Toronto: The Author, 1945, 128 pp.

1259. Hadsel, Winifred N., "Czechoslovakia's Road to Socialism." FPR, XXII, 270-279.

1260. Hanc, Josef. "Czechoslovakia." Leonid I. Strakhovsky, Ed., Handbook of Slavic Studies, pp. 582-603.

1261. Harsch, Joseph C., "Show Window of the East: Czechoslovakia." Rept, I, vi, 28-29.

1262. Heisler, J. B., and J. E. Mellon. Czechoslovakia, Land of Dream and Enterprise. Pref. by Wickham Steed. Rev. impression. Forest Hills, New York: Transatlantic Arts, 1945.

1263. Hindus, Maurice. The Bright Passage. Garden City, New York: Doubleday and Company, 1947.

1264. Hrobak, Philip Anthony, ed. Czecho-Slovakia:

Victim of Communist Agression. Middletown, Pennsylvania: Jednota Press, 1945, 64 pp.

1265. Hrusovsky, Francis. This Is Slovakia, A Country You Do Not Know. Scranton, Pennsylvania: Obrana Press, 1953, 110 pp.

1266. Josten, Josef. Oh, My Country. New York: MacDonald, 1949, 256 pp.

1267. Kerner, Robert Joseph, ed. Czechoslovakia. (United Nations Series.) Berkeley: University of California Press, 1948.

1268. Kohn, Hans, "Romanticism and Realism Among Czechs and Slovaks." RPol, XIV, 25-46.

1269. Lattimore, Owen, "Challenge at the Bridgehead." NR, CXVII, iv, 14.

1270. _____, "The Czech Exception Disproves the Rules." NR, CXVII, xii, 6-7.

1271. Lockhart, Sir Robert Bruce, "Report on Czechoslovakia." FA, XXXIII, 484-499.

1272. Mann, Klaus, "In Free Czechoslovakia." Nation, CLX, 717-718.

1273. Palmer, Gretta Brooker. God's Underground. New York: Appleton-Century-Crofts, 1949.

1274. Papanek, Jan. Czechoslovakia. New York: International Universities Press, 1945, 136 pp.

1275. Pirkova-Jakobson, Svatava, "Prague and the Purple Sage." HSS, III, 247-288.

1276. Radio Free Europe. Information and Reference Department. Inside Czechoslovakia. (Special Report, No. 25.) New York: Radio Free Europe, 1952, 7 pp.

1277. Ripka, Hubert. East and West. Forest Hills, New York: Transatlantic Arts, 1945, 151 pp.

1278. Roucek, Joseph S., "American Czechoslovaks and World War II." WAI, XVII, 85-90.

1279. Seton-Watson, Robert William, ed. Prague Essays. New York: Oxford University Press, 1949.

1280. Wechsberg, Joseph. Homecoming. New York: Alfred A. Knopf, 1946.

1281. Werth, Alexander, "Brave New World in Czechoslovakia." Nation, CLXXVIII, 208-209, 241-242.

1282. _____, "Czechoslovakia Revisited." Nation, CLXX, 7-8, 35-36, 56.

GEOGRAPHY AND POPULATION

1283. Anon. "Population." Vratislav Busek and Nicolas Spulber, Eds., Czechoslovakia, pp. 20-37. (East-Central Europe under the Communists).

1284. Capek, Milic. Key to Czechoslovakia, the Territory of Kladsko (Glatz): A Study of a Frontier Problem in Middle Europe. New York: R. Vogel, 1946, 153 pp.

1285. Melezin, Abraham. "The Land." Vratislav Busek and Nicolas Spulber, Eds., Czechoslovakia, pp. 2-19. (East-Central Europe under the Communists).

1286. Nuttonson, Michael Y. Agricultural Climatology of Czechoslovakia and its Agro-climatic Analogues in North America. (International Agro-climatological Series, Study No. 3.) Washington, D.C.: American Institute of Crop Ecology, 1947.

1287. Shute, John, "Czechoslovakia's Territorial and Population Changes." EG, XXIV, 35-44.

1288. United States. Army Map Service. Gazetteer to AMS I: 25,000 Maps of Czechoslovakia. (AMS Series M872 and M873.) Washington, D.C.: United States Government Printing Office, 1955, 438 pp.

1289. Wanklyn, Harriet Grace (Mrs. James Alfred Steers). Czechoslovakia. New York: Praeger, 1954, 445 pp.

1290. Wynne, Waller. The Population of Czechoslovakia. (Census Bureau. International Population Statistics, P-90, No. 3.) Washington, D.C.: United States Government Printing Office, 1953, 72 pp.

HISTORY

1291. Anon., "Anniversary of Liberation of Czechoslovakia; Correspondence Between SHAEF and Soviet High Command Concerning Decisions to Halt Allied Forces in Czechoslovakia." DSB, XX, 665-667.

1292. Auty, Robert, "Jan Kollar, 1793-1852." SEER, XXX, 74-91.

1293. Benes, Eduard. Eduard Benes in His Own Words: Three Score Years of a Statesman, Builder and Philosopher. Comp. by Karel Hudec. Long Island City, New York: Czech-American National Alliance, Eastern Division, 1945, 136 pp.

1294. _____. Memoirs: From Munich to New War and New Victory. Boston: Houghton Mifflin, 1956; London, Allen, Unwin, 1954.

1295. _____, "Post-war Czechoslovakia." FA, XXIV, 397-411.

1296. Benes, Vaclav, "Bohemia and the Nineteenth Century Polish Revolutions." CEF, V, ii, 5-11.

1297. _____, "Pan-Slavism and Czechoslovak Policy During World War II." ISS, I, 137-164.

1298. Brock, Peter. Political and Social Doctrines of the Unity of Czech Brethern in the Fifteenth and Early Sixteenth Centuries. (Slavistic Printings and Reprintings, 11.) New York: Lounz, 1957, 302 pp.

1299. del Vayo, J. Alvarez, "Czechoslovakia's Rebirth." Nation, CLXII, 529-530, 570, 600.

1300. Ehrich, Robert W., "Homolka: A Fortified Neolithic Village in Bohemia." Arch, IX, 233-240.

1301. _____, "Jaroslav Boehm: 'Zaklady Hallstattske Periody v Cechach'(Foundations of the Hallstatt Period in Bohemia)." AJA, LV, 400-402.

1302. Jaszi, Oscar, "The Significance of Thomas G. Masaryk for the Future." JCEA, X, 1-8.

1303. Kaminsky, Howard, "Chiliasm and the Hussite Revolution." ChH, XXVI, 43-71.

1304. Kennan, George F., "The Czechoslovak Legion." RusR, XVI, 3-16.

1305. Kisch, Guido. In Search of Freedom: A History of American Jews from Czechoslovakia. Foreword by Jan Masaryk. New York: Bloch Publishing Co., 1949, 373 pp.

1306. Kohn, Hans, "The Heritage of Masaryk." AAAPSS, CCLVIII, 70-73.

1307. Konirsh, Suzanne G., "Constitutional Aspects of

the Struggle Between Germans and Czechs in the Austro-Hungarian Monarchy." JMH, XXVII, 231-262.

1308. Kybal, Vlastimil, "Czechoslovakia and Italy: My Negotiations with Mussolini, 1922-1923." JCEA, XIII, 352-368; XIV, 65-76.

1309. Lettrich, Jozef. History of Modern Slovakia. New York: Praeger, 1955, 329 pp.

1310. Lockhart, Sir Robert Hamilton Bruce. Jan Masaryk. New York: Philosophical Library, 1951, 80 pp.

1311. Moravec, Frantisek. Memoirs. New York: Scribner's, 1949. [Autobiography by former Chief of Intelligence in Czech Army.]

1312. Muran, J. B. We Fight on: Slovak Rising in the German Rear. New York: Czechoslovak Government Information Service, [1945], 44 pp.

1313. Odlozilik, Otakar, "The Czechs on The Eve of the 1848 Revolution." HSS, I, 179-218.

1314. _____, "Eduard Benes in Munich Days." JCEA, XVI, 384-393.

1315. _____, "Eduard Benes Memoirs." JCEA, VIII, 412-420.

1316. _____, "Enter Masaryk: A Prelude to His Political Career." JCEA, X, 21-36.

1317. _____, "From Velehrad to Olomouc." HSS, II, 75-90.

1318. _____, "Modern Czechoslovak Historiography." SEER, XXX, 376-392.

1319. Opocensky, Jan, ed. Edward Benes: Essays and Reflections Printed on the Occasion of his Sixtieth Birthday by Sir Ernest Barker and others. Toronto: Thomas Nelson and Sons, 1945.

1320. Palickar, Stephen J. Slovakia: From Hungarian Despotism to Atheistic Czech Communism. Cambridge, Massachusetts: The Hampshire Press Inc., 1948, 138 pp.

1321. Pech, Stanley Zdenek, "F. L. Rieger: The Road from Liberalism to Conservatism." JCEA, XVII, 3-23.

1322. _____, "The Role of Frantisek L. Rieger in Nineteenth Century Czech Political Development." DA, XVII, 609.

1323. Roucek, Joseph S., "General Patton's Stopped Invasion of Czechoslovakia and the Role of Vlasov." UQ, XIII, 144-149.

1324. _____, "The Memoirs of President Benes. WAI, XX, 178-189.

1325. Schwarz, Henry F. "Bohemia under the Hapsburgs." Leonid I. Strakhovsky, Ed., Handbook of Slavic Studies, pp. 243-270.

1326. Seton-Watson, Robert William. Czechoslovakia in its European Setting: An Inaugural Lecture Delivered before the University of Oxford on Feb. 6, 1946. New York: Oxford University Press, 1946, 20 pp.

1327. Spinka, Matthew, "Paul Kravar and the Lollard-Hussite Relations." ChH, XXV, 16-26.

1328. Stankiewicz, Edward, "The Idea of Czech-Polish Unity Before and during the Renaissance." CEF, V, i, 4-7.

1329. Thomson, S. Harrison. Czechoslovakia in European History. 2nd ed. Princeton, New Jersey: Princeton University Press, 1953, 485 pp.

1330. _____, "Eduard Benes—1884-1948." JCEA, VIII, 239-241.

1331. _____, "Kamil Krofta." JCEA, V, 288-289.

1332. _____. "Medieval Bohemia." Leonid I. Strakhovsky, Ed., Handbook of Slavic Studies, pp. 97-121.

1333. _____, "T. G. Masaryk and Czech Historiography." JCEA, X, 37-52.

1334. Trinka, Zdena. Little Village Called Lidice. Special limited ed. Lidgerwood, North Dakota: International Book Publishers, Western Office, 1947, 128 pp.

1335. Wheeler-Bennett, John W. Munich: Prologue to Tragedy. New York: Duell, Sloan and Pearce, 1948.

1336. Yurchak, Peter P. The Slovaks, Their History and Traditions. Rev. ed. Whiting, Indiana: J. J. Lach, 1947.

1948 COUP AND SOVIET RULE

1337. Anon., "West Wind Over Prague." NBIC, II, viii, 22-26.

1338. Beck, Curt. "Biographical Sketches of Leading Figures of the Communist Regime." Vratislav Busek and Nicolas Spulber, Eds., Czechoslovakia, pp. 418-432. (East-Central Europe under the Communists).

1339. Czechoslovakia Under the Hammer and Sickle. New York: Council of Free Czechoslovakia, 1953.

1340. Dean, Vera Micheles, "Czech Coup Tests U. S. 'Containment' Policy." FPB, XXVII, xxi, 1-2.

1341. Duchacek, Ivo, "The February Coup in Czechoslovakia." WP, II, 511-532.

1342. _____, "The Strategy of Communist Infiltration: Czechoslovakia, 1944-1948." WP, II, 345-372.

1343. _____. Strategy of Communist Infiltration: The Case of Czechoslovakia. New Haven, Connecticut: Yale Institute of International Studies, 1949, 47 pp.

1344. Feierabend, Ladislav, "The Gottwald Era in Czechoslovakia." JCEA, XIII, 246-256.

1345. Friedman, Otto. The Break-up of Czech Democracy. Pref. Gilbert Murray. Toronto: Longmans, Green and Co., 1950, 176 pp.

1346. Gadourek, Ivan. Political Control of Czechoslovakia: A Study in Social Control of a Soviet Satellite State. (Leyden. Ryksuniversiteit. Sociologisch Inst. Publicaties, 1.) New York: Praeger, 1955, 285 pp.

1347. Gordey, Michel, "Gottwald Wastes No Time." NR, CXVIII, xvi, 19-21.

1348. Hadsel, Winifred N., "Communists Seize Power in Czechoslovakia." FPB, XXVII, xx, 1-2.

1349. Lockhart, Sir Robert Bruce, "The Czechoslovak Revolution." FA, XXVI, 632-645.

1350. Mares, Vaclav E., "Could the Czechs Have Remained Free?" CH, XXIII, 150-157.

1351. _____, "Czechoslovakia under Communism." CH, XXVI, 347-354.

1352. Ripka, Hubert. Czechoslovakia Enslaved. New York: Macmillan, 1950, 339 pp.

1353. Schmidt, Dana Adams. Anatomy of a Satellite. (Atlantic Monthly Press Book.) Boston: Little, Brown and Co., 1952, 512 pp.

1354. Scott, David, "Czech Rubber Stamp." NR, CXVIII, xxiii, 13-14.

1355. Storm, Walter. People's Victory in Czechoslovakia. Introd. John Stuart. New York: New Century Pubs., 1948, 63 pp.

1356. Stransky, Jan. East Wind Over Prague. New York: Random House, 1951. [A personal account of communist methods in Czechoslovakia.]

1357. Taborsky, Edward, "Czechoslovakia in the Khrushchev-Bulganin Era." ASEER, XVI, 50-65.

1358. United States. Library of Congress. Legislative Reference Service. Tensions Within the Soviet Captive Countries. Czechoslovakia, Pt. 4, pp. 85-115. Prepared at the request of the Committee on Foreign Relations. Washington, D.C.: United States Government Printing Office, 1954.

1359. Vucinich, Wayne S., "Czechoslovakia: Three Communist Years." CH, XX, 266-271.

1360. Zinner, Paul, "Marxism in Action: The Seizure of Power in Czechoslovakia." FA, XXVIII, 644-659.

1361. _____, "Problems of Communist Rule in Czechoslovakia." WP, IV, 112-129.

GOVERNMENT AND POLITICS

1362. Anon., "Czechoslovakia: National Party Conference." NBIC, V, viii, 15-21.

1363. _____, "Czechoslovakia: Short History of the Communist Party." NBIC, V, viii, 7-14.

1364. Beck, Curt F., "Can Communism and Democracy coexist? Benes's Answer." ASEER, XI, 189-206.

1365. _____. "The Government." Vratislav Busek and Nicolas Spulber, Eds., Czechoslovakia, pp. 80-100. (East-Central Europe under the Communists).

1366. _____. "Politics and Political Organizations." Vratislav Busek and Nicolas Spulber, Eds., Czechoslovakia, pp. 60-79. (East-Central Europe under the Communists).

1367. Black, Robert E., "Leftists Distorted Press Laws to Capture Czech Newspapers." JQ, XXVI, 181-185.

1368. Chudoba, Bohdan, "Czechoslovakia: A Study in Disintegration." Thought, XXV, 79-99.

1369. Dall, Robert, "Behind the Czech Purge." Rept, V, 24-27.

1370. Free Europe Committee. Czechoslovak Section. Research and Publications Service. The Czechoslovak National Assembly. New York: Free Europe Committee, 1952, 15 pp.

1371. _____. Czechoslovak Section. Research and Publications Service. The Pattern of the Purge. An Analytic Essay. New York: Free Europe Committee, 1952, 12 pp.

1372. Gadourek, Ivan. The Communist Party of Czechoslovakia in the Post-Stalinist Period. (Czechoslovak Foreign Institute in Exile, Studies.) Chicago: The Author, 1957, 39 pp.

1373. Hulicka, Karel, "The Communist Anti-Masaryk Propaganda in Czechoslovakia." ASEER, XVI, 160-174.

1374. Hunt, Richard, "The Denigration of Masaryk." YR, XLIII, 414-426.

1375. Kocvara, Stephen. "The Constitutional System." Vratislav Busek and Nicolas Spulber, Eds., Czechoslovakia, pp. 40-59. (East-Central Europe under the Communists).

1376. Kohn, Hans, "Democracy in the Soviet Orbit: Czechoslovakia's Struggle." CH, XIV, 67-70.

1377. Korbel, Pavel. The Development of Slovakia's Constitutional Position. New York: Free Europe Committee, 1953, 41 pp.

1378. _____. Parliamentary Elections in Czechoslovakia. New York: Free Europe Committee, 1952.

1379. _____. The Supreme Organs of the Communist Party of Czechoslovakia. New York: Free Europe Committee, 1952.

1380. _____, and V. Vagassky. Forced Labor, Population Transfers and Deportations in Czechoslovakia. (Second Supplement.) New York: Free Europe Committee, 1952.

1381. _____, and V. Vagassky. Purges in the Communist Party of Czechoslovakia. New York: Free Europe Committee, 1952.

1382. Odlozilik, Otakar. Masaryk's Idea of Democracy. New York: Masaryk Institute, Inc., 1952, 13 pp.

1383. Sadlik, Joseph, "Purge in Prague." America, LXXXVIII, 323-324.

1384. Skala, Hugo M., "The Terror in Czechoslovakia"; NR, CXXII, xvi, 21-22.

1385. Skilling, H. Gordon, "The Czechoslovak Constitutional System: The Soviet Impact." PSQ, LXVII, 198-224.

1386. _____, "Czechoslovakia: Government in Communist Hands." JPol, XVII, 424-447.

1387. _____, "The Formation of a Communist Party in Czechoslovakia." ASEER, XIV, 346-358.

1388. _____, "People's Democracy, the Proletarian Dictatorship and the Czechoslovak Path to Socialism." ASEER, X, 100-116.

1389. Sturm, Rudolf. "Propaganda." Vratislav Busek and Nicolas Spulber, Eds., Czechoslovakia, pp. 101-127. (East-Central Europe under the Communists).

1390. Taborsky, Edward, "Local Government in Czechoslovakia, 1918-1948." ASEER, X, 205-215.

1391. _____, "Slovakia Under Communist Rule, Democratic Centralism versus National Autonomy." JCEA, XIV, 255-263.

1392. Wellek, Rene, "The Philosophical Basis of Masaryk's Political Ideas." Ethics, LV, 298-304.

LAW

1393. Anon., "Trial of William N. Oatis." DSB, XXV, 283-289.

1394. _____, "The Ways of Tyranny; The Slansky Trial." NBIC, I, xii, 3-4; 6-22.

1395. Barlowe, Raleigh, "Czechoslovakia's Law on Subdivision of Farm Holdings." LE, XXVI, 81-83.

1396. Benes, Vaclav, "The Legal Profession in Czechoslovakia: Its Status Under the Communists." ABAJ, XL, 487-490; 518.

1397. _____, "The New Legal System of Czechoslovakia." JCEA, XII, 215-235.

1398. Concerning the Registration of Deposits, Securities

and Insurance Policies. Tr. of Degree No. 95 of the President of the Czechoslovak Republic, October 20, 1945. Washington, D.C.: Library of Congress, Mid-European Law Project, 1952, 12 pp.

1399. Kalhous, Rudolf, "Recent Literature in the Field of Legal History in Czechoslovakia." AJCL, III, 111-114.

1400. Mayda, Jaroslav, "Lawyers under Communism: A 'New' Legal Order in Czechoslovakia." ABAJ, XXXIX, 1071-1074.

1401. Prochazka, Adolf. Changes in the Philosophy of Czechoslovak Law Since the Prague coup d'etat of February, 1948. Washington, D.C.: National Committee for a Free Europe, Mid-European Studies Center, 1953.

1402. Rado, Alan R., "Czechoslovak Nationalization Decrees: Some International Aspects." AJIL, XLI, 795-806.

1403. Reiner, Paul, "New Czechoslovak Law on Intermarriage with Foreigners." AJIL, XLVII, 314.

1404. _____, "New Czechoslovak Legislation on Nationality." AJIL, XLIV, 387-389.

1405. Taborsky, Edward, "Administrative Jurisdiction in Czechoslovakia." AJCL, IV, 435-438.

1406. United States. Library of Congress. Law Library. Czechoslovakia: Catalogue of Sources of Legal Information. Washington, D.C.: Library of Congress, 1952, 30 pp.

1407. Zenkl, Peter, "On 'Human Rights' in Czechoslovakia." JCEA, XIV, 264-269.

INTERNATIONAL AFFAIRS

1408. Anon., "U. S. Asks Czechoslovakia for Evidence on Aircraft Incident." DSB, XXIX, 180-183.

1409. _____, "U. S.-Czechoslovak Relations: Suspension of Trade Concessions; Refugee Train Episode; Sudeten German Population." DSB, XXV, 621-630.

1410. _____, "U. S. Demands Payment From Czechoslovakia in Plane Incident." DSB, XXXI, 302-3-5; 308; 648-650.

1411. Briggs, Lucy B., "Czechoslovakia and Korea." JAAUW, XLVII, 215-217.

1412. Hechinger, Fred M., "Moscow, Prague, and Israel." Rept, VIII, ii, 28-30.

1413. Kasparek, Jiri, "Negotiating the Czech-Soviet Aviation Agreement." ASEER, XI, 207-214.

1414. _____, "Soviet Russia and Czechoslovakia's Uranium." RusR, XI, 97-105.

1415. Rose, William J., "Czechs and Poles As Neighbors." JCEA, XI, 153-171.

1416. Soroka, Waclaw, "Cooperation of Agrarian Parties as a Factor of Czechoslovak-Polish Rapprochement." CEF, IV, ii, 11-19.

1417. Taborsky, Edward, "Benes and Stalin-Moscow 1943 and 1945." JCEA, XIII, 154-181.

1418. _____, "Benes and the Soviets." FA, XXVII, 302-314.

1419. Talmadge, I. D. W., "Czechoslovakia: Moscow's Reluctant Ally." CH, XIII, 270-272.

1420. Wandycz, Piotr S., "The Benes-Sikorski Agreement." CEF, I, i, 3-9.

1421. _____, "Czechoslovak-Polish Confederation and the Great Powers 1940-43." IUGSEES, III, 1-152.

1422. _____, "Wilson, Czechoslovaks and Poles in Paris 1919." CEF, IV, i, 3-7.

THE ECONOMY

1423. Ames, Edward. "Domestic Trade, Banking, and Finance." Vratislav Busek and Nicolas Spulber, Eds., Czechoslovakia, pp. 367-391. (East-Central Europe under the Communists).

1424. Anon. "Consumer Goods Industries." Vratislav Busek and Nicolas Spulber, Eds., Czechoslovakia, pp. 329-347. (East-Central Europe under the Communists).

1425. _____, "Czechoslovak Balance Sheet." NBIC, IV, v, 3-14.

1426. _____, "The Czechoslovak Currency Reform: A Survey of its Background, Provisions and Popular Reaction." NBIC, II, vii, 17-24.

1427. _____, "Czechoslovakia: Second Five Year Plan." NBIC, V, viii, 22-27.

1428. _____, "Foreign Trade and Finance." Vratislav Busek and Nicolas Spulber, Eds., Czechoslovakia, pp. 348-366. (East-Central Europe under the Communists).

1429. _____, "Internal Trade and Consumer Goods in Czechoslovakia." NBIC, III, vii, 12-20.

1430. _____, "Transportation in Czechoslovakia." NBIC, V, i, 13-21.

1431. Bolles, Blair, "Will U. S. Trade Ban Move Czechs?" FPB, XXXI, iii, 3.

1432. Brzorad, Vilem J. The Economy of Czechoslovakia. (Economic Research Department. Chamber of Commerce of the United States.) Washington, D.C.: Council for Economic and Industry Research, 1955.

1433. _____. "Fuel, Power, and Producer Goods Industries." Vratislav Busek and Nicolas Spulber, Eds., Czechoslovakia, pp. 294-328. (East-Central Europe under the Communists).

1434. _____. "Mining." Vratislav Busek and Nicolas Spulber, Eds., Czechoslovakia, pp. 268-293. (East-Central Europe under the Communists).

1435. Duchacek, Ivo, "Czechoslovakia's Need: Trade Not Aid." CH, XXXIII, 22-28.

1436. Feierabend, Ladislav. Agricultural Cooperatives in Czechoslovakia. (Mid-European Studies Center Series No. 5). New York: Mid-European Studies Center, 1952, 125 pp.

1437. _____. Agricultural Production in Czechoslovakia in 1953. (Mimeo. Series No. 33.) Mid-European Studies Center, 1954, 35 pp.

1438. Flaningam, M. L., "A Survey of Czechoslovak-Austrian Tariff and Commercial Treaty Relations." JCEA, VI, 30-42.

1439. Gibian, George, "The Czechoslovak Two-Year Plan." JCEA, VI, 375-391.

1440. Hadsel, Winifred N., "U. S. Halts Loans to Gain Economic Concessions from Czechs." FPB, XXVI, ii, 4.

1441. Horbaly, William. Agricultural Conditions in Czechoslovakia 1950. (Department of Geography, University of Chicago Research Paper No. 18.) University of Chicago Press, 1951, 104 pp.

1442. Hulicka, Karel, "Land Reform and Politics in Czechoslovakia: 1945-1952." LE, XXIX, 233-247.

1443. Kocvara, Stefan. The Sovietization of Czechoslovak Farming. Standing Charter of a Unified Agricultural Cooperative in Czechoslovakia of February 17, 1953. Washington, D.C.: Mid-European Law Project, Library of Congress, 1954, 42 pp.

1444. Koenig, Ernest. "Agriculture." Vratislav Busek and Nicolas Spulber, Eds., Czechoslovakia, pp. 245-267. (East-Central Europe under the Communists).

1445. _____, "Planning in Czechoslovak Agriculture." FAgr, XVI, 157-160.

1446. Mares, Vaclav E., "The Disrupted Czech Economy." CH, XXIV, 356-360.

1447. _____. "Transportation and Communications." Vratislav Busek and Nicolas Spulber, Eds., Czechoslovakia, pp. 392-416. (East-Central Europe under the Communists).

1448. Mehr, Stanley, "The Farmer and His Land in Communist Czechoslovakia." FAgr, XIV, 156-160.

1449. Meissner, Frank, "Economies of Scale in Relation to Agrarian Reforms in Czechoslovakia." ASEER, XIV, 67-83.

1450. _____, "Mandatory Delivery Quotas in Czechoslovak Agriculture." JCEA, IV, 30-48.

1451. _____, "The Socialization Process in Czechoslovak Agriculture." JFE, XXXV, 88-98.

1452. Oatman, Miriam E., "The Nationalization Program in Czechoslovakia." DSB, XV, 1027-1031.

1453. Rudzki, Adam, "Czechoslovak-Polish Transport Cooperation." CEF, II, iii-iv, 19-21.

1454. Skala, Hugo, "Czechoslovakia: Glittering Bankrupt." Rept, I, ix, 34-35.

1455. Spulber, Nicolas. "The Economy, Retrospect and Prospect: 1954-1960." Vratislav Busek and Nicolas Spulber, Eds., Czechoslovakia, pp. 220-226. (East-Central Europe under the Communists).

1456. _____. "National Income and Product."

Vratislav Busek and Nicolas Spulber, Eds., Czechoslovakia, pp. 227-244. (East-Central Europe under the Communists).

1457. Stepan, Ladislav. The Coal Industry in Czechoslovakia. (Mimeo. Series No. 32.) New York: Mid-European Studies Center, 1954, 40 pp.

1458. Trend, Harry. "Public Health and Welfare." Vratislav Busek and Nicolas Spulber, Eds., Czechoslovakia, pp. 198-218. (East-Central Europe under the Communists).

1459. Wechsberg, Joseph, "Czechoslovakia's Reconstruction." YR, XXXV, 502-514.

LANGUAGES

1460. Auty, R., "Language and Society in the Czech National Revival." SEER, XXV, 241-248.

1461. Harkins, William Edward, and Marie Hnykova. Modern Czech Grammar. (Columbia University Department of Slavic Languages. Columbia Slavic Studies.) New York: King's Crown Press, 1953, 338 pp.

1462. Horecky, Paul L. Czech and Slovak Abbreviations. Washington, D.C.: United States Government Printing Office, 1956, 164 pp.

1463. Hrobak, Philip Anthony. Slovak for Beginners. Middletown, Pennsylvania: The Author, 1952. [Three books.]

1464. Jonas, Karel. Complete Pronouncing Dictionary of the English and Bohemian Languages for General Use. 4th ed. 2 vols. Chicago: F. Pancner, 1945.

1465. Kovac, Edward, Jr. Slovak and English Interpreter. (Slovensko-Anglicky Tlmac.) 2nd ed. Scranton, Pennsylvania: Obrana Press, 1951.

1466. Kraus, David, "Statistical Aid in Language Teaching." AATSEEL, IX, 7-10.

1467. Kucera, Henry, "Phonemic Variations in Spoken Czech." Word, XI, 575-602.

1468. _____, Jindrich, "Notes on the Czech Conjugation." Word, VIII, 378-386.

1469. Kupcek, Joseph R., "Foreign Influences and the Preservation and Purification of Literary Slovak." AATSEEL, X, 26.

1470. Matejka, Ladislav, "R. M. Rilke and the Czech Language." ASEER, XIII, 588-596.

1471. Rubenstein, Herbert, "The Czech Conjugation." Word, VII, 144-154.

1472. Schwarz, J. Colloquial Czech: An Easy Course for Beginners. (Trubner's Colloquial Manuals.) Forest Hills, New York: Transatlantic Arts, 1946. [A revised edition.]

THE ARTS

1473. Bradac, Olga, "Aesthetic Trends in Russia and Czechoslovakia." JAAC, IX, 97-105.

1474. Fles, Barthold. Slavonic Rhapsody: The Life of Anton Dvorak. New York: Allen, Towne and Health, 1948, 231 pp.

1475. Horecky, Paul L., "The Czech Renaissance, Viewed Through Rare Books." LQ, XIV, 95-107.

1476. Lewis, Flora, "A Polish Puppet Show in Prague." Rept, XVI, v, 34-36.

1477. Matejcek, Antonin, and Jaroslav Pesina. Czech Gothic Painting, 1350-1450. Tr. by J. C. Houra. New York: George Efron, 1951, 76 pp.

1478. Obolensky, Dimitri, "Father Francis Dvornik." HSS, II, 1-10.

1479. Palickar, Stephen I. Slovakian Culture in the Light of History, Ancient, Medieval, and Modern. Cambridge, Massachusetts: Hampshire Press, Inc., 1954, 283 pp.

1480. Plicka, Karel. Praha (Prague). Two hundred and eight photographs. Introd. Zdenek Wirth. New York: Heinman, 1947. [Captions in English, French, Czech and Russian.]

1481. Purdy, Clair Lee. Antonin Dvorak, Composer from Bohemia. New York: Julian Messner, 1950, 200 pp.

FOLKLORE

1482. Deutsch, Leonhard, ed. Treasury of Slovak Folk Songs. Published under the sponsorship and general editorship of John J. Lach. Introds. by Milos K. Mlynarovich and Adam P. Lesmesky. New York: Crown Publishers, 1950, 127 pp.

1483. Frantisek, Rehor. Waggishtails of Czechs: Gesta Czechorum. New York: Seven Sirens Press, 1948. [Anecdotes.]

1484. Hollander, Hans, "The Music of Leos Janacek— Its Origin in Folklore." MQ, XLI, 171-176.

1485. Kubina, Frank. Bohemian Collection of Folk Songs. Chicago: Chart Music Publishing House, n.d.

1486. Lubinova, Mila. Dances of Czechoslovakia. Published under the auspices of the Royal Academy of Dancing and the Ling Physical Education Association. (Handbooks of European National Dances.) New York: Chanticleer Press, 1949, 40 pp.

1487. Ryan, Lawrence V., "Some Czech-American Forms of Divination and Supplication." JAF, LXIX, 281-285.

1488. Seckar, Alvena V., "Slovak Wedding Customs." NYFQ, III, 189-204.

1489. Spacek, Anna, and N. L. Boyd. Folk Dances of Bohemia and Moravia. Chicago: H. T. FitzSimons Co., n.d.

1490. Yurchak, Peter. Slovak Proverbs and Sayings. Scranton, Pennsylvania: Obrana Press, 1947.

LITERATURES

1491. Cech, Edward, "The Modern Czech Catholic Writers." CEF, V, i, 8-11.

1492. Eisner, Pavel, "Franz Kafka and Prague." BA, XXI, 264-273.

1493. Harkins, William Edward. Anthology of Czech Literature. (Columbia Slavic Studies.) New York: Columbia University Press, 1953.

1494. _____. The Russian Folk Epos in Czech Literature 1800-1900. (Columbia Slavic Studies.) New York: King's Crown Press, 1951, 282 pp.

1495. _____, and Klement Simoncic. Czech and Slovak Literature. (Slavic Bibliography Series, Columbia University.) New York: King's Crown Press, 1950, 50 pp.

1496. Hostovsky, Egon. Midnight Patient. Tr. from the Czech by Philip H. Smith, Jr. New York: Appleton-Century Crofts, 1954, 278 pp.

1497. Kucera, Henry, and Emil Kovtun. "Literature." Vratislav Busek and Nicolas Spulber, Eds., Czechoslovakia, pp. 173-197. (East-Central Europe under the Communists).

1498. Pirscenok, Anna, "Czech Literature in the Moravian Archives in Bethlehem, Pennsylvania." DA, XVI, 2447-2448.

1499. Politzer, Heinz, "Prague and the Origins of Rainer Maria Rilke, Franz Kafka, and Franz Werfel." MLQ, XVI, 49-62.

1500. Radl, Otto. "Czech and Slovak Literature." Leonid I. Strakhovsky, Ed., Handbook of Slavic Studies, pp. 484-511.

1501. Souckova, Milada, "The Critical Years in Czech Literature." BA, XXX, 21-26.

1502. _____, "The First Stirrings of Modern Czech Literature." HSS, II, 225-239.

1503. _____. A Literature in Crisis: Czech Literature 1938-1950. New York: Mid-European Studies Center, 1953.

1504. _____, "Marxist Theory in Czech Literature." HSS, I, 335-362.

1505. Sturm, Rudolf, "America in the Life and Work of the Czech Poet Josef Sladek." HSS, II, 287-296.

1506. Wellek, Rene. "Czech Literature." Horatio Smith, Ed., Columbia Dictionary of Modern European Literature, pp. 185-191.

1507. _____, "Modern Czech Criticism and Literary Scholarship." HSS, II, 343-358.

1508. _____. "Slovak Literature." Horatio Smith, Ed., Columbia Dictionary of Modern European Literature, pp. 757-759.

EDUCATION

1509. Czechoslovak Universities II. New York: Free Europe Press, Free Europe Committee, 1954.

1510. Duchacek, Ivo. "Education." Vratislav Busek and Nicolas Spulber, Eds., Czechoslovakia, pp. 154-172. (East-Central Europe under the Communists).

1511. Fischer, George, "Russian Studies in Czechoslovakia." AATSEEL, VI, 84-85.

1512. A Group of Czech Refugee Students, "The Present Situation in the Universities of Czechoslovakia." HER, XX, 83-90.

1513. Korbel, Pavel. Czechoslovak Universities. New York: Free Europe Committee, 1952.

1514. _____. Sovietization of the Czechoslovak School System. New York: Free Europe Committee, 1954, 53 pp.

1515. Matthiessen, Francis Otto. From the Heart of Europe. New York: The Oxford University Press, 1948, 194 pp. [Diary of notes while teaching at Prague.]

1516. Mostecky, Vaclav, "The Library Under Communism: Czechoslovak Libraries from 1948 to 1954." LQ, XXVI, 118-127.

PHILOSOPHY AND RELIGION

1517. Bohmer, Alois, Stephan Kocvara, and Jindrich Nosek. "Church and State in Czechoslovakia." Vladimir Gsovski, Ed., Church and State Behind the Iron Curtain, pp. 1-68.

1518. Busek, Vratislav. "Church and State." Vratislav Busek and Nicolas Spulber, Eds., Czechoslovakia, pp. 130-153. (East-Central Europe under the Communists).

1519. Cecilia, Sister. Deliverance of Sister Cecilia. New York: Farrar, Straus and Cudahy, 1954, 360 pp.

1520. Nemec, Ludvik. Church and State in Czechoslovakia. New York: Vantage, 1955, 588 pp.

1521. _____. Episcopal and Vatican Reaction to the Persecution of the Catholic Church in Czechoslovakia. (Catholic University of America Studies in Sacred Theology, 2nd. Series.) Washington, D.C.: Catholic University of America Press, 1953, 94 pp. [Thesis.]

1522. United States. Library of Congress. Law Library. Czechoslovakia: Churches and Religion. Digest-Index of Eastern European Law. Washington, D.C.: Library of Congress, 1951, 54 pp.

1523. Zubek, Theodoric J. Church of Silence in Slovakia. Whiting, Indiana: J. J. Lach, 1956, 310 pp.

SOCIOLOGY

1524. Chicago University. Division of Social Sciences. Jan Hajda, ed. A Study of Contemporary Czechoslovakia. Chicago: University of Chicago for Human Relations Area Files, 1955, 63 pp.

1525. Elias, T., "Two Studies: Hajda, Jan, 'A Study of Contemporary Czechoslovakia.'" CEF, IV, ii, 22-30.

1526. Jirasek, Alois. Some Aspects of Czech Culture. Tr. by Richard Neuse (Behavior Science Translations.) New Haven, Connecticut: Human Relations Area Files, 1953, 54 pp.

1527. Karpf, Ruth, "Slovakia Forms New Habits." NR, CXIX, viii, 10-11.

VIII. FINLAND

GENERAL

1528. Aaron, Daniel, "The Helsinki the Athletes Didn't See." Rept, VII, v, 24-27.

1529. Ashcroft, Diana. Journey to Finland. Toronto: S. J. Reginald Sanders, 1952, 292 pp.

1530. Bell, Henry McGrady. Land of Lakes: Memories Keep Me Company. Pref. Sir Paul Dukes. Toronto: Ryerson Press, 1950.

1531. Era-Esko, Aarni, "Sutton Hoo and Finland." Spec, XXXI, 514-515.

1532. Finland Today. Illustrated with Reproductions of Paintings by Gallen-Kallela. New York: Heinman, 1948, 112 pp.

1533. Fodor, Eugene, ed. Scandinavia in 1952: With Finland and Olympic Games. Associate editors: Lawrence R. Devlin and Frederic R. G. Sanborn. (Fodor's Modern Guides. Travel Publications Book, Vol. 1.) New York: David McKay Co., 1952, 427 pp.

1534. Gervasi, Frank, "Next Door to the Soviets; Finland's postwar comeback." Rept, I, xiv, 22-24.

1535. Hadsel, Winifred N., "Finns Negotiate With Moscow." FPB, XXVII, xxii, 3.

1536. Hinshaw, David. An Experiment in Friendship. New York: Putnam, 1947, 147 pp. [A description of Quaker relief work in Finland.]

1537. _____. Heroic Finland. New York: Putnam, 1952, 306.

1538. Huizinga, J. H., "Finland: Freedom under the Guns." Rept, XIII, iv, 20-22.

1539. Ogrizek, Dore. Scandinavia: Denmark, Norway, Finland and Iceland. Tr. by Paddy O'Hanlon and H. Tredale Nelson. (World in Color Series.) New York: McGraw-Hill Book Co., 1952, 438 pp.

1540. Royal Institute of International Affairs. The

Scandinavian States and Finland: A Political and Economic Survey. London and New York: Royal Institute of International Affairs, 1951, 312 pp.

1541. Stokes, Gordon, ed. Finland. Tr. and adapted by Florence Christie. (Nagel Travel Guide Series.) New York: Praeger, 1953, 167 pp.

1542. Strode, Hudson. Finland Forever. New York: Harcourt, Brace and Co., 1952, 472 pp.

1543. Sulkin, Sidney, "The Finnish Paradox." NR, CXIV, xiii, 433-434.

1544. Toimittaneet. This is Finland. Ensio Rislakki, et al., Eds. New York: Hafner Publishing Co., 1946. [Story in pictures about Finland. Text in English, Finnish and Swedish.]

1545. Wallenius, Kurt M. Men from the Sea. Tr. from the Finnish by Alan Blair. New York: Oxford University Press, 1955, 268 pp.

1546. Wuorinen, John H. "Finland." Stephen D. Kertesz, Ed., The Fate of East-Central Europe, pp. 321-337.

1547. _____, "Finland Stands Guard." FA, XXXII, 651-661.

GEOGRAPHY AND POPULATION

1548. Foye, Isabel, "A Journey Thru Lapland in Finland and Norway." JG, XLVIII, 298-302.

1549. Ifkonen, T. I., "The Lapps of Finland." SJA, VII, 32-68.

1550. Platt, Raye Roberts, ed. Finland and Its Geography. New York: Duell, Sloan and Pearce, 1955, 510 pp.

1551. Van Cleef, Eugene, "Raye R. Platt, ed., 'Finland and Its Geography.'" AAAG, XLVI, 285-286.

1552. _____, "Finland—Bridge to the Atlantic." JG, XLVIII, 99-104.

HISTORY

1553. Anderson, Albin T., "Origins of the Winter War: A Study of Russo-Finnish Diplomacy." WP, VI, 169-189.

Finland: History

1554. Heideman, Bert R. Mortimer, "A Study of the Causes of Finland's Involvement in World War II at Three Separate Times: November, 1939; June, 1941; September, 1944." DA, XIII, 778.

1555. Joesten, Joachim. Finland's Road to Disaster. (News Background Reports, No. 9.) New York: News Background, n.d.

1556. Kalijarvi, Thorsten V., "Finland Since 1939." RPol, X, 84-99.

1557. Kersten, Felix. Kersten Memoirs, 1940-1945. Introd. H. R. Trevor-Roper. Tr. from the German by Constantine Fitzgibbon and James Oliver. New York: Macmillan, 1957, 314 pp.

1558. Lundin, C. Leonard. Finland in the Second World War. (Slavic and East European Series, VI.) Bloomington: Indiana University Press, 1954, 288 pp.

1559. Mannerheim, Carl Gustaf Emil, friherre. Memoirs. Tr. by Eric Lewenhaupt. New York: E. P. Dutton, 1954, 540 pp.

1560. Mazour, Anatole. Finland Between East and West. Princeton, New Jersey: Van Nostrand, 1956, 298 pp.

1561. Olin, Saul Chalmer. Finlandia: The Racial Composition, the Language, and a Brief History of the Finnish People. Hancock, Michigan: Book Concern, 1957, 198 pp.

1562. Pallo, A., "Post-war Finland." BR, I, 105-109.

1563. Pelto, Pertti J., "The Mesolithic Combware Culture of Finland." KASP, No. 13, pp. 32-54.

1564. Shearman, Hugh. Finland: the Adventures of a Small Power. (The Library of World Affairs, No. 13.) New York: Praeger, 1950, 114 pp.

1565. Smith, C. Jay Jr., "Russia and the Origins of the Finnish Civil War of 1918." ASEER, XIV, 481-502.

1566. Tanner, Vaino. The Winter War: Finland Against Russia, 1939-1940. Stanford: Stanford University Press, 1957, 276 pp.

1567. Wuorinen, John H., ed. and tr. Finland and World War II, 1939-1944. New York: The Ronald Press, 1948, 228 pp.

GOVERNMENT AND POLITICS

1568. Bellquist, Eric C., "Finland: Democracy in Travail." WPQ, II, 217-227.

1569. Leiser, Ernest, "Finland—Another Czechoslovakia?" Rept, IV, vii, 17-20.

1570. Spencer, Arthur, "Finland Maintains Democracy." FA, XXXI, 301-310.

1571. Swan, Marshall W. S., "Sparks on Finland." AFSJ, XXVII, vi, 23.

1572. Wuorinen, John H., "Democracy Gains in Finland." CH, XXI, 208-211; 327-330.

THE ECONOMY

1573. Englund, Eric, "Finland's Agriculture Looks Toward Recovery." FAgr, XII, 126-134.

1574. Laatinen, S., and William Mead, "The Intensification of Finnish Farming." EG, XXXIII, 31-40.

1575. Mead, William R., "The Cold Farm in Finland: Resettlement of Finland's Displaced Farmers." GR, XLI, 529-543.

1576. _____. Farming in Finland. New York: De Graff, 1954, 248 pp.

1577. Pesola, Vilho A., "Plant Breeding in Finland." FAgr, XII, 192-194.

1578. Pihkala, Kaarlo Volevi, "The Land Settlement Program of Finland." LE, XXVIII, 147-159.

1579. Reese, Elmer A., "Reindeer in Finland." FAgr, XVI, 211-215.

1580. Van Cleef, Eugene, "Farming in Finland." EG, XXX, 180-181.

1581. Yohe, Ralph S., "Finland Resettles its War-Displaced Farmers." FAgr, XVII, 76-80.

LANGUAGE AND LITERATURE

1582. Harms, Robert T., "The Finnish Genitive Plural." Language, XXXIII, 533-537.

1583. Kolehmainen, John I., "When Finland's Tolstoy Met His Russian Master." ASEER, XVI, 534-541.

1584. Olli, John B. "Finnish Literature." Horatio Smith, Ed., <u>Columbia Dictionary of Modern European Literature</u>, pp. 265-266.

1585. Sahlman, Selma Siiri, "The Finnish Language in the United States." ASp, XXIV, 14-24.

1586. Sarajas, Annamari, "Contemporary Finnish Writing." BA, XXIX, 149-154.

1587. Sebeok, Thomas A., "Finnish Adverbial Nonce-Forms." Word, I, 281-283.

1588. _____. Spoken Finnish. Indiana University, Bloomington, Indiana: The Author, 1949, 479 pp.

1589. Stocker, Clara. Finnish Folk Songs: For Soprano and Alto (or Tenor) Recorders, Arranged. (Earls Court Repertoire.) Boston: E. C. Schirmer Music Co., n.d.

1590. Waldrop, A. Gayle, "The Daily Newspaper Press in Finland." JQ, XXXIV, 228-238.

1591. Whitney, Arthur Harold. Teach Yourself Finnish. New York: David McKay, 1956.

1592. Wuolle, Aino. English-Finnish Dictionary. 4th ed. New York: Heinman, 1952.

1593. _____. Finnish-English Dictionary. 3rd ed. New York: Heinman, 1951.

THE ARTS

1594. Anon., "15 Contemporary Finnish Designers." DQ, XXXVII, 1-25.

1595. Arnold, Elliott. Finlandia: The Story of Sibelius. (Holt Musical Biography Series.) New York: Henry Holt and Co., 1950, 247 pp.

1596. Heikel, Yngvar Sigurd, and Anni Collan. Dances of Finland. Published under the auspices of the Royal Academy of Dancing and the Ling Physical Education Association. (Handbooks of European National Dances.) New York: Chanticleer Press, 1948, 40 pp.

1597. Neuenschwander, Eduard and Claudia. Finnish Architecture and Alvar Aalto. New York: Praeger, 1954, 192 pp.

1598. Okkonen, Onni. Finnish Art. Tr. by Helen Goldthwait-Väänänen. New York: Hafner Publishing Co., 1946, 41 pp.

PHILOSOPHY AND RELIGION

1599. Kantonen, T. A., "The Finnish Church and Russian Imperialism." ChH, XX, ii, 3-13.

1600. Lutz, Howard TenBroeck, "The Protestant Reformation in Finland to 1539." DA, XVII, 2582-2583.

SOCIOLOGY

1601. Chamblis, Rollin, "Contributions of the Vital Statistics of Finland to the Study of Factors that Induce Marriage." ASoR, XXII, 38-48.

1602. Croog, Sidney H., "Premarital Pregnancies in Scandinavia and Finland." AJS, LVII, 358-365.

1603. Pehrson, Robert N. The Bilateral Network of Social Relations in Könkämäs Lapp District. (Indiana University Publications. Slavic and East European Series.) Bloomington, Indiana: Indiana University Press, 1956, 128 pp.

1604. Verkko, Veli Kaarle. Homicides and Suicides in Finland and Their Dependence on National Character. New York: Stechert-Hafner, 1951.

IX. HUNGARY

GENERAL

1605. Anon., "Developments in Hungary." UNR, III, vii, 5-12.

1606. _____, "The Hungarian Course." NBIC, III, ix, 3-15.

1607. _____, "Hungarian Journalism." NBIC, IV, iv, 38-42.

1608. Bennett, Paula Pogany, and V. R. Clark. Art of Hungarian Cooking: Two Hundred and Twenty-two Favorite Recipes. Drawings by Willy Pogany. New York: Doubleday, 1954, 223 pp.

1609. De Biro, Elisabeth. Hungarian Cooking: Simple and Economical Recipes. Ed. Katalin Frank. New York: British Book Centre, 1953, 143 pp.

1610. Fabian, Bela. Cardinal Mindszenty: The Story of a Modern Martyr. New York: Scribner, 1949.

1611. Free Europe Committee. Hungarian Section. Research and Publications Service. Miscellaneous Statistical Data on Hungary, 1950-1952. As Reported by the Budapest Central Bureau of Statistics. New York: Free Europe Committee, 1952.

1612. Free Europe Press Research Staff. Chronology of Events in Hungary, 1952. New York: Free Europe Press, 1953.

1613. _____. Chronology of Events in Hungary, 1953. New York: Free Europe Press, 1954.

1614. _____. Hungary in the Year 1951. New York: Free Europe Press, 1952.

1615. Gedye, G. E. R., "The New Course in Hungary: Promise and Performance." PoC, III, vi, 1-9.

1616. Green, Rosa. Hungarian-American Cook Book: Culinary Gems from World Famous Hungarian Recipes, Especially Adapted to American Tastes. 2nd rev. ed. New York: Tudor, 1949, 351 pp.

1617. Gyorgy, Andrew, "Postwar Hungary." RPol, IX, 297-321.

1618. Helmreich, Ernst C., ed. Hungary. (East-Central Europe Under the Communists: Mid-European Studies Center Series.) New York: Frederick A. Praeger for the Mid-European Studies Center of the Free Europe Committee, 1957.

1619. Jaszi, Oscar, "The Choices in Hungary." FA, XXIV, 453-466.

1620. Karasz, Arthur. Hungary in the Danubian Basin. Washington, D.C.: Mid-European Studies Center, 1953.

1621. Kendrick, Alexander, "Hungary: Showplace of Communism." NR, CXIX, xiii, 7-8.

1622. Kertesz, Stephen D. "Hungary." Stephen D. Kertesz, Ed., The Fate of East Central Europe, pp. 219-248.

1623. Lehrman, Hal, "Hungary-Rumania: Crime and Punishment; Pages from a Correspondent's Notebook." Com, II, 327-335.

1624. Maciuszko, George J., "In Memoriam Joseph Remenyi." BA, XXXI, 135-137.

1625. Major, Robert, "The Hungarian Press, 1914-1948: A Study of Vicissitudes." JQ, XXVI, 72-74.

1626. Montgomery, John Flournoy. Hungary: The Unwilling Satellite. New York: Devin-Adair, 1947, 251 pp.

1627. Nagy, Ferenc. The Struggle Behind the Iron Curtain. Tr. by Stephen K. Swift. New York: Macmillan, 1948, 471 pp.

1628. Orme, Alexandra, pseud. By the Waters of the Danube. Tr. Norbert Guterman. New York: Duell, Sloan and Pearce, 1951, 360 pp.

1629. Radio Free Europe. Information and Reference Department. Situation in Hungary. (Special Report, No. 28.) New York: Free Europe Committee, 1952, 6 pp.

1630. Schweng, Lorand D. Political, Social and Economic Developments in Post-War Hungary. Washington, D.C.: Free Europe Committee, 1950.

1631. Vajda, Paul, "Janos and the Conquerors." Rept, II, 11-13.

1632. Vambery, Rusztem. Hungarian Problem. Introd. Oscar Jaszi. New York: Nation, n.d., 47 pp.

1633. _____. Hungary—To Be or Not To Be. New York: Ungar, 1946, 208 pp.

1634. Vogeler, Robert A. I Was Stalin's Prisoner. By the author with Leigh White. New York: Harcourt Brace and Co., 1952.

1635. Willen, Paul, "Communist Hungary: The Locust and the Briefcases." Rept, XI, vii, 31-33.

1636. Winslow, Anne, ed., "Hungary." IC, No. 514, pp. 4-23.

GEOGRAPHY AND POPULATION

1637. Ladik, George. Water Supply in Hungary. (Publication of the Mid-European Studies Center, No. 20.) New York: Mid-European Studies Center, 1954, 63 pp.

1638. LeNard, Leslie, "Land and Peasants in Hungary." Government, Law and Courts Behind the Iron Curtain. Part VIII, pp. 71-92. Washington, D.C.: International Commission of Jurists, 1955.

1639. Lengyel, Emil. Americans from Hungary. Philadelphia: L. B. Lippincott Company, 1948, 319 pp.

1640. Pisky, Frederick S. "The People." Ernst Helmreich, Ed., Hungary, pp. 45-71. (East-Central Europe under the Communists).

1641. Rezler, Julius. "The Land." Ernst Helmreich, Ed., Hungary, pp. 34-44. (East-Central Europe under the Communists).

HISTORY

1642. Adamesteanu, Dinu, "Archeological News, Hungary 1939-1945." AJA, LV, 380-382.

1643. Borsody, Stephen, "Modern Hungarian Historiography." JMH, XXIV, 398-405.

1644. Brewster, Ralph Henry. Wrong Passport. New York: British Book Centre, 1955, 274 pp.

1645. Burks, Richard V., "Two Teleki Letters." JCEA, VII, 68-73.

1646. Capa, Robert. Slightly Out of Focus. New York: Henry Holt and Co., 1947.

1647. Cattell, David, "The Hungarian Revolution of 1919 and the Reorganization of the Comintern in 1920." JCEA, XI, 27-38.

1648. De Robeck, Nesta. Saint Elizabeth of Hungary: A Story of Twenty-four Years. Milwaukee: Bruce Publishing Co., 1954, 211 pp.

1649. Eppstein, John, ed. Hungary. (British Society for International Understanding. British Survey Handbooks, No. 4.) New York: Macmillan, 1945, 87 pp.

1650. Florinsky, Michael T., "The Case of Hungary." CH, XIII, 153-156.

1651. Helmreich, Ernst C. "Hungary in History." Ernst Helmreich, Ed., Hungary, pp. 1-16. (East-Central Europe under the Communists).

1652. Horthy, Admiral Nicholas. Memoirs. New York: Speller, 1957, 268 pp.

1653. Horvath, Peter, "Communist Tactics in Hungary Between June 1944 and June 1947; An Analysis and Appraisal." DA, XVI, 1273-1274.

1654. Juldanic, S. Guldescuv, "The Kossuth Tradition and Hungary's Delusion of Grandeur." SAQ, XLVII, 469-479.

1655. Kaczer, Illes. Siege. Tr. from the Hungarian by Lawrence Wolfe. New York: Dial Press, 1953, 594 pp.

1656. Kallay, Nicholas. Hungarian Premier: A Personal Account of a Nation's Struggle in the Second World War. New York: Columbia University Press, 1954, 517 pp.

1657. Karolyi, Mihaly, grof. Memoirs: Faith without Illusion. Tr. from the Hungarian by Catherine Karolyi. Introd. A. J. P. Taylor. New York: E. P. Dutton, 1956, 392 pp.

1658. Kelleher, Patrick J. Holy Crown of Hungary. (Papers and Monographs, Vol. XIII.) Rome and New York: American Academy in Rome, 1951, 124 pp.

1659. Kertesz, Stephen D. Diplomacy in a Whirlpool: Hungary Between Nazi Germany and Soviet Russia. Notre Dame, Indiana: Notre Dame Press, 1953.

1660. _____, "The Methods of Communist Conquest: Hungary 1944-1947." WP, III, 20-54.

1661. Kosa, John, "A Century of Hungarian Emigration, 1850-1950." ASEER, XVI, 501-514.

1662. _____, "The Early Period of Anglo-Hungarian Contact." ASEER, XIII, 414-431.

1663. Lelcai, T. J., "Historiography in Hungary, 1790-1848." JCEA, XIV, 3-18.

1664. Lengyel, Emil, "When Rome and Berlin Were in Flower; 'Hungary: The Unwilling Satellite' by John Flournoy Montgomery." SatR, XXXI, i, 12.

1665. Lukinich, Imre, "American Democracy As Seen by the Hungarians of the Age of Reform." JCEA, VIII, 270-281.

1666. Luthin, Reinhard H., "A Visitor From Hungary." SAQ, XLVII, 29-34. [Kossuth].

1667. Macartney, Carlile Aylmer. A History of Hungary, 1929-1945. 2 vols. New York: Praeger, 1957.

1668. _____. Medieval Hungarian Historians: A Critical and Analytical Guide. London and New York: Cambridge University Press, 1953, 190 pp.

1669. Madden, Henry Miller. Xantus, Hungarian Naturalist in the Pioneer West. Limited ed. Burlingame, California: W. P. Wreden, 1949, 312 pp.

1670. Moravcsik, Gyula, "Byzantine Christianity and the Magyars in the Period of Their Migration." ASEER, V, xiv, 29-45.

1671. _____, "The Role of the Byzantine Church in Medieval Hungary." ASEER, VI, xviii-xix, 134-151.

1672. Officinia Press, Budapest. Mutilated Budapest. New York: Heinman, 1946.

1673. Orme, Alexander. Comes the Comrade! New York: Morrow, 1950, 376 pp.

1674. Paloczy-Horvath, G. In Darkest Hungary. Forest Hills, New York: Transatlantic Arts, 1945, 158 pp.

1675. Pribram, A. F. Austria-Hungary and Great Britain, 1908-1914. New York: Oxford University Press, 1951.

1676. Remenyi, Joseph, "Klemens Mikes, Hungarian Exile (1690-1761)." Sym, XI, 123-126.

1677. Sebestyen, Endre. Kossuth, A Magyar Apostle of World Democracy. Pittsburgh: Expert Print Co., 1950, 218 pp.

1678. Sugar, Peter F., "The Influence of the Enlightenment and the French Revolution in Eighteenth Century Hungary." JCEA, XVII, 331-355.

1956 Revolution

1679. Anon., "Aggression in Hungary: A Soviet Definition Condemns Russia." ABAJ, XLIII, 928-929.

1680. _____, "Documents from Budapest." JCEA, XVII, 174-180.

1681. _____, "General Assembly Action on the Hungarian Question." DSB, XXXV, 867-874.

1682. _____, "The Hungarian Revolt." EE, VI, i, 16-25.

1683. _____, "Hungarian Youth in Revolt." EE, VI, i, 26, 28-37.

1684. _____, "Hungary After the Revolt; The First Six Months." EE, VI, vii, 28-36.

1685. _____, "New Action on Hungary." UNR, III, viii, 6-13.

1686. _____, "Preliminary Findings of Hungary Committee." UNR, III, x, 52-53.

1687. _____, "The Report on Hungary." UNR, IV, ii, 4-17.

1688. _____, "Witnesses Before Committee on Hungary." UNR, III, ix, 43.

1689. Aptheker, Herbert. Truth about Hungary. New York: Masses and Mainstream, 1957, 256 pp.

1690. Bailey, George, "The Road to Dishonor that Ended in Budapest." Rept, XVI, viii, 10-13.

1691. Bain, Leslie B., "Aftermath in Hungary." Rept, XVI, vi, 25-29.

1692. _____, "Budapest: Interview in a Basement Hideaway." Rept, XV, x, 13-15.

1693. _____, "How We Failed in Hungary." Rept, XVI, ii, 26-28.

1694. _____, "Hungary: The First Six Days." Rept, XV, viii, 20-21.

1695. _____, "Hungary: Guilty Consciences and Rehabilitated Corpses." Rept, XV, v, 18-21.

1696. Beke, Laszlo, pseud. Student's Diary: Budapest, October 16-November 1, 1956. Ed. and tr. Leon Kossar and Ralph M. Zoltan. New York: Viking Press, 1957, 125 pp.

1697. Berle, Adolf A. Jr., "Hungary and Human Dignity." America, XCVI, 222-226.

1698. Buhler, Neal V. "Hungarian Revolution." Ernst Helmreich, Ed., Hungary, pp. 352-389. (East-Central Europe under the Communists).

1699. Cherne, Leo, "Thirty Days That Shook the World." SatR, XXXIX, ii, 22-23; 31.

1700. Coffin, Tris, "Revolt in the Soviet Satellites." NR, CXXV, xiii, 10-12.

1701. Dean, Vera Micheles, "Hungarian Coup Widens East-West Rift." FPB, XXVI, xxxiv, 1-2.

1702. Dobriansky, Lev E., "After Hungary What?" UQ, XII, 339-346.

1703. Fejto, Francois. Behind the Rape of Hungary. Foreword by Jean-Paul Sartre. Tr. Norbert Guterman. New York: David McKay, 1957, 335 pp.

1704. _____, "The Revolt of the Hungarian Writers." PR, XXIV, 71-83.

1705. Free Europe Committee. Revolt in Hungary: A Documentary Chronology of Events Based Exclusively on Internal Broadcasts by Central and Provincial Radios, Oct. 23, 1956-Nov. 4, 1956. New York: Free Europe Committee, 1957, 112 pp.

1706. Fryer, Peter, "Revolution and Counterrevolution." PoC, VI, ii, 49-51.

1707. Garthoff, Raymond L., "The Tragedy of Hungary." PoC, VI, i, 3-11.

1708. Gleitman, Henry. Youth in Revolt: The Failure of Communist Indoctrination in Hungary. (Studies in Contemporary Communism, 2.) New York: Free Europe Press, 1957, 46 pp.

1709. Heller, Andor. No More Comrades. Chicago: Regnery, 1957, 157 pp.

1710. Hoffman, Stanley, "Sisyphus and the Avalanche: The United Nations, Egypt and Hungary." IO, XI, 446-469.

1711. International Conference of Free Trade Unions. Four Days of Freedom. New York: The Confederation, 1957.

1712. Jonas, Pal, "Josef Dudas; Key Figure in the Hungarian Revolt." EE, VI, ix, 3-9.

1713. _____, "My Generation; A Personal Account of Hungarian Youth in Revolt." EE, VI, vii, 17-27.

1714. Jones, Sally Ferris, "The 'Lost' Convoy from Budapest." AFSJ, XXXIV, ix, 22.

1715. Kiss, Sandor, "Parties and Programs in the Revolution." PoC, VI, ii, 47-49.

1716. Landy, Paul, "Hungary since the Revolution." PoC, VI, v, 8-15.

1717. Lasky, Melvin J., ed. The Hungarian Revolution. New York: Praeger, 1957.

1718. Lengyel, Emil, "The Hungarian Revolution and the UN." FPB, XXXVI, xxiv, 185-186.

1719. _____, "Rebellion in Budapest; 'The Hungarian Revolution,' edited by Melvin J. Lasky." SatR, XL, xxxiv, 19-20.

1720. _____, "Why Hungary Resists." FPB, XXXVI, vii, 57-58.

1721. Lowenthal, Richard, "Hungary—Were We Helpless?" NR, CXXXV, xxii, 10-15.

1722. Moor, Paul, "A Quick Trip to Budapest." Rept, XIV, viii, 36-39.

1723. Paloczy-Horvath, G. "A Meeting of Two Young Men; A Hungarian Intellectual Discusses Youth's Dilemma before the Revolt." EE, VI, i, 27-37.

1724. Rees, Elfan, "Lessons of the Hungarian Crisis." IC, No. 515, pp. 234-237.

1725. Schmid, Peter, "Budapest Under Fire; The Conspiracy of Freedom." Com, XXIII, 25-33.

1726. Stillman, Edmund O. The Ideology of Revolution: The People's Demands in Hungary, October-November, 1956. (Studies in Contemporary Communism, 1.) New York: Free Europe Press, 1957, 37 pp.

1727. Taylor, Edmond, "The Lessons of Hungary." Rept, XV, xi, 17-21.

1728. _____, "The Short Career of Poet Istvan." Rept, XV, viii, 22-23.

1729. United Nations. General Assembly. Report of the Special Committee on the Problem of Hungary. United Nations, General Assembly, Official Records: Eleventh Session, Supplement No. 18 (A/3592). New York, 1957.

1730. Zinner, Paul E., "Should U.S. Have Helped Hungary More?" FPB, XXXVI, xvii, 132, 134-135.

Hungarian Refugees

1731. Anon., "Athletes on the Run." NBIC, V, v, 40-41.

1732. _____, "The Exodus from Hungary." UNR, III, vii, 13-18.

1733. _____, "Repatriation and Treatment of Refugees from Hungary." UNR, III, ix, 38-41.

1734. Bailey, George, "The Fate of the Hungarian Refugees." Rept, XVI, v, 22-26.

1735. Dobos, Istvan, "Two Hundred Thousand Refugees." CEF, V, ii, 12-18.

1736. Major, Robert, "The Hungarian Emigrant Press." JQ, XXXII, 205-208.

1737. Michener, James A. The Bridge at Andau. New York: Random House, 1957, 270 pp.

1738. Warren, George L., "Meeting the Challenge of Moving Hungarian Refugees." DSB, XXXVI, 743-745.

GOVERNMENT AND POLITICS

1739. Anon. "The Constitutional System and Government." Ernst Helmreich, Ed., Hungary, pp. 74-103. (East-Central Europe under the Communists).

1740. _____, "German Documents on Hungary." DSB, XIV, 984-986.

1741. _____, "Hungarian Party: Propaganda, Education and Agitation." NBIC, IV, vii, 3-15.

1742. _____, "The Hungarian Press." EE, VI, viii, 3-17.

1743. _____, "Janos Kadar—A Profile." PoC, VI, v, 15-18.

1744. _____. "The Party and Political Organizations." Ernst Helmreich, Ed., Hungary, pp. 104-131. (East-Central Europe under the Communists).

1745. _____. "Propaganda and Information Media." Ernst Helmreich, Ed., Hungary, pp. 151-165. (East-Central Europe under the Communists).

1746. Braham, Randolph. "State Security." Ernst Helmreich, Ed., Hungary, pp. 132-150. (East-Central Europe under the Communists).

1747. Brunauer, Sandor. Communist Use of the Franchise in Hungary. (Mimeo. Series No. 24.) New York: Mid-European Studies Center, 1954, 16 pp.

1748. Fabian, Bela, "Hungary's and Rumania's Nazis-in Red; Hitler's Graduates Staff Stalin's New Order." Com, XI, 470-474.

1749. _____, "Red Quadrille in Budapest." America, LXXXIX, 455-456.

1750. Free Europe Committee. Hungarian Section. Research and Publications Service. Bolshevization Tactics in Hungary: Matyas Rakosi's Speech "The Way of Our People." Introd. Paul Fabry. New York: Free Europe Committee, 1952, 43 pp.

1751. _____. Hungarian Section. Research and Information Center. The Hungarian People's Republic. 2nd rev. ed. New York: Free Europe Committee, 1951.

1752. Free Europe Press Research Staff. Hungarian Party Congress, May 24-30, 1954. New York: Free Europe Press, 1954.

1753. Gabor, Robert. Organization and Strategy of the Hungarian Workers (Communist) Party. Hungarian Section. Research and Publications Service. New York: Free Europe Committee, 1952, 25 pp.

1754. Ignotus, Paul, "The AVH: Symbol of Terror." PoC, VI, v, 19-25.

1755. Kertesz, Stephen D., "A Political Solution for Hungary." CH, XXXIII, 7-15.

1756. Lehrman, Hal, "Hungary Samples Democracy." Nation, CLXI, 622-623.

1757. E. M., "Janos Kadar: A Profile." PoC, VI, v, 15-18.

1758. Nagy, Imre. Imre Nagy on Communism: In Defense of the New Course. New York: Praeger, 1957, 306 pp.

1759. _____. Imre Nagy on National Integrity and Coexistence. Chapters II and III from Imre Nagy On Communism. West New York, New Jersey: International Press Service, 1957.

1760. _____, "My Beliefs." EE, VI, vii, 3-16, 57.

1761. Nemes, Joseph. Signs In The Storm. Nashville, Tennessee: Abingdon, 1957.

1762. Putnam, Eva, "Foreign Press: Hungary." NR, CXVIII, i, 33-34.

1763. Racz, Istvan B., "The Smallholders' Party in the Revolt: The Rebirth of a Democratic Party." EE, VI, xi, 7-13.

1764. Revai, Jozsef, "Ideological Purity." EE, VI, v, 50-56.

1765. Ridder, Walter, "Our Propaganda in Hungary." NR, CXXXV, xxv, 12-13.

1766. United States. Congress. House. Select Committee on Communist Aggression. Communist Takeover and Occupation of Hungary. (Special Report No. 10. 83rd. Congress.) Washington, D.C.: United States Government Printing Office, 1954.

1767. _____. Library of Congress. Legislative Reference Service. Tensions Within the Soviet Captive Countries. Hungary, Pt. 7, pp. 173-205. Prepared at the request of the Committee on Foreign Relations. Washington, D.C.: United States Government Printing Office, 1954.

INTERNATIONAL RELATIONS

1768. Anon., "International Relief Inside Hungary." UNR, IV, ii, 53.

1769. _____, "The 'Obliging' Bear." NBIC, II, xii, 3-7.

1770. _____, "Release of Robert A. Vogeler by the Hungarian Government." DSB, XXIV, 723-725.

1771. _____, "U. S. Takes Serious View of Hungary's Conduct in Trial of Robert A. Vogeler." DSB, XXII, 323-326.

1772. _____, "A Young Hungarian Exile Speaks About Federation in East-Central Europe." CEF, V, ii, 23-26.

1773. Baross, George, "Hungary's Place in Europe." JCEA, IX, 167-172.

1774. Cottrell, Alvin J., and James E. Dougherty, "Hungary and the Soviet Idea of War." RusR, XVI, 17-26.

1775. Free Europe Committee. Hungarian Section. Information Service. Russian Cultural Penetration in Hungary. Ed. Istvan Csicsery-Ronay. 2nd supplemented ed. New York: Free Europe Committee, 1951.

1776. Hadsel, Winifred N., "U. S. Protests Soviet Actions in Hungary." FPB, XXVI, xxiii, 4.

1777. Hogye, Michael. The Paris Peace Conference of 1946: Role of the Hungarian Communists and of the Soviet Union. (Publication of the Mid-European Studies Center, No. 19.) New York: Mid-European Studies Center, 1954.

1778. Homonnay, Elemer. Wilson's Principles and the Southern Hungarian Question. Tr. Jo McKinney. Cleveland, Ohio: The Author, 1957.

1779. Kertesz, Stephen D. "Hungary in International Affairs Since 1945." Ernst Helmreich, Ed., Hungary, pp. 17-31. (East-Central Europe under the Communists).

1780. _____, "Soviet and Western Politics in Hungary, 1944-1947." RPol, XIV, 47-74.

1781. Nyaradi, Nicholas. My Ringside Seat in Moscow. New York: Crowell, 1952, 320 pp.

1782. Paikert, G. C., "Hungarian Foreign Policy in Intercultural Relations, 1919-1944." ASEER, XI, 42-65.

1783. Schoenfeld, H. F. Arthur, "Soviet Imperialism in Hungary." FA, XXVI, 554-566.

1784. United States. Department of State. America's Interest in Hungarian Struggle for Independence. (Documents and State Papers, Vol. I., No. 5.) Washington, D.C.: United States Government Printing Office, 1948.

1785. de Valpine, Jean E., "Soviet Power in Hungary and the Myth of the State." BBJ, I, 7-18.

1786. Wadsworth, James J., "Hungary: Our Continuing Responsibility." DSB, XXXVII, 192-195.

1787. Young, Richard, "The Development of International Law: Hungarian Plane Incident in the World Court." ABAJ, XL, 637-639.

LAW

1788. Arato, Istvan, "Hungarian Jurisprudence Relating to the Application of International Law by National Courts." AJIL, XLIII, 536-541.

1789. Bedo, Alexander Kalnoki. Laws on Nationalization in Hungary. Washington, D.C.: Library of Congress, 1955, 18 pp.

1790. _____, "Worker and Factory." Government, Law and Courts Behind the Iron Curtain. Pt. VII, Hungary, pp. 91-108. Washington, D.C.: International Commission of Jurists, 1955.

1791. _____, and George Torzsay-Biber. Legal Sources and Bibliography of Hungary. (Vladimir Gsovski, ed. Legal Sources and Bibliography of Eastern Europe). New York: Praeger, for the Free Europe Committee, 1956, 157 pp.

1792. Bone, Edith. Seven Years' Solitary. New York: Harcourt Brace, 1952.

1793. Brunauer, Alexander. The Right to Work in Hungary: An Outline of Labor Laws and Social Security in Today's Hungary. New York: Free Europe Committee, 1951, 19 pp.

1794. Gorove, Stephen, "Hungary: International Aspects of the New Penal Code." AJCL, III, 82-87.

1795. Torzsay-Biber, George. "New Substantive Criminal Law." Government, Law and Courts Behind the Iron Curtain. Preliminary ed. Pt. III, Hungary, pp. 75-104. Washington, D.C.: International Commission of Jurists, 1955.

1796. United States. Library of Congress. Law Library. Hungary: Labor Law (prior to labor code). Historical and Legal Background. Digest Index of East European Law. Washington, D.C.: Library of Congress, 1951, 13 pp.

THE ECONOMY

1797. Anon. "Agriculture." Ernst Helmreich, Ed., Hungary, pp. 229-258. (East-Central Europe under the Communists).

1798. _____, "Consumer Goods and Internal Trade in Hungary." NBIC, III, xii, 15-27.

1799. _____, "Hungarian Balance Sheet." NBIC, III, xii, 3-13.

1800. _____, "Hungary's Relief Needs and Economic Situation." UNR, III, ix, 41-42.

1801. _____, "Hungary's Second Five Year Plan (1956-1960)." NBIC, V, vi, 40-43.

1802. Bernatsky, Kornel. The Economics of the Individual Production Units in Hungary. Washington, D.C.: Mid-European Studies Center, 1953.

1803. _____. Organization of the Farming Industry. Washington, D.C.: Mid-European Studies Center, 1953.

1804. _____. Production Systems in Hungarian Agriculture. (Mimeo. Series No. 34.) New York: Mid-European Studies Center, 1954.

1805. Eckstein, Alexander, "Land Reform and the Transformation of Agriculture in Hungary." JFE, XXXI, 456-468.

1806. European Gas and Electric Company. Standard Oil Company (New Jersey) and Oil Production in Hungary by MAORT, 1931-1948. New York: Standard Oil Company of New Jersey, 1949.

1807. Free Europe Committee, Hungarian Research and Publication Center. The Position of the Hungarian Worker Between January 1, 1950 and November 1952. Ed. Laszlo Varga. New York: Free Europe Committee, 1953.

1808. Free Europe Press. Communist Land Policy in Hungary. New York: Free Europe Press, 1954.

1809. Free Europe Press Research Staff. The New Hungarian Economic Policy—Three Speeches by Imre Nagy and Matyas Rakosi. New York: Free Europe Press, 1953.

1810. Gabor, Robert. The Bolshevization of the Hungarian Trade-Unions (1945-1951). New York: Free Europe Committee, 1952.

1811. _____, and Bela Gyorky. "Public Health and Social Security." Ernst Helmreich, Ed., <u>Hungary</u>, pp. 334-349. (East-Central Europe under the Communists).

1812. Hilton, Howard J., Jr., "Hungary: A Case Story of Soviet Economic Imperialism." DSB, XXV, 323-327.

1813. _____. Hungary; A Case History of Soviet Economic Imperialism. (European and British Commonwealth Series, 29.) Washington, D.C.: Office of Public Affairs, Department of State, 1951.

1814. The Hungarian Oil Industry. (Publication of the Mid-European Studies Center, No. 15). New York: Mid-European Studies Center, 1954, 106 pp.

1815. Kemeny, Gyorgy. Economic Planning in Hungary, 1947-9. New York: Royal Institute of International Affairs, 1952, 146 pp.

1816. Kovacs, Imre. Agrarian Problems in Hungary. New York, 1950.

1817. Major, Robert. Failure of the Forint. New York: Research and Publication Service, Hungarian Section, Free Europe Committee, 1951.

1818. Nogaro, Bertrand, "Hungary's Recent Monetary Crisis and Its Theoretical Meaning." AER, XXXVIII, 526-542.

1819. Pisky, Frederick S. "Labor." Ernst Helmreich, Ed., <u>Hungary</u>, pp. 259-283. (East-Central Europe under the Communists).

1820. _____. Labor Discipline in Hungary. (Mimeo. Series No. 11.) New York: Mid-European Studies Center, 1954.

1821. Racz, Gabriel. "Transportation and Communications." Ernst Helmreich, Ed., <u>Hungary</u>, pp. 316-333. (East-Central Europe under the Communists).

1822. Schweng, Lorand D. Economic Planning in Hungary Since 1938. (Publication of the Mid-European Studies Center, No. 1.) New York: Mid-European Studies Center, 1951, 80 pp.

1823. Spulber, Nicolas. "National Income and Its Distribution." Ernst Helmreich, Ed., <u>Hungary</u>, pp. 214-228. (East-Central Europe under the Communists).

1824. Stowe, Leland, "Hungary's Agrarian Revolution." FA, XXV, 490-503.

1825. Vajk, Raoul. "Oil and Gas in Hungary in 1946." Transactions of the American Institute of Mining and Metallurgy and Engineers, 1947, 433-439.

1826. Vegh, Jeno. Foreign Trade and Agriculture of Hungary. Washington, D.C.: Mid-European Studies Center, 1953.

1827. 'Veritas,' "Hungary's 1955 Crude Output Best Yet." WO, CLXIII, 188-191.

1828. _____, "Production in Hungary, 17,280 or 14,550 BPD?" WO, CXXXIX, 234-238.

1829. Wszelaki, Jan. "Industry." Ernst Helmreich, Ed., Hungary, pp. 291-315. (East-Central Europe under the Communists).

1830. _____, "Mining." Ernst Helmreich, Ed., Hungary, pp. 284-290. (East-Central Europe under the Communists).

LANGUAGE

1831. Bernolak, Imre, ed. Modern English-Hungarian and Hungarian-English Dictionary. (Modern angol-magyar es magyar-angol szotar.) 4th ed. Ottawa: The Editor, 1957, 375 pp.

1832. Bizonfy, Ferencz. Angol-Magyar Szotar. (English-Hungarian Dictionary.) 8th enl. ed. Cleveland, Ohio: Szabadsag, 1952, 480 pp.

1833. Bobula, Ida Miriam. Sumerian Affiliations: A Plea for Reconsideration. Washington: Margaret Hanna, 1951.

1834. Columbia University. American Language Center. English as a Second Language, with Special Application to Hungarians. New York: Rinehart and Co., 1957.

1835. Fono, Lajos. English-Hungarian Technical Dictionary. Technical terminology revised by Imre Razso. New York: Heinman, 1951, 976 pp.

1836. Garvin, Paul L., "Pure-Relational Suffixes and Past Positions in Hungarian." Language, XXI, 250-255.

1837. Green, Bela. American Language Master (Americai Nyelvmester): An English-Hungarian Grammar, Interpreter, and Dictionary. 5th rev. and enlarged ed. New York: Kerekes Bros. Inc., 1957, 287 pp.

1838. _____. English-Hungarian and Hungarian-English Pocket Dictionary. New York: Kerekes Bros. Inc., 1957, 287 pp.

1839. Lotz, John. "Etymological Connections of magyar 'Hungarian.'" Morris Halle, et al., comp., For Roman Jakobson, pp. 677-681.

1840. _____, "Vowel Frequency in Hungarian." Word, VIII, 227-235.

1841. Orszagh, Laszla. Concise Hungarian-English Dictionary. New York: Heinman, 1955, 749 pp.

1842. _____. Hungarian-English Dictionary. New York: Heinman, 1953, 1444 pp.

1843. Sebeok, Thomas A., "Linguist, Informant and Units." MLJ, XXIX, 376-381.

1844. _____. Spoken Hungarian. 2nd ed. Indiana University, Bloomington, Indiana: The Author, 1948, 482 pp.

1845. Weiss, Edward. Paprikas Magyar-Angol Gyors Tanitomester (Hungarian-English Rapid Teaching Master.) New York: Paprikas Phono Corp., 1956, 157 pp.

1846. _____. Paprikas Magyar-Angol Zsebszotar. (Hungarian-English Pocket Dictionary.) New York: Paprikas Phono Corp., 1956, 160 pp.

THE ARTS

1847. Anon., "Bela Bartok." NBIC, IV, x, 29-41.

1848. Babbitt, Milton, "The String Quartets of Bartok." MQ, XXXV, 377-385.

1849. Bartok, Bela, "Music, Gypsy or Hungarian Music." MQ, XXXIII, 240-257.

1850. Gergely, Emro Joseph. Hungarian Drama in New York: American Adaptations, 1908-1940. Philadelphia: University of Pennsylvania Press, 1947, 197 pp.

1851. Gombosi, Otto, "Bela Bartok (1881-1945)." MQ, XXXII, 1-11.

1852. Remenyi, Joseph, "Aladar Schopflin: Hungarian Critic." Sym, I, iii, 20-30.

1853. _____, "Deszo Kosztolanyi, Hungarian 'Homo Aestheticus' (1885-1936)." ASEER, V, xii-xiii, 180-203.

1854. _____, "Ferenc Kazinczy, Hungarian Critic and Neologist." SEER, XXIX, 233-243.

1855. Saygun, A. Adnan, "Bartok in Turkey." MQ, XXXVII, 5-9.

1856. Starkie, Walter Fitzwilliam. Raggle-taggle: Adventures with a Fiddle in Hungary and Roumania. (Albemarle Library.) Hollywood-by-the-Sea, Florida: Transatlantic Arts, 1949, 324 pp.

1857. Strem, George G., "Cultural Life in Satellite Hungary." PS, VII, 78-89.

LITERATURE

1858. Ady, Endre. Selections of poems from [his] writings. Tr. by Antal Nyerges. Washington, D.C.: American Hungarian Federation, 1946.

1859. Cushing, George Frederick, ed. Hungarian Prose and Verse [in Hungarian]: A Selection with an Introductory Essay. (London, University. School of Slavonic and East European Studies. Dept. of Language and Literature. London East European Series: Language and Literature.) New York: De Graff, 1956, 197 pp.

1860. Kirkconnell, Watson, ed. Little Treasury of Hungarian Verse. (American Hungarian Library.) Washington, D.C.: American Hungarian Federation, 1947, 55 pp.

1861. Kormendi, Ferenc, "Hungary's Rebellious Muse." PoC, V, iii, 31-36.

1862. _____. "Literature and the Arts." Ernst Helmreich, Ed., Hungary, pp. 168-189. (East-Central Europe under the Communists).

1863. Remenyi, Joseph, "Aron Tamasi, the Transylvanian Regionalist (1897-)." ASEER, V, xiv-xv, 135-149.

1864. _____, "Daniel Berzenyi (1776-1836), Hungarian Horatian Poet." SEER, XXIV, 174-179.

1865. _____, "Ferenc Herczeg: Hungarian Playwright and Novelist." SEER, XXX, 175-184.

1866. _____, "Ferenc Mora, Hungarian Regionalist." SAQ, LV, 349-358.

1867. _____, "Geza Gardonyi, Hungarian Novelist and Playwright." SEER, XXXIII, 17-24.

1868. _____, "Gyula Juhasz; Great Hungarian Lyrist." BA, XX, 13-18.

1869. _____, "A Hungarian Exponent of French Realism, Zoltan Ambrus, 1861-1933." Sym, II, ii, 261-274.

1870. _____. Hungarian Literature. (American Hungarian Library, No. 2.) Washington, D.C.: American Hungarian Federation, 1946, 48 pp.

1871. _____, "Hungarian Literature in the Past Three Decades." BA, XXX, 13-20.

1872. _____, "Hungarian Publications in English." ASEER, VI, xvi-xvii, 179-180.

1873. _____, "Janos Kidolanyi: Hungarian Novelist and Playwright." SAQ, XLIX, 74-81.

1874. _____, "Jeno Peterfy, Hungarian Critic, Essayist and Monographer." Sym, IV, i, 107-119.

1875. _____, "J. Jeno Teransky." SAQ, LII, 391-398.

1876. _____, "Kalman Mikszath (1847-1910)." ASEER, VIII, 214-225.

1877. _____, "Lajos Aprily, Transylvanian Poet." BA, XXV, 21-23.

1878. _____, "Lajos Kassak, Hungarian 'Avant-Garde' Writer and Poet." MLJ, XXXV, 119-123.

1879. _____, "Mihaly Vorosmarty, Hungarian Poet, Playwright and Critic." SEER, XXXI, 353-363.

1880. _____, "Pal Gyulai, Hungarian Critic." MLJ, XXXVII, 393-397.

1881. _____, "Poetes Miseres; Three 19th-Century Hungarian Poets." Sym, IX, i, 91-105.

1882. _____, "Sandor Marai, 'Blender of Dreams and Substance.'" BA, XXIII, 339-344.

1883. _____, "Sandor Remenyik, Transylvanian Regionalist, 1890-1942." SAQ, LI, 94-102.

1884. _____, "The Transylvanian Poet Jeno Dsida (1907-1938)." SEER, XXXV, 249-254.

1885. _____, "Three Twentieth Century Hungarian Poets." ASEER, VI, xvi-xvii, 36-55.

1886. _____, "Two Hungarian Men of Letters." SEER, XXVII, 489-502.

1887. _____, "Two 19th-Century Hungarian Men of Letters, Janos Arany and Baron Jozsef Eotvos." Sym, VI, i, 157-180.

1888. _____, "Zsigmond Moricz, Hungarian Realist (1872-1942)." ASEER, IV, viii-ix, 165-181.

FOLKLORE

1889. Buday, Gyorgy. Dances of Hungary. Published under the auspices of the Royal Academy of Dancing and the Ling Physical Education Association. (Handbooks of European National Dances, No. 11.) New York: Chanticleer Press, 1950, 40 pp.

1890. Halpert, Herbert, "Hungarian Lying-Contest Tales about America." NYFQ, I, 236-237.

1891. Newman, Olga. Hungarian Folk Art. (Home Craft Course Series.) Plymouth Meeting, Pennsylvania: Mrs. C. Naaman Keyser, 1947.

1892. Pasti, Barbara, ed. Memoires of Hungary (Magyarorszag Legszabb Dalai): A Collection of its Best-loved Songs. With original Hungarian words. English lyrics by Olga Paul. New York: Edward B. Marks Music Corporation, n.d.

1893. Roheim, Geza. Hungarian and Vogul Mythology. (American Ethnological Society Monograph.) New York: J. J. Augustin, 1954, 86 pp.

1894. Scheiber, Alexander, "Additions to the History of the Legend of the Wandering Jew in Hungary." MF, VI, 155-158.

1895. Sebeok, Thomas A., "A New Collection of Hungarian Folktales." HF, VIII, 50-66.

EDUCATION

1896. Bako, Elemer, "Past and Present Hungarian Archival Collections." AA, XX, 201-207.

1897. Csicsery-Ronay, Istvan. Current Developments in Higher Education in Hungary. New York: Research and Publication Service, Hungarian Section, Free Europe Committee, 1951.

1898. Free Europe Committee. Hungarian Section. Research and Publication Service. Curricula of Hungarian Schools. New York: Free Europe Committee, 1952, 8 pp.

1899. _____. Hungarian Section. Research and Publication Service. Hungary's Bolshevized Pedagogy in 1951-1952. New York: Free Europe Committee, 1952, 16 pp.

1900. Fugedi, Erik, "The War Losses of Hungarian Private Archives." JCEA, VIII, 282-284.

1901. Juhasz, William. Blueprint for a Red Generation. The Philosophy, Methods and Practices of Communist Education as Imposed on Captive Hungary. (Publication of the Mid-European Studies Center, No. 7.) New York: Mid-European Studies Center, 1952, 101 pp.

1902. _____. "Education." Ernst Helmreich, Ed., Hungary, pp. 190-211. (East-Central Europe under the Communists).

1903. _____. "Pedagogical News from Bolshevik Hungary." Weekly Digest of News from Hungary. New York: Research and Publication Service, Hungarian Section, Free Europe Committee, 1951.

PHILOSOPHY AND RELIGION

1904. Bedo, Alexander Kalnoki, Hugo Kalnoky, Leslie LeNard, and George Torzsay-Biber. "Church and State in Hungary." Vladimir Gsovski, Ed., Church and State Behind the Iron Curtain, pp. 69-158. (Mid-European Studies Center of the Free Europe Committee).

1905. Brunauer, Sandor. Religion under the Hungarian Communist Regime. Washington, D.C.: Mid-European Studies Center, 1953.

1906. Hungarian People's Republic. Washington Legation. The Relationship Between Church and State in the Hungarian People's Republic. Washington, D.C.: n.d.

1907. Kertesz, Stephen D., "Church and State in Hungary: The Background of the Cardinal Mindszenty Trial." RPol, XI, 208-219.

1908. Kovach, Francis J., "The Philosophy of Bela von Brandenstein." RM, XI, 315-336.

1909. Mindszenty, Jozsef Cardinal. Cardinal Mindszenty

Speaks. Introd. Akos Zombory. New York: Longmans, Green and Co., 1949.

1910. Shuster, George N. In Silence I Speak. New York: Farrar, Straus, 1956, 296 pp.

1911. _____, "A Stand and a Fight for a Faith; 'Cardinal Mindszenty Speaks' by Joseph Cardinal Mindszenty, and 'Cardinal Mindszenty' by Bela Fabian." SatR, XXXII, xxxi, 19-20.

1912. Swift, Stephen K. The Cardinal's Story. New York: Macmillan, 1949. [A biography of Cardinal Mindszenty.]

SOCIOLOGY

1913. Gleitman, Henry, and Joseph J. Greenbaum. Preliminary Results of Depth Interviews and Attitude Scales. Inquiry into Political and Social Attitudes in Hungary of the Free Europe Press. Edmund O. Stillman, Project Chief. New York: Free Europe Committee, 1957, 157 pp.

1914. Kosa, John, "Hungarian Society in the Time of the Regency, (1920-1944)." JCEA, XVI, 254-266.

1915. Sebeok, Thomas A. Data on Nakedness and Related Traits in Hungary. Indiana University, Bloomington, Indiana: The Author, 1949, 212 pp.

1916. _____, "Work and Cult Among the Hungarian Peasants." SJA, III, 147-182.

X. POLAND

GENERAL

1917. Anon., "Letters from Poland." NBIC, I, xii, 34-39.

1918. _____, "Poland Revisited." NBIC, V, ii, 21-27.

1919. Bolek, Francis, and Ladislaus J. Siekaniec. Polish American Encyclopedia. Advisory ed. Alphonse S. Wolanin. Vol. I. New York: Polish Book Import Company Inc., n.d.

1920. Brant, Irving, "Eyewitness in Poland." NR, CXIV, i, 15-18.

1921. _____. New Poland. New York: International Universities Press, 1946, 116 pp.

1922. Bregman, Alexander, "The Russian Army's Polish Cat's-paws." Rept, IV, vi, 26-28.

1923. Cary, William Harris. Poland Struggles Forword. New York: Greenberg, 1949, 192 pp.

1924. Czapski, Joseph. The Inhuman Land. [Translated from French. Foreword by Daniel Haleig. Introduction by Edward Crankshaw]. New York: Sheed and Ward, 1952, 301 pp.

1925. Davies, Raymond Arthur. Truth About Poland. Toronto: World News Co., 1946, 91 pp.

1926. Elias, T. "Two Studies: Iwanska, Alicja, 'Contemporary Poland, Society, Politics, Economy.'" CEF, IV, ii, 22-30.

1927. Fay, Sidney B., "No Peace for Poland." CH, IX, 7-11.

1928. Gross, Feliks, "The Fate of Poland." JCEA, VIII, 242-269.

1929. Halecki, Oscar. "Contemporary Poland." Leonid I. Strakhovsky, Ed., Handbook of Slavic Studies, pp. 560-581.

1930. _____, ed. Poland. (East-Central Europe Under the Communists: Mid-European Studies Center Series.) New York: Frederick A. Praeger for the Mid-European Studies Center of the Free Europe Committee, 1957.

1931. _____. "Poland." Stephen D. Kertesz, Ed., The Fate of East-Central Europe, pp. 129-149.

1932. _____, "Poland at the Tenth International Congress of Historical Sciences." PolR, I, i, 5-22.

1933. Harsch, Joseph C., "Poland: A Change Ahead?" Rept, I, viii, 28-29.

1934. Herling, Gustav. A World Apart. New York: New American Library, 1952, 256 pp.

1935. Iwanska, Alicja, ed. Contemporary Poland: Society, Politics, Economy. Chicago: University of Chicago, 1955, 578 pp.

1936. Kerstein, Edward S. Red Star over Poland: A Report from behind the Iron Curtain. Introd. by Szymon St. Deptula. Appleton, Wisconsin: Nelson Publishing Co., 1947, 174 pp.

1937. Korab, Alexander, "Poland: The Search for Independence." PoC, V, vi, 10-16.

1938. Kott, Jan, "Night and Day in Warsaw." PR, XXIV, 83-86.

1939. Maks, Leon. Russia by the Back Door. Tr. from the Polish by Rosamond Batchelor. London and New York: Sheed and Ward, 1954, 264 pp.

1940. Montias, John M., "Current Trends in Poland." FPB, XXXVI, xxii, 173-175.

1941. Murphy, Charles J. V., "The Polish Salient." Fortune, LV, vi, 124-127, 266-280.

1942. Nasakowski, Marian, "Poland." UNR, II, v, 39-40.

1943. Polanie Club, Minneapolis. Treasured Polish Recipes for Americans. Minneapolis, Minnesota: Polanie Club, 1948.

1944. Rose, William John. Poland Old and New. Toronto: Clarke, Irwin and Co., 1948.

1945. Schmitt, Bernadotte, et al. Poland. (United Nations Series, Robert J. Kerner, Ed.) Berkeley: University of California, 1945, 500 pp.

1946. Sharp, Samuel L. Poland. White Eagle on a Red Field. Cambridge, Massachusetts: Harvard University Press, 1953, 326 pp.

1947. _____, "Red and Black In Poland." NR, CXXIX, xi, 11-13.

1948. Smith, Harold Montauge. Polish Post Seven Years War: A Complete Record of All Stamps, Seals, Fieldposts and Labels Issued by the Polish Postal Authorities at Home and Abroad During the Six Years' War, from 1939 to 1945. Detroit: Pulaski Philatelic Club, 1946, 81 pp.

1949. Stern, Peter, "Poland." Focus, III, 1-6.

1950. _____. The Struggle for Poland. Washington, D.C.: Public Affairs Press, 1953, 79 pp.

1951. Strong, Anna Louise. Inside Liberated Poland. New York: National Council of American-Soviet Friendship, 1945, 47 pp.

1952. _____. I Saw the New Poland. Boston: Little, Brown and Co., 1946, 280 pp.

1953. Strzetelski, Stanislaw, "A Nation Struggles for Her Culture." PolR, I, i, 23-29.

1954. Super, Margaret Low (Stump) (Ann Su Cardwell, pseud.). Case for Poland. By Ann Su Cardwell. Introd. by R. H. Markham. Ann Arbor, Michigan: Ann Arbor Press, 1945.

1955. _____. Poland, Here is the Record: An American's View. By Ann Su Cardwell. Ann Arbor, Michigan: Michigan Committee of Americans for Poland, C. F. Wells, Chairman, 1945, 64 pp.

1956. Super, Paul. Twenty Five Years with the Poles. Brooklyn, New York: Paul Super Memorial Fund, 1950.

1957. Syers, Kenneth, "Letter from Poland." NR, CXV, xi, 325-326.

1958. Thomson, S. Harrison, "The New Poland." FPR, XXIII, 226-234.

1959. United States. Library of Congress. Legislative Reference Service. Tensions Within the Soviet Captive Countries. Poland, Pt. 5, pp. 117-147. Prepared at the request of the Committee on Foreign Relations. Washington, D.C.: United States Government Printing Office, 1954.

1960. Urban, Jerzy, "A Jug on My Head; Comments on a Visit to Lodz." EE, VI, ii, 16-20.

1961. Urs Graf, Basle, Switzerland. Warsaw 1945.

New York: Heinman, 1946. [Text in English, French, German and Polish], 80 pp.

1962. Valkenier, Elizabeth, "Soviet Impact on Polish Post-War Historiography, 1946-1950." JCEA, XI, 372-396.

1963. Warfield, Hania, and Gaither Warfield. Call Us to Witness: A Polish Chronicle. Chicago: Ziff-Davis, 1945, 434 pp.

1964. Weintraub, Wiktor. "Soviet Cultural Imperialism in Poland." Waldemar Gurian, Ed., Soviet Imperialism: Its Origins and Tactics, pp. 91-113.

1965. Werth, Alexander, "Poland, 1949." Nation, CLXXVIII, 583-584, 610-611.

1966. Wittlin, Joseph, "The Perception of Hell." SatR, XXX, xxiv, 7-8.

GEOGRAPHY AND POPULATION

1967. Gorczynski, Wladyslaw. Comparison of Climate of the United States and Europe with Special Attention to Poland and her Baltic Coast. (Polish Institute of Arts and Sciences in America. Polish Institute Series, No. 7.) New York: Herald Square Press, 1945, 288 pp.

1968. Goudy, A. P. "Racial Origins." W. F. Reddaway, Ed., Cambridge History of Poland, I, pp. 1-15.

1969. Horak, S., "Why Western Ukranian Territories Were Annexed to Poland." JG, I, i, 51-68; II, i-ii, 49-67.

1970. Hordynsky, Sviatoslav, "Stubborn Polish Claims to Western Ukraine." UQ, VI, 265-269.

1971. Kelly, Eric P. Land of the Polish People. Rev. ed. (Portraits of the Nations Series.) Philadelphia: Lippincott, 1952, 84 pp.

1972. Koehl, Robert L., "The Deutsche Volksliste in Poland." JCEA, XV, 354-366.

1973. Leszczycki, Stanislaw, "The Geographical Bases of Contemporary Poland." JCEA, VII, 357-373.

1974. J. M. M. "The People." Oscar Halecki, Ed., Poland, pp. 44-69. (East-Central Europe under the Communists).

1975. Maudlin, W. Parker, and D. S. Akers. The

Population of Poland. Washington, D.C.: United States Bureau of the Census, 1954, 198 pp.

1976. Roucek, Joseph S., "Geopolitical Problems of Poland." WAI, XVII, 420-427.

1977. Schechtman, Joseph B., "The Polish-Soviet Exchange of Population." JCEA, IX, 289-314.

1978. V. H. W., and Abraham Melezin. "The Land." Oscar Halecki, Ed., Poland, pp. 17-43. (East-Central Europe under the Communists).

1979. Werth, Alexander, "Poland Today: The New Lands." Nation, CLXV, 308-309.

1980. Zielinski, Henryk. Population Changes in Poland, 1939-1950. (Publication of the Mid-European Studies Center, No. 16.) New York: Mid-European Studies Center, 1954, 101 pp.

HISTORY

1981. Beck, Jozef. Final Report. New York: Robert Speller and Sons, 1957.

1982. Black, Cyril E., "Poznan and Europe In 1848." JCEA, VIII, 191-206.

1983. Blackburn, Edwin Charles. "Stanislas Leszczynski: A Study in the Enlightenment." DA, XVII, 132-133.

1984. Bonatt, Edward, "International Law and the Plebiscites In Eastern Poland, 1939." JCEA, V, 378-393.

1985. Boswell, A. Bruce. "Jagiello's Successors: the Thirteen Years' War and the Knights, 1434-1466." W. F. Reddaway, Ed., Cambridge History of Poland, I, pp. 232-249.

1986. _____. "Territorial Division and the Mongol Invasions." W. F. Reddaway, Ed., Cambridge History of Poland, I, pp. 85-107.

1987. _____. "The Twelfth Century: from Growth to Division." W. F. Reddaway, Ed., Cambridge History of Poland, I, pp. 43-59.

1988. Brock, Peter, "The Birth of Polish Socialism." JCEA, XIII, 213-231.

1989. _____, "Boleslaw Wyslouch, Founder of the Polish Peasant Party." SEER, XXX, 139-163.

1990. _____, "The Early Years of the Polish Peasant Party, 1895-1907." JCEA, XIV, 219-235.

1991. _____, "Joseph Cowen and the Polish Exiles." SEER, XXXII, 52-69.

1992. _____, "Polish Democrats and English Radicals, 1832-1862: A Chapter in the History of Anglo-Polish Relations." JMH, XXV, 139-156.

1993. _____, "Zeno Swietoslawski, A Polish Forerunner of the 'Narodniki.'" ASEER, XIII, 566-587.

1994. Chandler, Alvin Duke, "The Poles at Jamestown." PolR, II, iv, 3-6.

1995. Columbia University, Klub Polski. Polish Insurrection of 1863: A Study of New York Editorial Opinion Concerning this Conflict. New York: Columbia University, Klub Polski, n.d., 131 pp.

1996. Czaplinski, W. "The Reign of Wladyslaw." W. F. Reddaway, Ed., Cambridge History of Poland, I, pp. 488-501.

1997. Dyboski, Roman. Poland in World Civilization. (Ludwik Krzyzanowski, ed.) New York: Barrett, 1950.

1998. Dziewanowski, M. K., "Appeasement at Vienna." CH, XVI, 16-21; 83-85.

1999. _____, "Czartoryski: European Federalist." CH, XIX, 21-28.

2000. _____, "Czartoryski—A European Federalist." CEF, III, ii-iii, 21-24.

2001. _____, "Herzen, Bakunin, and the Polish Insurrection of 1863." JCEA, VIII, 58-78.

2002. _____, "Pilsudski's Federal Policy, 1919-1921." JCEA, X, 113-128, 270-287.

2003. _____, "The Polish Revolutionary Movement and Russia, 1904-1907." HSS, IV, 375-394.

2004. _____, "Revolution of 1904-05 and the Marxist Movement of Poland." JCEA, XII, 259-275.

2005. _____, "Social Democrats Versus 'Social Patriots': The Origins of the Split of the Marxist Movement in Poland." ASEER, X, 14-25.

2006. _____, "World War I and the Marxist Movement of Poland." ASEER, XII, 72-92.

2007. Forst-Battaglia, Otto. "Jan Sobieski." W. F. Reddaway, Ed., Cambridge History of Poland, I, pp. 532-556.

2008. Gasiorowski, Zygmunt, "The Conquest Theory of the Genesis of the Polish State." Spec, XXX, 550-560.

2009. _____, "Did Pilsudski Attempt to Initiate a Preventive War in 1935?" JMH, XXVII, 135-152.

2010. _____, "A Note on Louis L. Gerson's 'Woodrow Wilson and the Rebirth of Poland, 1914-1920.'" PolR, II, iv, 89-94.

2011. _____, "Polish-Czechoslovak Relations, 1918-1922." SEER, XXXV, 172-193.

2012. _____, "Polish-Czechoslovak Relations, 1922-1926." SEER, XXXV, 473-504.

2013. Gerson, Louis. Woodrow Wilson and the Rebirth of Poland, 1914-1920: A Study in the Influence on American Policy of Minority Groups of Foreign Origin. New Haven: Yale University Press, 1953, 166 pp.

2014. Gorka, Olgierd Aleksander. Outline of Polish History, Past and Present. 2nd rev. and enlarged ed. Forest Hills, New York: Transatlantic Arts, 1945, 140 pp.

2015. Gronowicz, Antoni. Piasts of Poland. Tr. by Joseph Vetter. New York: Scribner, 1945, 199 pp.

2016. Halecki, Oscar. "Casimir the Great." W. F. Reddaway, Ed., Cambridge History of Poland, I, pp. 167-187.

2017. _____. "From the Union with Hungary to the Union with Lithuania: Jadwiga, 1374-1399." W. F. Reddaway, Ed., Cambridge History of Poland, I, pp. 188-209.

2018. _____. "Historical Background." Oscar Halecki, Ed., Poland, pp. 2-16. (East-Central Europe under the Communists).

2019. _____. History of Poland. Tr. by Monica Gardner and Mary Corbridge-Patkaniowska. 2nd ed. New York: Roy Publishers, 1956, 359 pp.

2020. _____. "Medieval Poland." Leonid I. Strakhovsky, Ed., Handbook of Slavic Studies, pp. 77-96.

2021. _____. "Modern Poland until the Partitions (1509-1795)." Leonid I. Strakhovsky, Ed., Handbook of Slavic Studies, pp. 223-242.

2022. _____. "Partitioned Poland (1795-1918)." Leonid I. Strakhovsky, Ed., Handbook of Slavic Studies, pp. 326-345.

2023. _____. "Problems of the New Monarchy: Jagello and Vitold, 1400-1434." W. F. Reddaway, Ed., Cambridge History of Poland, I, pp. 210-231.

2024. _____, "Wilson and Poland Today." PolR, I, ii-iii, 6-11.

2025. Hechinger, Fred M., "'I Saw Poland Betrayed' by Arthur Bliss Lane." SatR, XXXI, x, 11-12.

2026. Hepner, Benoit P. "History and the Future: The Vision of August Cieszkowski." RPol, XV, 328-349.

2027. Jarecka, Louise Llewellyn, "Archaeological News; Poland." AJA, LIV, 423-424.

2028. Jedlicki, M. Z. "German Settlement in Poland and the Rise of the Teutonic Order." W. F. Reddaway, Ed., Cambridge History of Poland, I, pp. 125-147.

2029. Jedrzejewicz, Waclaw, ed. Poland in the British Parliament 1939-1945. Volume I: British Guarantees to Poland to the Atlantic Charter (March 1939-August 1941). New York: Jozef Pilsudski Institute of America, 1946, 493 pp.

2030. Kaeckenbeeck, Georges S., "Upper Silesia Under the League of Nations." AAAPSS, CCXLIII, 129-133.

2031. Kaplan, Herbert H., "The Election of the Last King of Poland; Stanislas Augustus Poniatowski." PolR, II, i, 27-49.

2032. Komarnicki, Titus. Rebirth of the Polish Republic: A Study in the Diplomatic History of Europe 1914-1920. Toronto: William Heinemann Ltd., 1957, 776 pp.

2033. Konopczynski, Wladyslaw. Casimir Pulaski. Tr. from the Polish by Irena Makarewicz. Milwaukee, Wisconsin: Polish Roman Catholic Union of America, 1947, 62 pp.

2034. _____, "England and the First Partition of Poland." JCEA, VIII, 1-23.

2035. Korduba, M. "The Reign of John Casimir: Part I, 1648-54." W. F. Reddaway, Ed., Cambridge History of Poland, I, pp. 502-517.

2036. Kostrzewski, Jozef, "Post-War Prehistory in Poland." AJA, LIII, 355-356.

2037. Kukiel, Marion. Czartoryski and European Unity,

1770-1861. Princeton: Princeton University Press, 1955, 354 pp.

2038. Kulski, W. W., "A Statesman of the Middle Zone of Europe." JCEA, X, 9-20.

2039. Kusielewicz, Eugene, "The Jefferson-Niemcewicz Correspondence." PolR, II, iv, 7-21.

2040. _____, "New Light on the Curzon Line." PolR, I, ii-iii, 82-88.

2041. _____, "Wilson and the Polish Cause at Paris." PolR, I, i, 64-79.

2042. Lane, Arthur Bliss. I Saw Poland Betrayed: An American Ambassador Reports to the American People. Indianapolis: Bobbs-Merrill, 1948, 344 pp.

2043. Laserson, Max M., and James T. Shotwell. Poland and Russia, 1919-1945. New York: King's Crown Press, Columbia, 1945, 114 pp.

2044. Leslie, R. F. Polish Politics and the Revolution of November 1830. (London. University Historical Studies, 3.) New York: De Graff, 1956, 307 pp.

2045. Levytsky, Orest, "Socinianism in Poland and South-West Rus." AUA, III, i, 485-508.

2046. Luciv, W. "Ukrainians and the Polish Revolt of 1863." EEProb, I, i, 22-34.

2047. Malara, Jean, "Poland after the Death of Stalin." PoC, IV, ii, 12-19.

2048. Malinowski, Wladyslaw R., "The Pre-War Unionization of Polish Workers." JCEA, V, 176-185.

2049. Manning, Clarence A. Soldier of Liberty, Kasimir Pulaski. New York: Philosophical Library, 1945.

2050. Marcinkowski, Karol. The Crisis of the Polish-Swedish War, 1655-1660. Wilberforce, Ohio: The Author, 1952, 98 pp.

2051. Mikolajczyk, Stanislaw. Rape of Poland: Pattern of Soviet Aggression. (Whittlesey House Publication.) New York: McGraw-Hill, 1948.

2052. Morley, Charles, "Alexander I and Czartoryski." SEER, XXV, 405-426.

2053. _____, "Czartoryski's Attempts at a New Foreign Policy Under Alexander I." ASEER, XII, 463-485.

2054. _____, "The European Significance of the November Uprising." JCEA, XI, 407-416.

2055. Nowak, Frank. "The Interregna and Stephen Batory, 1572-86." W. F. Reddaway, Ed., Cambridge History of Poland, I, pp. 369-391.

2056. _____. "Sigismund III, 1587-1632." W. F. Reddaway, Ed., Cambridge History of Poland, I, pp. 451-474.

2057. Pajewski, J. "Zygmunt August and the Union of Lublin." W. F. Reddaway, Ed., Cambridge History of Poland, I, pp. 348-368.

2058. Papee, F. "Imperial Expansion and the Supremacy of the Gentry, 1466-1509." W. F. Reddaway Ed., Cambridge History of Poland, I, pp. 250-272.

2059. Petrovich, Michael B., "Russian Pan-Slavists and the Polish Uprising of 1863." HSS, I, 219-248.

2060. Pociecha, W. "Zygmunt (Sigismund) I, 1506-1548." W. F. Reddaway, Ed., Cambridge History of Poland, I, pp. 300-321.

2061. Porskyj, Volodymyr, "The Decembrist Milieu in the Diary of Pelagja Rosciszewska." AUA, I, 29-35.

2062. Reddaway, W. F., et. al., eds. The Cambridge History of Poland: From the Origins to Sobieski. Vol. I. Cambridge and New York: Cambridge University Press, 1950.

2063. Rodes, John E., "The Welfare State of Stanislas Leszczynski." Hist, XIX, i, 39-47.

2064. Rutkowski, J. "The Social and Economic Structure in the Fifteenth and Sixteenth Centuries." W. F. Reddaway, Éd., Cambridge History of Poland, I, pp. 441-450.

2065. Sass, Charles, "The Election Campaign in Poland in the Years 1696-1697." JCEA, XII, 111-127.

2066. Sobieski, Zygmunt, "Reminiscences from Lwow." JCEA, VI, 351-374.

2067. Staniewska, Anna, "Roman Dyboski, 1883-1945." BA, XX, 140-142.

2068. Straus, Hannah Alice. The Attitude of the Congress of Vienna Toward Nationalism in Germany, Italy, and Poland. New York: Columbia University Press, 1949, 164 pp.

2069. Taborsky, Edward, "A Polish-Czechoslovak Confederation." JCEA, IX, 379-395.

2070. Tomkiewicz, W. "The Reign of John Casimir: Part II, 1654-68." W. F. Reddaway, Ed., Cambridge History of Poland, I, pp. 518-531.

2071. von Torne, P. O. "Poland and the Baltic in the First Half of the Seventeenth Century." W. F. Reddaway, Ed., Cambridge History of Poland, I, pp. 475-487.

2072. Tymieniecki, K. "The Reunion of the Kingdom, 1295-1333." W. F. Reddaway, Ed., Cambridge History of Poland, I, pp. 108-124.

2073. Wandycz, Piotr S. Czechoslovak-Polish Confederation and the Great Powers, 1940-1943. (Indiana University Publications. Slavic and East European Series, Volume III.) Bloomington: Indiana University Publications, 1956.

2074. _____, "The Polish Precursors of Federalism." JCEA, XII, 346-355.

2075. Warvariv, C., "Polish-Ukrainian Relations, November 1916-November 1918." EEProb, I, i, 35-50.

2076. deWeerd, Hans, "Report of the Netherlands Ambassador to the Polish Court on Bohdan Khmelnytsky in 1654." UQ, XIII, 56-58.

2077. Ziffer, Bernard, "Gresham or Copernicus?" PolR, II, ii-iii, 71-77.

2078. Zyzniewski, Stanley J., "Miljutin and the Polish Question." HSS, IV, 237-248.

World War II
2079. Anders, Lt. Gen. Wladyslaw. An Army in Exile: The Story of the Second Polish Corps. New York: Macmillan, 1949, 319 pp.

2080. Anon. Dark Side of the Moon. Preface T. S. Eliot. New York: Scribner, 1947, 229 pp.

2081. Bolles, Blair, "Compromise on Poland Sought At San Francisco." FPB, XXIV, xxviii, 1-2.

2082. _____, "Polish Accord Reveals Efficacy at U. S. Intervention in Europe." FPB, XXIV, xxxvii, 4.

2083. Ciechanowski, Jan. Defeat in Victory. New York: Doubleday, 1947, 397 pp.

2084. Fields, Harold, "The Fight to Save Warsaw: 'Silent is the Vistula' by Irena Orska." SatR, XXIX, xxix, 26.

2085. Folkman, Adolf. Promise Hitler Kept. As told to Stefan Szende. New York: Roy Publishers, 1945, 218 pp.

2086. Friedman, Philip. Their Brothers' Keepers. New York: Crown Publishers, 1957, 224 pp.

2087. Gingerich, William Francis. The German Administration of the General Government of Poland, 1939-1941. Washington, D.C.: 1949.

2088. Goldstein, Bernard. Stars Bear Witness. Tr. and ed. Leonard Shatzkin. New York: Viking Press, 1949, 295 pp.

2089. Halecki, Oscar, "The Sixth Partition of Poland." RPol, VII, 142-155.

2090. Halpern, Ada. Conducted Tour. Foreword by Eleanor F. Rathbone. New York: Sheed and Ward, 1945.

2091. Janta, Aleksander. Bound with Two Chains. New York: Roy Publishers, 1945, 234 pp.

2092. Jones, Dorsey D., and Robert F. Smith, "The Katyn Forest Massacre." WAI, XXIII, 304-315.

2093. Komorowski, Tadeusz. Secret Army. New York: Macmillan, 1951, 407 pp.

2094. Korbonski, Stefan. Fighting Warsaw: The Story of the Polish Underground State, 1939-1945. Tr. from the Polish by F. B. Czarnomski. New York: Macmillan, 1956, 495 pp.

2095. Kulkielko, Renya. Escape from the Pit. Foreword by Ludwig Lewisohn. New York: Sharon, 1947.

2096. Orska, Irena. Silent is the Vistula. New York: Longmans, Green and Company, 1946, 295 pp. [An account of Warsaw uprising of 1944 by a woman officer in the underground Polish Home Army]

2097. Rawicz, Slavomir. The Long Walk. New York: Harper, 1956, 240 pp.

2098. Sharp, Samuel L., "Poland's Tragic Debacle; 'Fighting Warsaw,' by Stefan Korbonski." SatR, XL, iv, 30.

2099. Soltan, Christina. Under Strange Skies. New York: Macmillan, 1948.

2100. Standley, W.H., et al. "Katyn Forest Massacre: Muder or High Strategy?" USNIP, LXXVIII, 1053-1065.

2101. Stypulkowski, Zbigniew Francewicz. Invitation to Moscow. New York: David McKay, 1951, 359 pp.

2102. Swiecicki, Marek. With the Red Devils at Arnhem. Forest Hills, New York: Transatlantic Arts, 1945.

2103. Szmaglewska, Seweryna. Smoke over Birkenau. New York: Henry Holt and Co., 1947.

2104. Szoszkies, Henryk J. No Traveler Returns. Ed. with a prologue and epilogue by Curt Riess. New York: Doubleday, 1945. [At head of title: The Story of Hitler's Greatest Crime.]

2105. United States. Congress. Select Committee to Conduct an Investigation of the Facts, Evidence and Circumstances of the Katyn Forest Massacre. 82nd Congress, 1st. and 2nd. Sess. Hearings Before the Select Committee to Conduct An Investigation of the Facts, Evidence and Circumstances of the Katyn Forest Massacre on Investigation of the Murder of Thousands of Polish Officers in the Katyn Forest near Smolensk, Russia. Washington, D.C.: United States Government Printing Office, 1950.

2106. Unseen and Silent: Adventures from the Underground Movement Narrated by Paratroops of the Polish Home Army. Tr. from the Polish by George Iranek-Osmecki. Foreword by Wladyslaw Anders and Sir Colin Gubbins. New York and London: Sheed and Ward, 1954, 350 pp.

2107. Virski, Fred. My Life in the Red Army. New York: Macmillan, 1949.

2108. Vucinich, Wayne S., "Poland's Fate; I. Munich to Yalta." CH, XVI, 331-336; II. "Yalta to Potsdam." XVII, 15-21.

2109. Wankowicz, Melchior, ed. Golgotha Road. New York: National Committee of Americans of Polish Descent, 1945, 62 pp.

2110. Woolsey, L..H., "Poland at Yalta and Dumbarton Oaks." AJIL, XXXIX, 295-300.

2111. Wright, Herbert, "Poland and the Crimea Conference." AJIL, XXXIX, 300-308.

2112. Zbyszewski, Karol. Fight for Narvik: Impressions of the Polish Campaign in Norway. 2nd ed. Forest Hills, New York: Transatlantic Arts, n.d.

2113. Zywulska, Krystyna. I Came Back. New York: Roy Publishers, 1951.

GOVERNMENT AND POLITICS

2114. Anon. "Constitution and Government." Oscar Halecki, Ed., Poland, pp. 72-96. (East-Central Europe under the Communists).

2115. _____, "Polish Balance Sheet." NBIC, IV, i, 3-17.

2116. _____, "The Polish Course." NBIC, III, i, 3-10.

2117. _____, "The Polish Election." EE, VI, iii, 3-12.

2118. _____. "Politics and Political Organizations." Oscar Halecki, Ed., Poland, pp. 97-126. (East-Central Europe under the Communists).

2119. _____. "Propaganda." Oscar Halecki, Ed., Poland, pp. 127-148. (East-Central Europe under the Communists).

2120. _____, "The Swiatlo Story." NBIC, IV, iii, 3-36.

2121. Bialer, Sewerin, "I Chose Truth; A Former Leading Polish Communist's Story." NBIC, V, x, 3-15.

2122. Bregman, Alexander, "The Urge to Confess." Rept, II, ix, 15-16.

2123. Brock, Peter, "The Politics of the Polish Peasant." IRSH, I, 210-222.

2124. Brzezinski, Zbigniew, "Poland—A Political Glimpse." PoC, VI, v, 26-30.

2125. Deutscher, Isaac, "Rokossovsky: Pole, or Russian?" Rept, XVI, i, 27-29.

2126. Dziewanowski, M. K. "Biographical Sketches of Leading Figures of the Communist Regime." Oscar Halecki, Ed., Poland, pp. 516-534. (East-Central Europe under the Communists).

2127. _____, "The Foundation of the Communist Party of Poland." ASEER, XI, 106-122.

2128. _____. "Poland, 1950-1954. 'New Course' or 'New Look.'" JCEA, XV, 380-393.

2129. Free Europe Committee. Polish Section. Research and Publications Service. A Special Report on the Draft Constitution for Poland. New York: Free Europe Committee, 1952, 6 pp.

2130. _____. Polish Section. Research and Publications Service. The Text of the Polish Communist New Draft Constitution.

Published in Warsaw on January 27, 1952. New York: Free Europe Committee, 1952, 23 pp.

2131. Ebon, Martin, "'The Rape of Poland'; 'Struggle Behind the Iron Curtain.'" SatR, XXXI, ii, 13.

2132. Fay, Sidney B., "Poland's Troubled Elections." CH, XII, 212-219.

2133. Gwozdz, Jozef, and Kazimierz Glabisz. "The Armed Forces and National Security." Oscar Halecki, Ed., Poland, pp. 149-175. (East-Central Europe under the Communists).

2134. Jones, Ralph A., "Polish Local Government Reorganized on Soviet Model." ASEER, X, 56-68.

2135. Korab, Alexander, "Strange Alliance: Piasecki and the Polish Communists." PoC, VI, vi, 33-38.

2136. Kulikowsky, D., "A Picture of Polish Imperialism." EEProb, I, i, 69-77.

2137. R., "The Fate of Polish Socialism." FA, XXVIII, 125-143.

2138. Rudzinski, Aleksander Witold. Polish Public Administration Before World War II. (Mimeo. Series No. 30.) New York: Mid-European Studies Center, 1954.

2139. Rudzka, Walentyna, "Federal Ideas of Romuald Traugutt." CEF, III, i, 13-15.

2140. Siemienski, J. "Constitutional Conditions in the Fifteenth and Sixteenth Centuries." W. F. Reddaway, Ed., Cambridge History of Poland, I, pp. 416-440.

2141. Sorensen, R. C., and L. L. Meyer, "Local Uses of Wired Radio in Communist Ruled Poland." JQ, XXXII, 343-348.

2142. Staar, Richard F., "The Central Committee of the United Polish Workers' Party (PZPR)." JCEA, XVI, 371-383.

2143. _____, "The Polish Communist Party 1918-1948." PolR, I, ii-iii, 41-58.

2144. _____, "The Political Bureau of the United Polish Workers' Party." ASEER, XV, 206-215.

2145. _____, "The Political Framework of Communist Poland." DA, XIV, 703.

2146. _____, "Regimentation of Youth in Satellite Poland." SSSQ, XXXVII, i, 7-19.

2147. _____, "The Secretariat of the United Polish Workers' Party (PZPR)." JCEA, XV, 272-285.

2148. Stedman, Murray S. Jr., "Theory of the Polish People's Democracy." WPQ, IX, 835-849.

2149. Ulam, Adam B., "The Crisis in the Polish Communist Party." RPol, XII, 83-98.

2150. United States. Congress. House of Representatives, 83rd Congress, 2nd. session, Select Committee on Communist Aggression. Communist Take-over and Occupation of Poland. Washington: United States Government Printing Office, 1954, 37 pp.

2151. _____. Congress. House of Representatives, 83rd Congress, 2nd session, Select Committee on Communist Aggression. Polish Documents. Appendix to Committee Report on Communist Take-over and Occupation of Poland. Washington: United States Government Printing Office, 1954, 176 pp.

2152. Wagner, W. J., "The New Constitution of Poland." AJCL, II, 59-63.

Since October, 1956

2153. Anon., "Ferment in Poland." NBIC, V, iii, 3-14.

2154. _____, "Gomulka's Keynote Speech." NBIC, V, xi, 4-5; 42-43.

2155. _____, "Insurrection in Poznan." NBIC, V, viii, 3-6.

2156. _____, "Poland's October Revolution." EE, VI, i, 3-15; ii, 3-16.

2157. _____, "Poland's 'Road to Socialism.'" PoC, VI, i, 1-3.

2158. _____, "Upheaval in Poland." NBIC, V, xi, 3, 6.

2159. _____, "Youth in Ferment; A Survey of Current Problems in Poland." NBIC, V, x, 16-21; 24-26; xi, 19-27.

2160. Bain, Leslie B., "Can Gomulka Reconcile the Irreconcilable?" Rept, XVI, xi, 23-26.

2161. Deutscher, Isaac, "October Revolutions, New Style." Rept, XV, viii, 14-17.

2162. Dziewanowski, M. K., "Gomulka and Polish National Communism: A Brief Historical Sketch." PoC, VI, i, 43-46.

2163. Sharp, Samuel L., "Gomulka: A Pole Apart." Rept, II, ix, 12-15.

2164. Shneiderman, S. L., "Before the Earthquake in Poland." Rept, XV, viii, 18-19.

2165. _____, "The Four Days that Shook Poland." Rept, XV, x, 15-18.

2166. Strzetelski, Stanislaw, "The Background of the October Events in Poland." PolR, I, iv, 68-79.

2167. _____, "The True Force Behind the October Revolution in Poland." PolR, II, ii-iii, 19-31.

LAW

2168. Bloch, Josef. Labour Legislation and Social Insurance in Poland. Foreword by H. Samuels. Toronto: Carswell, 1945, 55 pp.

2169. Grzybowski, Kazimierz. Poland's Labor Law. Washington: Mid-European Law Project, Library of Congress, 1951, 41 pp.

2170. Gwozdz, Jozef, and Rosada, Stefan, "Sources of Legal Information in Poland." LLJ, XLVI, 120-130.

2171. Nagorski, Zgymunt, Sr., ed. Legal Problems Under Soviet Domination. (Studies of the Association of Polish Lawyers in Exile in the U. S. Volume I.) New York: Association of Polish Lawyers in Exile in U. S. A., 1956, 132 pp.

2172. Rudzinski, Aleksander Witold, "Sovietization of Civil Law in Poland." ASEER, XV, 216-243.

2173. Semmes, Harry H., "Justice Behind the Iron Curtain: Polish Lawyers Fight for the Criminally Accused." ABAJ, XLIII, 697-698.

2174. Studies in Polish and Comparative Law: A Symposium of Twelve Articles. Foreword by H. C. Gutteridge. Toronto: Carswell Co., 1945, 274 pp.

2175. United States. Library of Congress. Law Library. Poland: Catalogue of Sources of Legal Information. Washington, D.C.: Library of Congress, 1951, 19 pp.

2176. _____. Library of Congress. Law Library. Poland: Labor Law—Introduction: General Survey. Digest Index of East European Law. Washington, D.C.: Library of Congress, 1951, 41 pp.

INTERNATIONAL AFFAIRS

2177. Arciszewski, Franciszek, "Some Remarks about the Strategical Significance of the New and Old Soviet Polish Border." PolR, I, ii-iii, 89-96.

2178. Arski, Stefan. New Polish-German Border. Washington: Polish Embassy, 1947.

2179. Budz, Andrew I., Jr. The Oder-Neisse Border: Weapon in Communist Domination over Poland. New York: Columbia University. R. I. Certificate Essay, 1954, 80 pp.

2180. Co-ordinating Committee of American-Polish Associations in the East. Polish-Russian Problem. New York: The Committee, n.d., 67 pp.

2181. Czubatyi, Nicholas, "Ukraine—Between Poland and Russia." RPol, VII, 331-353.

2182. _____, "The Ukrainians and the Polish Russian Border Dispute." UQ, I, 57-71.

2183. Dean, Vera Micheles, "Polish Border Issue Highlights State of U. S.-Russian Relations." FPB, XXVI, xxvii, 1-3.

2184. Gronowicz, Antoni. Pattern for Peace: The Story of Poland and Her Relations with Germany. New York: Paramount Publishing Company, 1951, 215 pp. [A defense of the Oder-Neisse line as Poland's German frontier]

2185. Halecki, Oscar, and Rothfels, Hans, "Comment and Answer—German Polish Relations." RPol, VIII, 255-257.

2186. _____, "The United States and Poland." RPol, XVI, 91-110.

2187. Hogan, W.C., et al., "Soviet Faith, A Case Study of Poland." USNIP, LXXX, 869-881.

2188. Koehl, Robert Lewis, "The Eternal Polish Question." CH, XIX, 340-347.

2189. Konovalov, Serge, ed. Russo-Polish Relations. Princeton: Princeton University Press, 1945.

2190. Kridl, Manfred, "Poland and Russia in the Past and in the Future." JCEA, V, 143-165.

2191. Krzesinski, Andrew John. Poland, Germany—A Lasting Peace?" New York: Renaissance Center Co., 1948.

2192. _____. Poland's Rights to Justice. New York: Devin-Adair, 1946, 120 pp.

2193. Kulski, W. W., "The Lost Opportunity for Russian-Polish Friendship." FA, XXV, 667-685.

2194. Kusielewicz, Eugene, "A Reader's Guide to Polish-American Studies." PolR, I, 155-165.

2195. Mason, John Brown. The Danzig Dilemma. Stanford University, California: Stanford University Press, 1946, 377 pp.

2196. Michalowski, Roman, "Poland and Europe: A German Appraisal." PolR, II, iv, 65-87.

2197. Mikolajczyk, Stanislaw, "Soviet Problems in Poland." CH, XXVI, 327-338.

2198. Sherman, Harold J. Social Impact of the Warsaw Convention: A Critique of the Lee Decisions on the Warsaw Convention and a Plea for Early Rectification. New York: The Exposition Press, 1952, 156 pp.

2199. Struve, Gleb, "A Chapter in Russo-Polish Relations." RusR, VI, 56-68.

2200. Thomson, S. Harrison, et al., "Problems of Polish Foreign Policy." FPR, XXIII, 234-235.

THE ECONOMY

2201. Alton, Thad Paul. Polish Postwar Economy. (Columbia University Russian Institute Studies.) New York: Columbia University Press, 1955, 330 pp.

2202. _____, "Polish Postwar Planning." DA, XIV, 43-44.

2203. Anon. "Agriculture." Oscar Halecki, Ed., Poland, pp. 289-320. (East-Central Europe under the Communists).

2204. _____. "Consumers' Goods Industries." Oscar Halecki, Ed., Poland, pp. 384-405. (East-Central Europe under the Communists).

2205. _____, "Ferment and the Polish Economy." NBIC, V, iv, 3-10.

2206. _____, "I'm from Nowa Huta!" NBIC, II, vi, 34-36.

2207. _____, "Internal Trade and Consumer Goods in Poland." NBIC, III, vi, 15-19.

2208. _____, "Poland's Five Year Plan (1956-1960)." NBIC, V, ix, 26-30.

2209. _____, "Polish Grain Balance." NBIC, V, ii, 31-37.

2210. _____, "Survey of Food Conditions in Poland." DSB, XVII, 223-224.

2211. _____, "Transportation in Poland." NBIC, IV, xii, 15-27.

2212. Dean, Vera Micheles, "Poland's Economy Revives Despite Political Conflicts." FPB, XXVI, xvi, 2-3.

2213. _____, "Poles, Czechs Face Different Recovery Problems." FPB, XXVIII, xxix, 3-4; xxx, 2-3; xxxi, 3-4.

2214. Dolina, Joseph, and Bogdan Mieczkowski. "Domestic Trade and Finance." Oscar Halecki, Ed., Poland, pp. 424-443. (East-Central Europe under the Communists).

2215. _____. "Foreign Trade." Oscar Halecki, Ed., Poland, pp. 444-466. (East-Central Europe under the Communists).

2216. _____. "Labor." Oscar Halecki, Ed., Poland, pp. 467-490. (East-Central Europe under the Communists).

2217. _____, "Poland's Foreign Trade and Related Economic Treaties and Agreements, 1945-1955." PolR, I, iv, 50-65.

2218. Douglas, Dorothy Sybil (Wolff). Transitional Economic Systems: The Polish-Czech Example. (International Library of Sociology and Social Reconstruction.) New York: Humanities Press, 1953, 375 pp.

2219. Dziewanowski, M. K., "Aid for Poland: A Calculated Risk." CH, XXXIII, 43-48.

2220. Free Europe Committee. Land Policy in Poland 1944-1953. New York: Free Europe Committee, 1953.

2221. Fryde, Matthew M. Selected Works on Polish Agrarian History and Agriculture. (Publication of the Mid-European Studies Center, No. 6.) New York: Mid-European Studies Center, 1952, 87 pp.

2222. Gryziewicz, Stanislaw. Polish Fuel and Power

in the Soviet Economic Sphere. (Mimeo. Series No. 23.) Mid-European Studies Center, 1954, 10 pp.

2223. Grzybowski, Kazimierz, "Polish Workers' Councils." JCEA, XVIII, 272-286.

2224. _____, "Trade Unions in Communist Poland." PoC, V, v, 16-21.

2225. _____, "Workers' Councils in Poland." PoC, VI, iv, 16-19.

2226. Koc, Adam, and Wlodzimierz Baczynski. The Polish State Budget 1950: An Analysis. New York: Mid-European Studies Center, 1952.

2227. Koenig, Ernest, "Land Reform in Poland." FAgr, XVII, 139-144.

2228. _____, "A New Farm Policy for Poland." FAgr, XXI, 3-4.

2229. Kotiuznski, Antoni. Agricultural Insurance in Poland. (Mimeo. Series No. 16.) New York: Mid-European Studies Center, 1954, 19 pp.

2230. Kowalczyk, Leon S. Poland's Chemical Industry. (Mimeo. Series No. 9.) New York: Mid-European Studies Center, 1954.

2231. Lange, Oscar, "On the Emergency Program." NBIC, V, xi, 28-32.

2232. Minc, Hilary. Poland's Economy, Present and Future. New York: Polish Research and Information Service, 1949, 45 pp.

2233. Montias, John Michael, "The Polish Iron and Steel Industry." ASEER, XVI, 301-322.

2234. _____, "Price-Setting Problems in the Polish Economy." JPE, LXV, 486-505.

2235. _____, "Unbinding the Polish Economy." FA, XXXV, 470-485.

2236. Nuttonson, Michael Y. Agricultural Climatology of Poland and its Agro-climatic Analogies in North America. (International Agro-climatological Series, Study No. 2.) Washington, D.C.: American Institute of Crop Ecology, 1947.

2237. Pronin, Dimitrit, "Land Reform in Poland: 1920-1945." LE, XXV, 133-145.

2238. Rosu, G. G., "USSR Draws Poland Into 'Zonal' Planning." WO, CLXIII, 191-194.

2239. Rudzki, Adam. "Transportation." Oscar Halecki, Ed., Poland, pp. 406-423. (East-Central Europe under the Communists).

2240. Shneiderman, S. L., "Behind the Scenes in Poland's Model City." Rept, XV, v, 15-17.

2241. Siekanowicz, Peter. Legislation on Sovietization of Industry and Commerce in Poland. Washington: Mid-European Law Project, Library of Congress, 1954, 17 pp.

2242. Skrzypek, Stanislaw, "Agricultural Policies in Poland." JCEA, XVI, 45-70.

2243. _____, "The Principles of the Budgetary System in Poland." PolR, I, i, 30-55.

2244. _____, "Real Wages in Poland—A Footnote." PoC, V, v, 21-22.

2245. Spulber, Nicolas. "National Income and Product." Oscar Halecki, Ed., Poland, pp. 270-288. (East-Central Europe under the Communists).

2246. Stankiewicz, Wladislaw, and J. M. Montias. Institutional Changes in the Postwar Economy of Poland. (Publication of the Mid-European Studies Center, No. 21.) New York: Mid-European Studies Center, 1955, 125 pp.

2247. Strong, Anna Louise, "Polish Land Reform." Nation, CLX, 122.

2248. Taylor, Jack. The Economic Development of Poland, 1919-1950. Ithaca, New York: Cornell University Press, 1952, 222 pp.

2249. Trend, Harry, and Franciszek J. Proch. "Social Insurance and Health Service." Oscar Halecki, Ed., Poland, pp. 491-514. (East-Central Europe under the Communists).

2250. United Nations. Food and Agriculture Organization. Report of the FAO Mission for Poland. New York: Columbia University Press, 1948.

2251. V. H. W. "Mining." Oscar Halecki, Ed., Poland, pp. 321-349. (East-Central Europe under the Communists).

2252. Warne, Colston E., "Economic Planning in Poland." CH, XIII, 257-260.

2253. Werth, Alexander, "Poland: Collectivization and Crisis." Nation, CLXVII, 466-467.

2254. Winston, Victor H., "The Polish Bituminous Coal-Mining Industry." ASEER, XV, 38-70.

2255. Wszelaki, Jan. "Economic Background." Oscar Halecki, Ed., Poland, pp. 250-269. (East-Central Europe under the Communists).

2256. _____. "Industry." Oscar Halecki, Ed., Poland, pp. 350-383. (East-Central Europe under the Communists).

2257. _____. "The Manpower Problem in Poland and Czechoslovakia." CEF, I, ii, 8-12.

2258. Zawadzki, Michal I., "Ten Years of Communist Planning in Polish Agriculture." JFE, XXXVIII, 792-798.

LANGUAGE

2259. Baluta, Joseph Francis John. Practical Handbook of the Polish Language. New York: Polish Book Importing Co., 1947. [A new edition.]

2260. Bolanowski, Jerome Edwin. New Polish Grammar. 4th ed. Milwaukee, Wisconsin: Polonia Publishing Co., 1945.

2261. Corbridge-Patkaniowska, Mary. Teach Yourself Polish. (Teach Yourself Books.) New York: Roy Publishers, 1950, 276 pp.

2262. Eckersley, Charles E., and Mary Corbridge-Patkaniowska. Essential English Dictionary: English-Polish Version. New York: Longmans, Green and Co., 1951.

2263. _____, and Mary Corbridge-Patkaniowska. Essential English for Polish Students: An Introductory Course. New York: Longmans, Green and Co., 1951, 99 pp.

2264. Handy Technical Dictionary in Eight Languages: English, German, French, Italian, Portuguese, Spanish, Polish, Russian. New York: Heinman, 1952. [Subdivided into language groups with each group arranged in alphabetical order. First published in 1949 by Disce.]

2265. Kierst, Wladyslaw. Concise Dictionary: English-Polish and Polish-English. New York: Heinman, 1957.

2266. Mac Callum, Thomas W. English for Poles. New York: Roy Publishers, n.d.

2267. Polish American Encyclopedia. Vol. I. New York: Polish Book Importing Company Inc., 1954.

2268. Polish-English and English-Polish Vest Pocket Dictionary, Complete with All Important Words, Nearly 30,000 Entries, Contains Rules for Polish Pronunciation, the Latest and the Best. Baltimore: Ottenheimer, 1955, 270 pp.

2269. Schenker, Alexander M., "Gender Categories in Polish." Language, XXXI, 402-408.

2270. _____, "Polish Conjugation." Word, X, 469-481.

2271. Scherer, Philip, "Derivation in Polish." Language, XXIV, 294-297.

2272. _____, "Juncture in Polish." Language, XXII, 353-357.

2273. Serech-Shevelov, Yury, "The Problem of Ukrainian-Polish Linguistic Relations from the Tenth to the Fourteenth Century." Word, VIII, 329-349.

2274. Stanislawski, Jan, ed. English-Polish and Polish-English Dictionary. 2nd ed. 2 vols. in 1. New York: Roy Publishers, 1948, 896 pp.

2275. _____. Newest Pocket English-Polish and Polish-English Dictionary. 2 vols. in 1. New York: Roy Publishers, 1948, 532 pp.

2276. Stankiewicz, Edward, "The Distribution of Morphemic Variants in the Declension of Polish Substantives." Word, XI, 554-574.

2277. _____, "Expressive Derivation of Substantives in Contemporary Russian and Polish." Word, X, 457-468.

2278. _____. "The Phonemic Patterns of the Polish Dialects: A Study in Structural Dialectology." Morris Halle, et al., comp., For Roman Jakobson, pp. 518-530.

2279. Tomaszewski, Wiktor. English-Polish and Polish-English Medical Dictionary. 2nd enl. ed. Baltimore: Williams and Wilkins, 1953, 304 pp.

2280. Trzaska, Evert & Michalski's Dictionary, English-Polish & Polish-English. New York: Heinman, 1946, 1140 pp.

2281. Wallenberg, Ernst, and M. Gorynski. 1000 Words in English: An Easy Way of Learning English for Poles. New York: Roy Publishers, n.d.

2282. Westfal, Stanislaw, "The Polish Adjective 'Radziecki,' 'Soviet.'" Word, VII, 168-176.

2283. _____. Study in Polish Morphology: The Genitive Singular Masculine. (Slavistic Printings and Reprintings, 8.) New York: Lounz, 1956, 399 pp.

2284. Wojcicka, Janina, ed. Polish Abbreviations, A Selective List. Washington, D.C.: Library of Congress, Slavic and East European Division, 1955, 122 pp.

2285. Zawacki, Edmund, "On Scientific Designation of Aspects in Russian and Polish." AATSEEL, XIII, 4-9.

THE ARTS

2286. Anon., "Polish 'Intelligentsia Clubs.'" EE, VI, ix, 15-26.

2287. _____, "The Polish Renaissance." BMC, LXXXVI-LXXXVII, 3-4.

2288. Balbin, Julius, "Leopold Staff, 1878-1957." PolR, II, ii-iii, 113-117.

2289. Boswell, A. Bruce. "Cultural and Social Conditions in the Middle Ages." W. F. Reddaway, Ed., Cambridge History of Poland, I, pp. 148-166.

2290. Bruckner, A. "Polish Cultural Life in the Seventeenth Century." W. F. Reddaway, Ed., Cambridge History of Poland, I, pp. 557-569.

2291. Conrad, Doda, "Re-evaluating a Major Polish Composer; 'The Life and Death of Chopin' by Casimir Wierzynski." SatR, XXXII, LXIV, 32-35.

2292. D'Otrange, M. L., "Polish Painting Surveyed in Detroit." Arts, XIX, xviii, 16.

2293. Estreicher, Karol, "Polish Renaissance Architecture." BMC, LXXXVI-LXXXVII, 4-9.

2294. Gronowicz, Antoni. Tchaikovsky. Tr. from the Polish by Joseph Vetter. New York: Thomas Nelson and Sons, 1946, 192 pp.

2295. Halecki, Oscar. "The Renaissance in Poland: Cultural Life and Literature." W. F. Reddaway, Ed., Cambridge History of Poland, I, pp. 273-286.

2296. Horniatkevych, Damian, "The Ukrainian Medieval Paintings on Polish Soil." UQ, VII, 162-169.

2297. Janta, Alexander, "Barriers into Bridges: Notes on the Problem of Polish Culture in America." PolR, II, ii-iii, 79-97.

2298. Jaspers, Karl, "Endurance and Miracle; 'The Captive Mind,' by Czeslaw Milosz." SatR, XXX, xxiii, 13, 30.

2299. Jelenski, K. A., "The Dilemma of the Polish Intellectuals." PR, XXIX, 247-260.

2300. Komornicki, S. S. "The Renaissance in Poland: the Fine Arts." W. F. Reddaway, Ed., Cambridge History of Poland, I, pp. 287-299.

2301. Krzyzanowski, Julian, "Stanislaw Wyspianski, 1869-1907." PolR, II, iv, 23-32.

2302. Mars, Anna Maria, "Polish Miniature Painters in the First Half of the 16th Century." BMC, LXXXVI-LXXXVII, 17-20.

2303. Michalkowa, J., "Dutch Portraits in Polish Collections." BMC, XCIX, 92-93.

2304. Milosz, Czeslaw. The Captive Mind. New York: Vintage Books, 1955, 250 pp.

2305. _____, "Poland: Voices of Disillusion." PoC, V, iii, 24-30.

2306. Morawski, Stefan, "Polish Theories of Art Between 1830 and 1850." JAAC, XVI, 217-236.

2307. Philipp, Hans, "Timbered Architecture in Poland." SOAHJ, VI, iii-iv, 14-17.

2308. Piotrowska, Irena. The Art of Poland. New York: Philosophical Library, 1947.

2309. Poznanski, C. Polish Artists in Great Britain. Forest Hills, New York: Transatlantic Arts, 1945.

2310. Savery, Frank, "Ceramic Art in Poland." BMC, LXXXVIII, 117-121.

2311. Soltynski, Roman. Glimpses of Polish Architecture. Tr. Peter Jordon. Foreword by W. G. Holford. 2nd. ed. Forest Hills, New York: Transatlantic Arts, 1945.

2312. Strakacz, Aniela. Paderewski as I Knew Him. Tr. from the Polish by Halina Chybowska. New Brunswick, New Jersey: Rutgers University Press, 1949, 338 pp.

2313. Tatarkiewicz, W. "Polish Art in the Seventeenth Century." W. F. Reddaway, Ed., Cambridge History of Poland, I, pp. 570-578.

2314. Topolski, Feliks. 88 Pictures. Introd. by Harold Acton. Forest Hills, New York: Transatlantic Arts, 1951, 96 pp. [Polish paintings.]

2315. Wallis, Mieczyslaw, "Polish Contributions to Aesthetics and Science of Art before 1939: A Selective Bibliography." JAAC, VII, 51-52.

2316. Zaborska, Stefania, "Popular Trends in Polish Renaissance Painting." BMC, LXXXVI-LXXXVII, 20-25.

2317. Zarnecki, Jerzy, "Renaissance Sculpture in Poland: Padovano and Michalowicz." BMC, LXXXVI-LXXXVII, 10-17.

LITERATURE

2318. Coleman, Arthur P. "Polish Literature." Horatio Smith, Ed., Columbia Dictionary of Modern European Literature, pp. 630-634.

2319. Coleman, Marion M., "Malczevski's 'Marja,' A Hundred and Twenty Years After (1825-1945)." ASEER, IV, viii-ix, 111-126.

2320. _____, ed. Wayside Willow: Prose and Verse Translated from the Polish by Members of the Klub Polski. Student ed. Loretta M. Bielawska. New York: Columbia University, Klub Polski, 1945, 50 pp.

2321. Columbia University, Klub Polski. Mazovian Melody: Translations of Prose and Verse on Mazovian Themes by Members [of the Club] together with a Mazovian Cantata by Henry Nagorka. Ed. by Marion Moore Coleman. Cheshire, Connecticut: A. P. Coleman, 1948, 57 pp.

2322. Folejewski, Zbigniew, "Jan Lechon's Poetic Work." PolR, I, iv, 3-7.

2323. _____, "Polish Poetry During the Last War." ASEER, X, 216-225.

2324. Gasiorowska, Xenia, "The Postwar Polish Historical Novel." CL, IX, 17-32.

2325. Jakobson, Roman, "Polish Scholarship and Pushkin." ASEER, V, xii-xiii, 88-92.

2326. Janta, Alexander, "A Conrad Family Heirloom at Harvard." PolR, II, iv, 41-64.

2327. Kridl, Manfred. Anthology of Polish Literature. (Columbia Slavic Studies.) New York: Columbia University Press, 1956.

2328. _____. A Survey of Polish Literature and Culture. Translated from the Polish by Olga Scherer-Virski. (Columbia Slavic Studies.) New York: Columbia University Press, 1956, 525 pp.

2329. _____, "Waclaw Borowy and His Role in Polish Literary Scholarship." ASEER, X, 282-293.

2330. Kruszewska, Albina I., and Marion M. Coleman, "The Wanda Theme in Polish Literature and Life." ASEER, VI, xvi-xvii, 19-35.

2331. Krynski, Magnus J., "Poland's Literary 'Thaw': Dialectical Phase or Genuine Freedom?" PolR, I, iv, 8-21.

2332. Krzyzanowski, Ludwik, "Joseph Conrad: A Bibliographical Note." PolR, II, ii-iii, 133-140.

2333. _____, "Joseph Conrad's 'Prince Roman': Fact and Fiction." PolR, I, iv, 22-62.

2334. _____. "Literature." Oscar Halecki, Ed., Poland, pp. 226-248. (East-Central Europe under the Communists).

2335. Lednicki, Waclaw, "Behind the Curtain of Indifference: Recent Polish Literature." JCEA, VII, 74-80.

2336. _____, "Goethe and the Russian and Polish Romantics." CL, IV, 23-43.

2337. _____. Henryk Sienkiewicz, 1846-1946. (Polish Institute Series.) New York: Polish Institute of Arts and Sciences in America, 1948.

2338. _____. Russia, Poland and the West: Essays in Literary and Cultural History. New York: Roy Publishers, 1954, 419 pp.

2339. Mills, Clark, "Five Poems by Jan Lechon." PolR, I, ii-iii, 3-5.

2340. Milosz, Czeslaw, "Murti-Bing." PR, XVIII, 540-556.

2341. Mollenhauer, Bernhard, "Lutoslawski and the Knight among Nations." ASEER, XIII, 245-251.

2342. Morska, Irena, ed. Polish Authors of Today and Yesterday. New York: S. F. Vanni Inc., 1947, 213 pp.

2343. Ordon, Edmund, "The Reception of the Polish Short Story in English: Reflections on a Bibliography." PolR, II, ii-iii, 125-132.

2344. Rey, Lucienne, "Intellectual and Literary Revival in Poland." PoC, VI, vi, 26-33.

2345. Scherer-Virski, Olga, "The Modern Polish Short Story." DA, XII, 614-615.

2346. Struve, Gleb, "Who was Pushkin's 'Polonophil.'" SEER, XXIX, 444-455.

2347. Wagner, Albert M., "Undivine Comedy: Zygmunt Krasinski and German Expressionism." ASEER, VI, xviii-xix, 95-109.

2348. Whitfield, Francis J. "Polish Literature." Leonid I. Strakhovsky, Ed., Handbook of Slavic Studies, pp. 452-483.

2349. Wierzynski, Kazimierz, "Selected Poems." PolR, II, iv, 33-40.

2350. Wittlin, Joseph, "Polish Literature: A Post Scriptum." BA, XXX, 170.

2351. _____, "A Quarter Century of Polish Literature." BA, XXX, 5-12.

2352. Ziffer, Bernard, "A Poem for Adults." PolR, I, i, 56-63.

Mickiewicz

2353. Bugelski, B. R., ed. Mickiewicz and the West: A Symposium. With an Introd. by the ed. (The University of Buffalo Studies, XXIII/1.) Buffalo: University of Buffalo, 1956.

2354. Coleman, Marion M. Young Mickiewicz. Cambridge Springs, Pennsylvania: Alliance College, 1956, 390 pp.

2355. _____, and Associates of Columbia University's Klub Polski. Mickiewiczana. Articles, Translations, Bibliographies, of Interest to Students of Mickiewicz. New York: Columbia University, 1946, 56 pp.

2356. Folejewski, Zbigniew. "Mickiewicz and the Poles in the West." B. R. Bugelski, Ed., Mickiewicz and the West, pp. 11-19.

2357. Keefer, Lubov, "The Influence of Adam Mickiewicz on the 'Ballades' of Chopin." ASEER, V, xii-xiii, 38-50.

2358. Kelly, Eric P. "Guidance for a Conquered People." B. R. Bugelski, Ed., Mickiewicz and the West, pp. 19-31.

2359. Kramer, Aaron, "Adam Mickiewicz's 'Concert of Concerts.'" PolR, I, iv, 63-67.

2360. Kridl, Manfred, "Adam Mickiewicz (1798-1855)." ASEER, VII, 340-360.

2361. _____, ed. Adam Mickiewicz: The Poet of Poland. (Columbia Slavic Studies.) New York: Columbia University Press, 1951.

2362. _____, "Two Champions of a New Christianity: Lamennais and Mickiewicz." CL, IV, 239-267.

2363. Kuncewicz, Maria, "Mickiewicz-Universal Humanist." PolR, I, ii-iii, 73-81.

2364. Lednicki, Waclaw, "Adam Mickiewicz 1855-1955, Some Comments About Three Letters of Mickiewicz Unpublished in the National Edition of Mickiewicz's Complete Works in Poland (Mickiewicz and Alfred de Vigny)." PolR, I, i, 80-91.

2365. _____, ed. Adam Mickiewicz in World Literature: A Symposium. Berkeley: University of California Press, 1956.

2366. _____. "Pushkin, Tyutchev, Mickiewicz, and The Decembrists: Legend and Facts." SEER, XXIX, 375-401.

2367. _____. "The Secret of Mickiewicz's Greatness." B. R. Bugelski, Ed., Mickiewicz and the West, pp. 63-75.

2368. Lee, Laurie, "The Uses of the Dead; Adam Mickiewicz: A Hundred Years After; A Wake in Warsaw." Encounter, VI, ii, 5-13.

2369. Mickiewicz, Adam. Adam Mickiewicz 1798-1855: In Commemoration of the Centenary of His Death. Paris: UNESCO; New York: Columbia University Press, 1955.

2370. _____. The Great Improvisation, from "Dziady" III. Tr. by Louise Varese. New York: Voyages, 1956.

2371. Mills, Clark, ed. Adam Mickiewicz, New Selected Poems. Introduction by George N. Shuster. New York: Voyages Press, 1957, 84 pp.

2372. _____, ed. Adam Mickiewicz 1798-1855: Selected

Poems. With a Critical Appreciation by Jan Lechon. New York: The Noonday Press, 1956.

2373. _____, "American Translations of Mickiewicz." PolR, I, i, 92-98.

2374. Milosz, Czeslaw, "Mickiewicz and Modern Poetry." ASEER, VII, 361-368.

2375. _____, "The Uses of the Dead: Adam Mickiewicz: A Hundred Years After; The Real Mickiewicz." Encounter, VI, ii, 14-24.

2376. Nagorski, Zygmunt, Sr., "The Adam Mickiewicz Year." PolR, I, i, 99-107.

2377. Ordon, Edmund. "Mickiewicz and Emerson." B. R. Bugelski, Ed., Mickiewicz and the West, pp. 31-55.

2378. Weintraub, Wiktor, "Adam Mickiewicz, the Mystic-Politician." HSS, I, 137-178.

2379. _____. "Mickiewicz, Lammenais and Biblical Prose." Morris Halle, et al., comp., For Roman Jakobson, pp. 644-652.

2380. Wellisz, Leopold. The Friendship of Margaret Fuller D'Ossoli and Adam Mickiewicz. New York: Polish Book Import Company, 1947, 40 pp. [Some 40 letters in French original and English translations]

2381. Zawacki, Edmund. "Mass Messianism, Mickiewicz versus Marx." B. R. Bugelski, Ed., Mickiewicz and the West, pp. 55-63.

2382. Zgorzelski, Czeslaw, "Adam Mickiewicz in the Light of Postwar Polish Criticism. A Bibliographical Survey." ASEER, VII, 369-373.

FOLKLORE

2383. Baretski, Charles Allan, "A Fateful Choice, A Polish Tale." NYFQ, VIII, 104-110.

2384. Benet, Sula. Song, Dance, and Customs of Peasant Poland. Pref. Margaret Mead. New York: Roy Publishers, 1951, 247 pp.

2385. Burczak, Helen, "A Fairy Tale From Poland." NYFQ, I, 110-111.

2386. Coleman, Marion M., ed. Polish Folklore, Vol. I, Nos. 1-2. Cambridge Springs, Pennsylvania: Alliance College, 1956.

2387. _____, "Polish Lore From Eastern New York." NYFQ, VI, 246-251.

2388. Jarecka, Louise (Llewellyn). Made in Poland: Living Traditions of the Land. New York: Alfred A. Knopf, 1949, 289 pp.

2389. Molski, Irene H., "The Christmas Season in Poland." NYFQ, IX, 261-267.

2390. Polanie Club, Minneapolis. Treasured Polish Songs with English Translations. Selected and ed. by Josepha K. Contaski. Minneapolis, Minnesota: Polanie Publishing Company, 1953, 352 pp.

2391. Portfolio of Polish Folk Art. (Folk Art Press Publication.) Plymouth Meeting, Pennsylvania: Mrs. C. Naaman Keyser, 1947.

2392. Rudnyckyj, J. B., "Goral Songs Recorded in Canada." SEEJ, XV, 34-40.

2393. Wolska, Helen. Dances of Poland. Published under the auspices of the Royal Academy of Dancing and the Ling Physical Education Association. (Chanticleer Ed., Handbooks of European National Dances, No. 22.) New York: Crown Publishers, 1952.

EDUCATION

2394. Eisenstein, Miriam. Jewish Schools in Poland, 1919-1939: Their Philosophy and Development. New York: King's Crown Press, 1950, 112 pp.

2395. Free Europe Committee. Polish Section. Research and information Center. Report on Higher Education. New York: Free Europe Committee, 1951.

2396. Hans, Nicholas, "Educational Reform in Poland in the Eighteenth Century." JCEA, XIII, 301-310.

2397. Hughes, Donald J., "Physics in Poland and Russia." PT, X, 10-15.

2398. Przedpelski, Boleslav J. Agricultural Extension Education in Poland. New York: King's Crown Press, 1948.

2399. Ruch Mas Pracujacych Polski. Proposed

Educational Reconstruction in People's Poland. Formulated by the Polish Underground Labor Movement and the Polish Teachers Underground Convention. Introd. by E. George Payne. Annotated by Reinhold Schairer. (Monograph, No. 1.) New York: Payne Educational Sociology Foundation, 1945, 31 pp.

    2400. Wojcicka, Janina. "Education." Oscar Halecki, Ed., Poland, pp. 178-197. (East-Central Europe under the Communists).

    2401. _____. Higher Education in Poland. (Mimeo. Series No. 12.) New York: Mid-European Studies Center, 1954, 20 pp.

    2402. _____. Libraries in Communist Poland. (Mimeo. Series No. 31.) New York: Mid-European Studies Center, 1954, 37 pp.

    2403. _____, "The Preservation of the State Records in Poland." AA, XX, 195-199.

    2404. Wojcicki, Antoni B. Adult Education in Poland During the Nineteenth and Twentieth Centuries. Cambridge, Massachusetts, 1951. [A Columbia University Thesis]

PHILOSOPHY AND RELIGION

    2405. Andrews, Theodore. Polish National Catholic Church in America and Poland. New York: Macmillan, 1954, 117 pp.

    2406. Anon. "Religion." Oscar Halecki, Ed., Poland, pp. 198-225. (East-Central Europe under the Communists).

    2407. David, Pierre. "The Church in Poland, from its Origin to 1250." W. F. Reddaway, Ed., Cambridge History of Poland, I, pp. 60-84.

    2408. Dolan, Edward, "Post-War Poland and the Church." ASEER, XIV, 84-92.

    2409. Dziewanowski, M. K., "Communist Poland and the Catholic Church." PoC, III, v, 1-8.

    2410. Fox, P. "The Reformation in Poland." W. F. Reddaway, Ed., Cambridge History of Poland, I, pp. 322-347.

    2411. Ketrzynski, S. "The Introduction of Christianity and the Early Kings of Poland." W. F. Reddaway, Ed., Cambridge History of Poland, I, pp. 16-42.

2412. Rosada, Stefan, and Jozef Gwozdz, "Church and State in Poland." Vladimir Gsovski, Ed., Church and State Behind the Iron Curtain, pp. 159-252. (Mid-European Studies Center of the Free Europe Committee).

2413. Staar, Richard F., "The Church of Silence in Communist Poland." CHR, XLII, 296-321.

2414. Szczesniak, Boleslaw, "The Mission of Giovanni de Plano Carpini and Benedict the Pole of Vratislavia to Halicz." JEccH, VII, 12-20.

2415. Uminski, J. "The Counter-Reformation in Poland." W. F. Reddaway, Ed., Cambridge History of Poland, I, pp. 392-415.

2416. United States. Library of Congress. Law Library. Poland: Churches and Religion. Digest Index of East European Law. Washington, D.C.: Library of Congress, 1951, 69 pp.

2417. Valkenier, Elizabeth, "The Catholic Church in Communist Poland, 1945-1955." RPol, XVIII, 305-326.

SOCIOLOGY

2418. Abel, Theodore, "Sociology in Postwar Poland." ASoR, XV, 104-106.

2419. Gross, Feliks. The Polish Worker: A Study in Social Stratum. New York: Roy Publishers, 1945, 274 pp.

2420. Mekarski, Stefan, "The Young Generation in Present-Day Poland." PolR, I, ii-iii, 22-40.

2421. Public Health in Poland. Fourth report on social developments in postwar Poland. New York: Polish Research and Information Center, 1949, 31 pp.

2422. Rooney, Elizabeth, "Polish-Americans and Family Disorganization." ACSR, XVIII, 47-51.

2423. Thomas, John L., "Marriage Prediction in 'The Polish Peasant.'" AJS, LV, 572-577.

2424. Wloszczewski, Dr. Stefan, "The Polish 'Sociological Group' in America." ASEER, IV, viii-ix, 142-157.

2425. Zaremba, Zygmunt. "Social Transformation in Poland." JCEA, XII, 276-289.

2426. _____, "Transformation in Contemporary Polish Society." JCEA, XII, 140-153.

2427. Znaniecki, Florian, "Comment (Marriage Prediction in 'The Polish Peasant')." AJS, LV, 577-578.

XI. RUMANIA

GENERAL

2428. Anon., " Roumania and the Red Thumb." WO, CXXXV, viii, 287.

2429. Brannen, Barry, "The Soviet Conquest of Rumania." FA, XXX, 466-488.

2430. Burillianu, Aristide. "Cultural Life." Alexandre Cretzianu, Ed., Captive Rumania, pp. 128-164.

2431. Carp, Mircea. "The Armed Forces." Alexandre Cretzianu, Ed., Captive Rumania, pp. 351-373.

2432. Ciurea, Emil. "The Background." Alexandre Cretzianu, Ed., Captive Rumania, pp. 3-76.

2433. Cretzianu, Alexandre, ed. Captive Rumania. Introd. Constantin Visoianu. New York: Praeger, 1956, 500 pp.

2434. Fischer-Galati, Stephen, ed. Romania. (East-Central Europe Under the Communists: Mid-European Studies Center Series.) New York: Frederick A. Praeger for the Mid-European Studies Center of the Free Europe Committee, 1957.

2435. Kliewer, Don, "Rumania Plunges Into Red 'Leftovers.'" WO, CXLIII, 162-166.

2436. Kormos, C. Rumania. (British Society for International Understanding. British Survey Handbooks, No. 2.) New York: Macmillan, 1945, 122 pp.

2437. Lehrman, Hal, "Rumanian Rhapsody in a Minor Key." Nation, CLXII, 540-541.

2438. Markham, Reuben Henry. Rumania Under the Soviet Yoke. Boston: Meador, 1949, 601 pp.

2439. Rubinstein, Alvin Z., "Stalinist Rumania." CH, XXXIII, 37-42.

2440. Stan, Anisoara. Romanian Cook Book. New York: Citadel Press, 1951, 256 pp.

2441. Wolff, Robert Lee. "Rumania." Stephen D. Kertesz, Ed., The Fate of East Central Europe, pp. 249-273.

GEOGRAPHY AND POPULATION

2442. Cornish, Louis C. Transylvania, the Land Beyond the Forest. Philadelphia: Dorrance, 1947, 258 pp.

2443. Melezin, Abraham. "The Land." Stephen Fischer-Galati, Ed., Romania, pp. 14-34. (East-Central Europe under the Communists).

2444. Pisky, Fred S. "The People." Stephen Fischer-Galati, Ed., Romania, pp. 35-58. (East-Central Europe under the Communists).

HISTORY

2445. Adamesteanu, Dinu, "Archaeological News: Rumania 1939-1945." AJA, LIV, 417-423.

2446. Callimachi, Annie-Marie (Vacaresco), Princess. Yesterday was Mine. New York: Whittlesey House, 1949, 267 pp.

2447. Campbell, John C., "Eighteen Forty-Eight in the Rumanian Principalities." JCEA, VIII, 181-190.

2448. _____, "Nicolas Jorga." SEER, XXVI, 44-59.

2449. Dvoichenko-Markov, Demetrius, "A Rumanian Priest in Colonial America." ASEER, XIV, 383-389.

2450. Fischer-Galati, Stephen. "Historical Background." Stephen Fischer-Galati, Ed., Romania, pp. 2-13. (East-Central Europe under the Communists).

2451. _____. Slavic-Romanian Relations in Modern Romanian Historiography. (Mimeo. Series No. 8.) New York: Mid-European Studies Center, 1953.

2452. Gafencu, Grigore. Last Days of Europe: A Diplomatic Journey in 1939. New Haven, Connecticut: Yale University Press, 1948.

2453. Ileana, Princess of Rumania. Hospital of the Queen's Heart. (Spitalul inima reginei.) New York: Rinehart and Co., 1954.

2454. _____. I Live Again. With the Collaboration of

Dorothy Kuenzli Hinckley. New York: Rinehart and Co., 1952, 374 pp.

2455. Lee, Arthur Stanley Gould. Crown Against Sickle: The Story of King Michael of Rumania. Toronto: Ryerson Press, 1950.

2456. Moats, Alice Leone. Lupescu. New York: Henry Holt and Co., 1955, 220 pp.

2457. Vucinich, Wayne S., "Soviet Rumania, 1944-51." CH, XXII, 85-91.

2458. Wolff, Leon. Low Level Mission: The Story of the Ploesti Raids. New York: Doubleday, 1957.

2459. Wolff, Robert Lee. "Romania: The Latin Empire of Constantinople." Spec, XXIII, 1-34.

GOVERNMENT AND POLITICS

2460. Anon., "The Rise and Fall of Ana Pauker." NBIC, I, vii, 16-21.

2461. _____, "The Romanian Course." NBIC, III, vii, 3-11.

2462. _____, "Romanian Party and Congress." NBIC, V, ii, 3-20.

2463. Aronovici, Serge H. "National Security." Stephen Fischer-Galati, Ed., Romania, pp. 120-130. (East-Central Europe under the Communists).

2464. Boila, Romulus. "Press and Radio." Alexandre Cretzianu, Ed., Captive Rumania, pp. 257-284.

2465. Braham, Randolph L. "The Government." Stephen Fischer-Galati, Ed., Romania, pp. 84-100. (East-Central Europe under the Communists).

2466. _____, "The New Constitution of Rumania." AJCL, III, 418-427.

2467. Brodney, Kenneth, "Rumania: A Communist Conquest." CH, XIII, 335-340.

2468. Fischer-Galati, Stephen. "The Constitutional System." Stephen Fischer-Galati, Ed., Romania, pp. 101-119. (East-Central Europe under the Communists).

2469. _____. "The Party and Political Organizations."

Stephen Fischer-Galati, Ed., Romania, pp. 60-83. (East-Central Europe under the Communists).

2470. A Former Member of the Bucarest Bar. "The R. P. R. Constitution." Alexandre Cretzianu, Ed., Captive Rumania, pp. 285-300.

2471. Gyorgy, Andrew, et al. Soviet Satellites: Studies of Politics in Eastern Europe. Notre Dame, Indiana: Review of Politics, University of Notre Dame, 1949, 64 pp.

2472. Ionescu, George. "The Pattern of Power." Alexandre Cretzianu, Ed., Captive Rumania, pp. 390-407.

2473. Roberts, Henry L. Rumania: Political Problems of an Agrarian State. New Haven, Connecticut: Yale University Press, 1951, 414 pp.

2474. Suppression of Human Rights in Rumania. Washington, D.C.: Rumanian National Committee, 1949, 163 pp.

2475. United States. Library of Congress. Legislative Reference Service. Tensions Within the Soviet Captive Countries. Rumania, Pt. 2, pp. 26-50. Prepared at the request of the Committee on Foreign Relations. Washington, D.C.: United States Government Printing Office, 1954.

INTERNATIONAL AFFAIRS

2476. Cretzianu, Alexandre, "Romanian Armistice Negotiations, Cairo, 1944." JCEA, XI, 243-258.

2477. _____, "The Soviet Ultimatum to Roumania." JCEA, IX, 396-403.

2478. Dvoichenko-Markov, Demetrius, "Transnistria: A Rumanian Claim in the Ukraine." SOF, XVI, 376-388.

2479. Ionnitziu, Mircea. "Foreign Relations." Alexandre Cretzianu, Ed., Captive Rumania, pp. 324-350.

2480. Szaz, Zoltan, "The Transylvanian Question: Romania and the Belligerents, July-October 1914." JCEA, XIII, 338-351.

2481. United States. Armistice Agreement with Romania, Signed at Moscow, September 12, 1944. (Executive Agreement Series 490.) Washington, D.C.: Department of State, 1946.

LAW

2482. United States. Library of Congress. Law Library. Rumania: Catalogue of Sources of Legal Information. Washington, D.C.: Library of Congress, 1952, 10 pp.

2483. _____. Library of Congress. Law Library. Rumania: Labor Code of 1950. Digest Index of East European Law. Washington, D.C.: Library of Congress, 1951, 53 pp.

2484. _____. Library of Congress. Law Library. Rumania: Trials. Digest Index of East European Law. Washington, D.C.: Library of Congress, 1951, 12 pp.

2485. Veniamin, Virgil. "The Judiciary." Alexandre Cretzianu, Ed., Captive Rumania, pp. 301-323.

THE ECONOMY

2486. Anon., "Consumer Goods and Internal Trade in Romania." NBIC, IV, iv, 14-27.

2487. _____, "Joint U.S.-Soviet Oil Commission in Rumania Dissolved." DSB, XVII, 225-227.

2488. _____, "Romanian Balance Sheet." NBIC, IV, iv, 3-13.

2489. _____, "Sovroms." NBIC, III, ix, 16-22.

2490. _____, "They Paid the Communists' Price." WO, CXXXVII, 234-235.

2491. _____, "Transportation in Rumania, Bulgaria and Albania." NBIC, V, iv, 11-23.

2492. Bossy, George H. "Agriculture." Stephen Fischer-Galati, Ed., Romania, pp. 196-231. (East-Central Europe under the Communists).

2493. _____. "Industry." Stephen Fischer-Galati, Ed., Romania, pp. 270-320. (East-Central Europe under the Communists).

2494. _____. "Mining." Stephen Fischer-Galati, Ed., Romania, pp. 232-247. (East-Central Europe under the Communists).

2495. _____. "Transportation and Communications." Stephen Fischer-Galati, Ed., Romania, pp. 321-342. (East-Central Europe under the Communists).

2496. Caranfil, Andrew G. "Labor." Stephen Fischer-Galiati, Ed., Romania, pp. 248-269. (East-Central Europe under the Communists).

2497. A Former Member of the Bucarest Bar. "Labor." Alexandre Cretzianu, Ed., Captive Rumania, pp. 374-389.

2498. Georgescu-Roegen, Otilia. Physical Factors of Romanian Agriculture. (Mimeo. Series No. 2.) New York: Mid-European Studies Center, 1953, 21 pp.

2499. Ionescu, George. "The Economic Field." Alexandre Cretzianu, Ed., Captive Rumania, pp. 77-101.

2500. _____. Social Legislation in Romanian Agriculture. (Mimeo. Series No. 18.) New York: Mid-European Studies Center, 1954, 20 pp.

2501. Jordan, Constantin. The Communization of the Romanian Oil Industry. (Mimeo. Series No. 24.) New York: Mid-European Studies Center, 1954, 20 pp.

2502. _____. The Romanian Methane Gas Industry. New York: Mid-European Studies Center, Free Europe Committee, 1955.

2503. _____. Romanian Oil Industry. New York: New York University Press, 1955, 357 pp.

2504. _____. The Romanian Oil Industry in 1947. (Mimeo. Series No. 22.) New York: Mid-European Studies Center, 1954, 23 pp.

2505. Nagel, Dumitru. Distribution of Agricultural Products in Romania. (Mimeo. Series No. 17.) New York: Mid-European Studies Center, 1954, 34 pp.

2506. _____. Romanian Agricultural Taxation. (Mimeo. Series No. 14.) New York: Mid-European Studies Center, 1954, 21 pp.

2507. _____, and Serban Constandaky. Insurance in Romanian Agriculture. (Mimeo. Series No. 21.) New York: Mid-European Studies Center, 1954, 27 pp.

2508. Norman, Daniel, "'New Course' in Rumanian Agriculture." PoC, IV, iv, 35-43.

2509. Plessia, Radu. "Financial Policy." Alexandre Cretzianu, Ed., Captive Rumania, pp. 102-127.

2510. Rosu, George, "Roumanian Oil Industry, a Soviet Carbon." WO, CXXXIX, 199.

2511. _____, "Time Running Out for Roumania's Oil." WO, CXXXIX, 224.

2512. Spulber, Nicolas, "The Danube-Black Sea Canal and the Russian Control over the Danube." EG, XXX, 236-245.

2513. _____. "National Income and Product." Stephen Fischer-Galati, Ed., Romania, pp. 184-195. (East-Central Europe under the Communists).

2514. _____. Statistical Abstract of the Roumanian Economy. Washington, D.C.: Council for Economic and Industry Research, 1956.

LANGUAGE

2515. Agard, Frederick B., "Noun Morphology in Romanian." Language, XXIX, 133-142.

2516. Nandris, Grigore. Colloquial Rumanian: Grammar, Exercises, Reader, Vocabulary. Forest Hills, New York: Transatlantic Arts, 1946, 340 pp.

2517. Schonkron, Marcel. Rumanian-English and English-Rumanian Dictionary, With Supplement of New Words, English-Rumanian. Rev. and enl. ed. New York: Ungar, 1952, 482 pp.

LITERATURE

2518. Anon. "Literature and the Arts." Stephen Fischer-Galati, Ed., Romania, pp. 165-181. (East-Central Europe under the Communists).

2519. Baerlein, Henry Philip Bernard, ed. Romanian Scene: Anthology on Romania and her People by Writers in English. Toronto: S. J. Reginald Saunders, 1945, 223 pp.

2520. Creanga, Ion. Folk Tales from Roumania. Tr. Mabel Nandris. New York: Roy Publishers, 1953.

2521. Feraru, Leon. "Rumanian Literature." Horatio Smith, Ed., Columbia Dictionary of Modern European Literature, pp. 693-694.

2522. Grindea, Miron, and Carola Grindea. Dances of Rumania. Published under the auspices of the Royal Academy of Dancing and the Ling Physical Education Association.

(Chanticleer ed., Handbooks of European National Dances.) New York: Crown Publishers, 1952, 40 pp.

2523. Luca, Remus, and Alexandru Oprea, "A Short Primer for Makers of Literature." NBIC, IV, i, 34-37.

2524. Munteano, B., "Contemporary Rumanian Literature: Triumph and Disaster." BA, XXX, 147-154.

2525. Tappe, Eric Ditmar, "The Centenary of I. L. Caragiale." ASEER, XI, 66-76.

2526. _____, "The Centenary of Mihai Eminescu." ASEER, X, 50-55.

2527. _____, ed. Rumanian Prose and Verse [in Rumanian]: A Selection with an Introductory Essay. (London University. School of Slavonic and East European Studies. Dept. of Language and Literature. London East European Series: Language and Literature.) New York: De Graff, 1956, 193 pp.

2528. Timiras, Nicholas, "Communist Literature in Romania." JCEA, XIV, 371-381.

2529. Vaiciulaitis, Antanas, "Jurgis Baltrusaitis 1873-1944." BA, XIX, 17-19.

EDUCATION

2530. Ciurea, Emil. "Education." Alexandre Cretzianu, Ed., Captive Rumania, pp. 204-256.

2531. Fischer-Galati, Stephen, "Communist Indoctrination in Rumanian Elementary Schools." HER, XXII, 191-202.

2532. _____. "Education." Stephen Fischer-Galati, Ed., Romania, pp. 148-165. (East-Central Europe under the Communists).

2533. The Perversion of Education in Rumania. Washington, D.C.: Rumanian National Committee, 1950, 96 pp.

PHILOSOPHY AND RELIGION

2534. Anon., "Sovrom Patriarch." NBIC, III, iv, 36-38.

2535. Bossy, Raoul, "Religious Persecutions in Captive Rumania." JCEA, XV, 161-181.

2536. Ciurea, Emil. "Religious Life." Alexandre Cretzianu, Ed., Captive Rumania, pp. 165-203.

2537. Fischer-Galati, Stephen. "Religion." Stephen Fischer-Galati, Ed., Romania, pp. 132-147. (East-Central Europe under the Communists).

2538. The Persecution of Religion in Rumania. Washington, D.C.: Rumanian National Committee, 1949, 37 pp.

2539. Rosu, George, Mircea Vasiliu, and George Crisan. "Church and State in Romania." Vladimir Gsovski, Ed., Church and State Behind the Iron Curtain, pp. 253-293. (Mid-European Studies Center).

2540. United States. Library of Congress. Law Library. Rumania: Churches and Religion. Digest Index of East European Law. Washington, D.C.: Library of Congress, 1951, 46 pp.

2541. Wilbur, Earl Morse. History of Unitarianism: In Transylvania, England, and America. Cambridge, Massachusetts: Harvard University Press, 1952, 518 pp.

XII. YUGOSLAVIA

GENERAL

2542. Adamic, Louis. The Eagle and the Roots. Garden City, New York: Doubleday, 1952, 531 pp.

2543. _____. Liberation. New York: United Committee of South Slavic Americans, 1945.

2544. Allen, Peter J., "On the Danube Frontier of Yugoslavia." Rept, VI, iii, 13-16.

2545. Anon., "Yugoslav Gift to Headquarters." UNR, I, vii, 34-35.

2546. Basic, Mark. It Happened in Yugoslavia—It Must Not Happen Here. Chicago: The Author, 1949.

2547. Byrnes, Robert F., ed. Yugoslavia. (East-Central Europe Under the Communists: Mid-European Studies Center Series.) New York: Frederick A. Praeger for the Mid-European Studies Center of the Free Europe Committee, 1957.

2548. Cesarich, George W. Croatia and Serbia: Why Is Their Peaceful Separation a European Necessity? Chicago: "Croatia" Cultural Publishing Center, 1954.

2549. Dean, Vera Micheles, "Military Problems of Yugoslavia." FPR, XXVII, 47-48.

2550. Dragnich, Alex N. Tito's Promised Land: Yugoslavia. New Brunswick, New Jersey: Rutgers University Press, 1954, 333 pp.

2551. _____. "Yugoslavia." Stephen D. Kertesz, Ed., The Fate of East Central Europe, pp. 358-373.

2552. Fotitch, Alexander Constantin. The War We Lost: Yugoslavia's Tragedy and the Failing of the West. New York: The Viking Press, 1948, 344 pp.

2553. Gayn, Mark, "Crisis in Yugoslavia." NR, CXXI, xiii, 14-16.

2554. Gedye, G. E. R., "Yugoslav Disillusion: The Culprit in Britain." Nation, CLXXVIII, 29.

2555. Gracalic, Ladislav. Yugoslavia. (Nagel Travel Guide Series.) New York: Praeger, 1954, 251 pp.

2556. Kos, Franc, "From Deepest Yugoslavia." AN, LIV, v, 43, 58-59.

2557. Krippner, Monica. Yugoslavia Invites: A Guide Book. Toronto: McGraw-Hill Book Co., 1954.

2558. Lehrman Hal, "Progress in Yugoslavia." Nation, CLXI, 156.

2559. ____, "Yugoslavia Revisited." Nation, CLXII, 713-714, 747-748.

2560. Logan, Milla Zenovich. Cousins and Commissars. New York: Scribner, 1949, 222 pp.

2561. Mannering, Henry, "Yugoslavia—Right Turn?" Rept, V, iii, 21-23.

2562. Mates, Leo, "The Contribution of Yugoslavia to Peace." AAAPSS, CCLXXXVIII, 105-113.

2563. Normand, Suzanne, and Jean Acker. Yugoslavia. Tr. Jean Penfold. (Les Beaux Pays.) New York: Essential Books, 1956, 144 pp.

2564. Ostovic, Pavle D. The Truth About Yugoslavia. New York: Roy Publishers, 1952, 300 pp.

2565. Pintar, John I. Four Years in Tito's Hell. New York: The Author, 1954, 300 pp.

2566. Popovic, Koca, "Yugoslavia." UNR, II, v, 28-29.

2567. Pridonoff, Eric Lionel. Tito's Yugoslavia. Introd. Brodie E. Ahlpart. Washington, D.C.: Public Affairs Press, 1955.

2568. Raditsa, Bogdan, "Yugoslavia Today." NR, CXV, x, 284-287, 318-321.

2569. St. John, Robert. The Silent People Speak. Garden City, New York: Doubleday, 1948, 397 pp.

2570. Strausz-Hupe, Robert, "Yugoslavia—Marx Without Stalin." CH, XIX, 267-270.

2571. Vucinich, Wayne, "Yugoslavia: Ally for Defense." CH, XX, 28-34.

2572. Werth, Alexander, "Yugoslavia Reappraised." Nation, CLXXI, 37-38, 59-60, 83-84, 147-148.

2573. _____, "Yugoslavia: Test of Nerves." Nation, CLXVII, 253-254.

GEOGRAPHY AND POPULATION

2574. Canada. Department of Mines and Technical Surveys, Geographical Branch. Yugoslavia: A Geographical Appreciation. (Foreign Geography Information Series.) Ottawa: Department of Mines and Technical Surveys, 1950.

2575. Kish, George. Yugoslavia. (Lands and Peoples Series.) New York: Holiday House, 1952. [Juvenile Literature.]

2576. _____, "Yugoslavia." Focus, I, vi, 1-4.

2577. Klancar, Anthony J., "Slovenia and the Slovenes." JCEA, VI, 1-20.

2578. Kostelski, Z. The Croats. Floreffe, Pennsylvania: "Kolo" Publishing Company, 1950, 64 pp.

2579. Mellen, Melrad. "The Land." Robert F. Byrnes, Ed., Yugoslavia, pp. 44-70. (East-Central Europe under the Communists).

2580. Poels, John. Without Let or Hindrance: A Journey to Jugoslavia. Hollywood-by-the-Sea, Florida: Transatlantic Arts, 1953, 181 pp.

2581. Sommelius, Torgny. Iron Gate of Illyria. Tr. from the Swedish by Naomi Walford. New York: Roy Publishers, 1955, 205 pp.

2582. United States. Bureau of the Census. The Population of Yugoslavia. (International Population Statistics, P-90, No. 5.) Washington, D.C.: United States Government Printing Office, 1954.

HISTORY

2583. Avakumovic, Ivan, "An Episode in the Continental System in the Illyrian Provinces." JEH, XIV, 254-261.

2584. Bilaikin, George. Tito. New York: Philosophical Library, 1950.

2585. Bonifacic, Antun F., and Clement S. Mihanovich, eds. The Croatian Nation in Its Struggle for Freedom and

Independence. Chicago: "Croatia" Cultural Publishing Center, 1955.

2586. Clarke, James F., "Serbia and the Bulgarian Revival (1762-1872)." ASEER, IV, x-xi, 141-162.

2587. Clissold, Stephen. Whirlwind: An Account of Marshal Tito's Rise to Power. New York: Philosophical Library, 1950, 245 pp.

2588. Dacie, Anne. Instead of the Brier. Hollywood-by-the-Sea, Florida: Transatlantic Arts, 1950, 318 pp.

2589. Govorchin, Gerald G., "The Emergence of the Radical Party in Serbian Politics." ASEER, XV, 511-526.

2590. Hammond, Thomas T. "A Brief History." Robert F. Byrnes, Ed., Yugoslavia, pp. 2-17. (East-Central Europe under the Communists).

2591. Inks, James M. Eight Bailed Out. Ed. by Lawrence Klingman. New York: Norton, 1954, 222 pp.

2592. Jelavich, Charles, "Nikola Pasic: Greater Serbia or Jugoslavia." JCEA, XI, 133-152.

2593. _____, "The Revolt in Bosnia-Hercegovina, 1881-1882." SEER, XXXI, 420-436.

2594. Kerner, Robert Joseph, ed. Yugoslavia. Chapters by Griffith Taylor and others. (United Nations Series.) Berkeley: University of California Press, 1949, 558 pp.

2595. Korosec, Josip, "Roman Family Tombs in Yugoslavia." Arch, X, 117-122.

2596. Kostelski, Z. The Yugoslavs: the History of the Yugoslavs and Their States to the Creation of Yugoslavia. New York: Philosophical Library, 1952, 498 pp.

2597. Macek, Vladko. In My Struggle for Freedom. New York: Robert Speller and Sons, 1957.

2598. Maclean, Fitzroy, H. Escape to Adventure. Boston: Little, Brown and Co., 1950, 419 pp.

2599. Martin, David. Ally Betrayed: The Uncensored Story of Tito and Mihailovich. New York: Prentice-Hall, 1946, 372 pp.

2600. Mestrovic, Matthew Mark, "Jugoslav Union and the Beginning of the Serb-Croat Conflict, 1918-1923." DA, XVII, 1993.

2601. Pandzic, Basil. A Review of Croatian History. Chicago: "Croatia" Cultural Publishing Center, 1954, 110 pp.

2602. Peter II, King of Yugoslavia. King's Heritage. (Limited autographed edition.) New York: Putnam, 1954, 304 pp. [Autobiography.]

2603. Petrovich, Michael B., "Catherine II and a False Peter III in Montenegro." ASEER, XIV, 169-194.

2604. _____, "The Rise of Modern Serbian Historiography." JCEA, XVI, 1-24.

2605. Preveden, Francis Ralph. A History of the Croatian People. Vol. I. Prehistory to 1397. New York: Philosophical Library, 1956, 129 pp.

2606. _____. Political and Cultural History of the Croatian People since Their Coming to the Adriatic Shores to the Present Day: With a Retrospect to the Gothic, Roman, Greek, Illyrian and Prehistoric Periods of the Ancient Illyricum and Pannonia. 7 Vols. Washington, D.C.: The Author, 1949.

2607. Rogers, Lindsay S. Guerrilla Surgeon. New York: Doubleday, 1957.

2608. Soulis, George C., "Tsar Stephen Dusan and Mount Athos." HSS, II, 125-140.

2609. Tomashevich, G. V., "Bozidar Knezevic: A Yugoslav Philosopher of History." SEER, XXXV, 443-461.

2610. Vucinich, Wayne S., "The Montenegrin Istoriski Zapisi, (1948-1953)." JCEA, XV, 394-399.

2611. _____, "Postwar Yugoslav Historiography." JMH, XXIII, 41-57.

2612. _____. Serbia Between East and West: The Events of 1903-1908. Stanford, California: Stanford University Press, 1954, 305 pp.

2613. _____, "The Yugoslav Lands in the Ottoman Period: Postwar Marxist Interpretations of Indigenous and Ottoman Institutions." JMH, XXVII, 287-306.

GOVERNMENT AND POLITICS

2614. Dean, Vera Micheles, "Yugoslavia: A New Form of Communism?" FPR, XXVII, 38-47.

2615. Djilas, Milovan, "The New Class." EE, VI, xi, 27-31.

2616. _____. The New Class. Eds. Morton Puner and Konrad Kellen. New York: Praeger, 1957, 214 pp.

2617. Djordjevic, Jovan, "Local Self-Government in Yugoslavia." ASEER, XII, 188-200.

2618. Douglas, William O., "Yugoslavia: A Wedge of Freedom in a One-Party State." Rept, VI, iii, 9-12.

2619. Dragnich, Alex N., "Recent Political Developments in Yugoslavia." JPol, XX, 114-126.

2620. _____, "Yugoslavia's New Constitution." CH, X, 420-423.

2621. Frankel, Joseph, "Communism and the National Question in Yugoslavia." JCEA, XV, 49-65.

2622. _____, "Federalism in Yugoslavia." APSR, XLIX, 416-430.

2623. Hammond, Thomas Taylor, "The Djilas Affair and Jugoslav Communism." FA, XXXIII, 298-316.

2624. _____, "Jugoslav Elections: Democracy in Small Doses." PSQ, LXX, 57-74.

2625. Handler, M. S., "Communist Dogma and Jugoslav Practice." FA, XXX, 426-444.

2626. Huot, Louis. Guns for Tito. New York: L. B. Fischer Publishing Co., 1945, 273 pp.

2627. Kardelj, Edvard, "Evolution in Jugoslavia." FA, XXXIV, 580-603.

2628. Lehrman, Hal, "Yugoslav Democracy, Limited." Nation, CLXI, 228-229.

2629. Lens, Sidney, "Yugoslavia's 'New Socialism.'" FPB, XXXIII, vi, 5-7.

2630. Markham, Reuben Henry. Tito's Imperial Communism. Chapel Hill: University of North Carolina Press, 1947, 292 pp.

2631. Martin, David. Tito: The History of a Fraud. New York: Prentice-Hall, 1946, 372 pp.

2632. Neal, Fred Warner. Certain Aspects of the New Reforms in Yugoslavia. Boulder, Colorado: University of Colorado, 1953.

2633. _____, "The Communist Party of Yugoslavia." APSR, LI, 88-111.

2634. _____, "The Reforms in Yugoslavia." ASEER, XIII, 227-244.

2635. _____, "The Reforms in Yugoslavia, 1948-1954: Titoism in Action." DA, XVII, 1797.

2636. Padev, Michael. Marshall Tito. Forest Hills, New York: Transatlantic Arts, 1945, 126 pp.

2637. Pawel, Ernst, "After the Yugoslav Elections." NR, CXIII, xxi, 671-673.

2638. Petrovich, Michael B., "The Central Government of Yugoslavia." PSQ, LXII, 504-530.

2639. Rudzinski, Alexander. "The Constitutional System." Robert F. Byrnes, Ed., Yugoslavia, pp. 92-111. (East-Central Europe under the Communists).

2640. _____. "The Government." Robert F. Byrnes, Ed., Yugoslavia, pp. 131-144. (East-Central Europe under the Communists).

2641. _____. "Politics and Political Organizations." Robert F. Byrnes, Ed., Yugoslavia, pp. 112-130. (East-Central Europe under the Communists).

2642. Ziffer, Bernard. "National Security." Robert F. Byrnes, Ed., Yugoslavia, pp. 145-165. (East-Central Europe under the Communists).

LAW

2643. Concerning Management of Governmental Enterprises. Tr. of Yugoslav Law No. 391 of July 2, 1950. 2nd ed. Washington: Mid-European Law Project, Library of Congress, 1953, 12 pp.

2644. Dragnich, Alex N., "The Mikhailovitch Trial." CH, XI, 114-117.

2645. Goldstajn, Aleksander, "Tort Liability and Insurance of Enterprise in Yugoslavia." AJCL, III, 247-249.

2646. _____, "Yugoslavia: Reform of Economic Courts." AJCL, IV, 600-603.

2647. Gsovski, Vladimir, ed. Agricultural Laws and Regulations in Yugoslavia, 1945-1953. (Publication of the

Mid-European Studies Center, Mid-European Law Project, Library of Congress No. 18.) New York: Mid-European Studies Center, 1954, 57 pp.

2648. Mid-European Studies Center. Translation of Yugoslav Laws on Agrarian Reform and Colonization. (Publication of the Mid-European Studies Center, Mid-European Law Project, Library of Congress No. 3.) New York: Mid-European Studies Center, 1952, 35 pp.

INTERNATIONAL AFFAIRS

2649. Anon., "U.S.-Yugoslav Claims Settlement; Summary of Agreements." DSB, XIX, 137-140.

2650. Ascoli, Max, "Our Belgrade Gamble." Rept, VI, iii, 5.

2651. _____, "Their Tito and Ours." Rept, II, iii, 4.

2652. Bartos, Milan, "Jugoslavia's Struggle for Equality." FA, XXVIII, 427-441.

2653. Challener, Richard D., "Montenegro and the U. S.: A Balkan Fantasy." JCEA, XVII, 236-242.

2654. Dean, Vera Micheles, "Will West's Warnings Protect Yugoslavia?" FPB, XXX, xx, 2-3.

2655. Fotitch, Constantin, "Tito and the Western Democracies." JCEA, XI, 353-371.

2656. Hadsel, Winifred N., "U. S. Backs Yugoslav Relief Despite Plane Incident." FPB, XXV, xLix, 4.

2657. Halperin, Ernest, "Helping Tito Help the West." Rept, VII, xi, 21-24.

2658. Hammond, Thomas Taylor. "Foreign Relations Since 1945." Robert F. Byrnes, Ed., Yugoslavia, pp. 18-41. (East-Central Europe under the Communists.)

2659. _____. Yugoslavia Between East and West. (Headline Series, Foreign Policy Association.) New York: Foreign Policy Association, 1954.

2660. Hodgkinson, Harry. West and East of Tito. Toronto: Longmans, Green and Co., 1952, 190 pp.

2661. Hoptner, J. B., "Yugoslavia as a Neutralist." JCEA, XVI, 156-176.

2662. Langer, Robert. The Austro-Yugoslav Problem. [New York?], 1951, 82 pp.

2663. Long, George W. Yugoslavia, Between East and West. Washington, D.C.: 1951.

2664. Meyer, Peter, "Tito's Threat to Stalin's Empire; The Role America Can Play." Com, IX, 515-524.

2665. Riggs, Fred W., "Tito Seeks Basis for Agreement With Neighbors." FPB, XXIX, xxxi, 3-4.

2666. Strausz-Hupe, Robert, "The United States and Yugoslavia: A Reappraisal." YR, XLV, 161-177.

2667. _____, "Yugoslav Counteroffensive in the Cold War." YR, XLI, 273-284.

2668. Vosnjak, Bogumil, "Yugoslavia and the United States." CH, XVIII, 23-27, 150-155.

2669. Vucinich, Wayne S., "Yugoslavia, Greece and Turkey." CH, XXIV, 103-108.

2670. Weller, George, "The Almighty Independence of Tito's Yugoslavia." Rept, XI, vi, 29-33.

2671. Werth, Alexander, "Yugoslavia: Neither East nor West. Tito's Odds for Survival." Nation, CLXVII, 600-601, 629-630.

Soviet Yugoslav Disputes since 1948

2672. Allen, Peter J., "Tito Trims his Sails." Rept, VI, i, 21-24.

2673. Armstrong, Hamilton Fish. Tito and Goliath. New York: Macmillan, 1951, 300 pp.

2674. _____, "Why the Soviet Woos that 'Mongrel' Tito." Rept, XIII, i, 15-20.

2675. Arnold, G. L., "Tito's Heresy." Nation, CLXVII, 65.

2676. Brown, Giles T., "The Dialectic Gulf Between Tito and Moscow." WAI, XXVIII, 377-397.

2677. Broz-Tito, Josip, "On Certain Current International Questions." FA, XXXVI, 68-77.

2678. Byrnes, Robert F., "Heresy in Yugoslavia." CH, XXXIII, 16-20.

2679. Caruthers, Osgood, "Tito On A Tightrope." NR, CXX, xvii, 18-20.

2680. Clarion, Nicolas, "Titoism and 'Titoslavia.'" SAW, XLIX, 431-440.

2681. Coblentz, Gaston, "The Plight of Tito." Rept, III, v, 27-29.

2682. Cooper, John Sherman, "Discussion of Tensions between Yugoslavia and U.S.S.R." DSB, XXV, 985-989.

2683. Dean, Vera Micheles, "Tito and Moscow: A Two-Way Bridge." FPB, XXXV, xx, 159-160.

2684. _____, "Tito's New Role." FPB, XXXIV, iii, 22-23.

2685. _____, "Tito's Stand Poses Dilemma for Both East and West." FPB, XXIX, iv, 3-4; XXXVIII, xlvi, 2-4.

2686. _____, "Tito: The Uses of Noncommitment." FPB, XXXV, vi, 44, 48.

2687. Dedijer, Vladimir. Tito. New York: Simon and Schuster, 1953.

2688. Dragnich, Alex N., "How Different is Tito's Communism?" APSR, LI, 112-114.

2689. _____, "Tito Withstands Russian Domination." CH, XXIII, 23-27.

2690. Draskovich, Slobodan M. Tito, Moscow's Trojan Horse. Chicago: Regnery, 1957, 357 pp.

2691. Ervin, Ellen W., "Problems of Titoism." CH, XXVI, 361-366.

2692. Farrell, Robert Barry. Jugoslavia and the Soviet Union 1948-1956: An Analysis With Documents. Hamden, Connecticut: Shoe String Press, 1956, 220 pp.

2693. Fast, Howard Melvin. Tito and His People. Winnipeg, Manitoba: Contemporary Pubs., n.d.

2694. Gervasi, Frank, "The Defense of the Tito Regime." NR, CXXI, xxv, 15-16.

2695. _____, "Tito's Revolution is Unique." NR, CXXI, xxiv, 12-15.

2696. Goldbloom, Maurice J., "Has Tito's Regime Gone Democratic?" Com, XV, 460-468.

2697. Guri, Dita, "The Tito-Stalin Struggle." WAI, XXIII, 159-165.

2698. Harsch, Joseph C., "Tito is not for Sale." Rept, I, x, 31-33.

2699. Haven, Andrew, "Tito and Gomulka: Contrasts and Comparisons." PoC, VI, iv, 8-15.

2700. Hodgkinson, Harry. Challenge to the Kremlin. New York: Praeger, 1952, 190 pp.

2701. Illyricus, "Tito's Brand of Communism." SAQ, LIV, 177-184.

2702. Kartun, Derek. Tito's Plot Against Europe: The Story of the Rajk Conspiracy. New York: International Publishers Co., 1950, 127 pp.

2703. Kendrick, Alexander, "Moscow's Courtship of Tito." NR, CXXXII, ii, 14-16.

2704. Korbel, Josef, "Titoism: An Evaluation." JCEA, XI, 1-9.

2705. _____. Tito's Communism. Denver: University of Colorado Press, 1951, 368 pp.

2706. Lash, Joseph P. "Titoism is More Than Balkan." NR, CXX, iii, 12-14.

2707. Lowenthal, Richard, "New Phase in Moscow—Belgrade Relations." PoC, IV, vi, 1-10.

2708. Maclean, Fitzroy. The Heretic. New York: Harper's, 1957.

2709. _____, "Tito: A Study." FA, XXVIII, 231-247.

2710. Macridis, Roy, "Stalinism and the Meaning of Titoism." WP, IV, 219-238.

2711. McVicker, Charles P. Titoism: Pattern for International Communism. New York: St. Martin's Press, 1957, 332 pp.

2712. Moritz, Johann, "Is Tito's Turn Next?" America, LXXXIV, 665-666.

2713. Mosely, Philip E., "Will Tito Turn East?" FPB, XXXIV, xx, 157-159.

2714. Neal, Fred Warner, "The Impact of Titoism on Eastern European Communism." WPQ, X, 444-445.

2715. Pribichevich, Stoyan, "Observer Finds Cominform Split Strengthens Tito." FPB, XXVIII, xv, 3-4.

2716. Roucek, Joseph S., "Tito-ism and the Growth of a New National Communistic Movement." WAI, XX, 233-240.

2717. Royal Institute of International Affairs. The Soviet-Yugoslav Dispute: Text of the Published Correspondence. New York: Royal Institute of International Affairs, 1949, 79 pp.

2718. Sheean, Vincent, "Grand Heresiarch; 'Tito and Goliath' by Hamilton Fish Armstrong." SatR, XXXIV, ii, 28-29.

2719. Shipler, Guy E., "Editor of 'The Churchman' on Tito's Rule." NR, CXVII, ix, 11-12.

2720. Sterling, Claire, "A Report on Titoism." Rept, XVI, vii, 17-21.

2721. Sternberg, Fritz, "Tito's Unique Yugoslavia." Nation, CLXXIV, 226-227.

2722. Talmadge, I. D. W., "Could Tito Hold Out." NR, CXXIII, xiv, 10-13.

2723. _____, "When the Devil Is Sick; 'Balkan Caesar: Tito vs. Stalin' by Leigh White." SatR, XXXIV, xxi, 11-12.

2724. Tennyson, Hallam. Tito Lifts the Curtain: The Story of Yugoslavia Today. Toronto: McGraw-Hill, 1955, 240 pp.

2725. Ulam, Adam B., "The Background of the Soviet-Yugoslav Dispute." RPol, XIII, 39-63.

2726. _____. Titoism and the Cominform. (Russian Research Center Studies, 5.) Cambridge: Harvard University Press, 1952, 243 pp.

2727. _____, "The Yugoslav-Russian Dispute and Its Implications." WP, I, 414-425.

2728. Vucinich, Wayne S., "Behind the Tito-Stalin Feud." CH, XV, 213-217.

2729. Werth, Alexander, "Can Tito Survive?" Nation, CLXXVIII, 473-474, 520-521.

2730. _____, "Tito, the Unrepentant." Nation, CLXVII, 147-418.

2731. White, Leigh. Balkan Caesar: Tito versus Stalin. New York: Scribner, 1951, 245 pp.

2732. Willen, Paul, "What Tito Wants." NR, CXXXV, xxiii, 7-10.

THE ECONOMY

2733. Alton, Thad P., "Postwar Changes in the Yugoslav Economic System and Methods of Planning." AER, XLVI, 380-388.

2734. Ames, Edward. "Domestic Trade and Finance." Robert Byrnes, Ed., Yugoslavia, pp. 326-350. (East-Central Europe under the Communists).

2735. Anon., "Food Shortages Threaten Yugoslavia's Political and Economic Survival." DSB, XXIII, 937-940.

2736. _____. "Health and Public Welfare." Robert F. Byrnes, Ed., Yugoslavia, pp. 389-408. (East-Central Europe under the Communists).

2737. Avsenek, Ivan. "Basic Industries." Robert F. Byrnes, Ed., Yugoslavia, pp. 282-309. (East-Central Europe under the Communists).

2738. _____. The Iron and Steel Industry in Yugoslavia, 1939-1953. (Mimeo. Series No. 25.) Mid-European Studies Center, 1953, 14 pp.

2739. _____. Yugoslav Metallurgical Industry. (Publication of the Mid-European Studies Center, No. 22.) New York: Mid-European Studies Center, 1955.

2740. Brashich, Ranko M. "Agriculture." Robert F. Byrnes, Ed., Yugoslavia, pp. 228-258. (East-Central Europe under the Communists).

2741. _____. Land Reform and Ownership in Yugoslavia, 1919-1953. (Publication of the Mid-European Studies Center, No. 17.) New York: Mid-European Studies Center, 1954, 169 pp.

2742. _____. Taxation in Yugoslav Agriculture. (Mimeo. Series No. 4.) New York: Mid-European Studies Center, 1953, 27 pp.

2743. Colbert, James L., "Continuation of Economic Assistance to Yugoslavia." DSB, XXVII, 825-826.

2744. Dolina, Joseph. "Foreign Trade." Robert F. Byrnes, Ed., Yugoslavia, pp. 351-369. (East-Central Europe under the Communists).

2745. Haggerty, John J., "Land Reclamation in Yugoslavia." FAgr, XIV, 191-195.

2746. Hoffman, George W., "Yugoslavia in Transition: Industrial Expansion Resource Bases." EG, XXXIII, 294-315.

2747. Howlett, Freeman S., "Fruit Production in Yugoslavia." FAgr, XVI, 12-16.

2748. Johnston, W. B., and I. Crkvencic, "Changing Peasant Agriculture in Northwestern Hrvatsko Primorje, Yugoslavia." GR, XLIV, 352-372.

2749. _____. "Examples of Changing Peasant Agriculture in Croatia, Yugoslavia." EG, XXXIII, 50-71.

2750. Knepfle, G. A., "More Bricks for Tito; Yugoslavia: economic uncertainty, political confidence." Rept, II, x, 26-28.

2751. Koeller, Harold L., "Yugoslavia Plans to Up Farm Output and Cut Imports." FAgr, XXI, 5-7.

2752. _____, "Yugoslavia to Push Cotton Production in Macedonia." FAgr, XXI, 14-15.

2753. Maldek, J. V., E. Sturc, and M. R. Wyczalkowsky. The Change in the Yugoslav Economic System. International Monetary Fund. Staff Papers, Vol. II, No. 3, November, 1952. [Washington, D.C.]

2754. Markon, George, and Melrad Mellen. "Mining." Robert F. Byrnes, Ed., Yugoslavia, pp. 259-281. (East-Central Europe under the Communists).

2755. Mellen, Melrad, and Victor H. Winston. The Coal Resources of Yugoslavia. New York: Praeger, 1957, 328 pp.

2756. Neuberger, Egon. "Consumer Goods." Robert F. Byrnes, Ed., Yugoslavia, pp. 310-325. (East-Central Europe under the Communists).

2757. _____. "General Survey of the Yugoslav Economy." Robert F. Byrnes, Ed., Yugoslavia, pp. 192-210. (East-Central Europe under the Communists).

2758. _____. "Transportation." Robert F. Byrnes, Ed., Yugoslavia, pp. 370-388. (East-Central Europe under the Communists).

2759. Nuttonson, Michael Y. Agricultural Climatology of Yugoslavia and its Agro-climatic Analogies in North America. (International Agro-climatological Series, Study No. 4.) Washington, D.C.: American Institute of Crop Ecology, 1947.

2760. Rodin, George. Economic Reconstruction in Yugoslavia. New York: King's Crown Press, 1946, 161 pp.

2761. Spulber, Nicolas. "National Income and Product." Robert F. Byrnes, Ed., Yugoslavia, pp. 211-227. (East-Central Europe under the Communists).

2762. Tinley, J. M., "Are Collective Farms on the Way Out in Yugoslavia?" FAgr, XXI, 6-7.

2763. Tomasevich, Jozo. Peasants, Politics, and Economic Change in Yugoslavia. Stanford, California: Stanford University Press, 1955, 743 pp.

2764. _____. Yugoslavia: Foreign Economic Relations 1918-1941. Reprinted from Yugoslavia. (United Nations Series.) Berkeley: University of California Press, 1949, pp. 169-528.

2765. Venables, Thomas M., et al., "Recent Changes in Yugoslav Agricultural Policy." FAgr, XVI, 134-139.

2766. _____, "Yugoslavia's New Farm Marketing Scheme." FAgr, XV, 175-176.

2767. Ward, Benjamin, "Workers' Management in Yugoslavia." JPE, LXV, 373-386.

2768. Yugoslavia. Office of Reconstruction and Economic Affairs, New York. Jugoslav Postwar Reconstruction Papers. Nicholas Mirkovich ed. New York: [n. pub.], 1942-1946.

LANGUAGES

2769. Bidwell, Charles E., et al. English for Yugoslavs. (American Council of Learned Societies. Program in English as a Foreign Language. Spoken English Textbooks.) Washington, D.C.: American Council of Learned Societies, 1955, 366 pp.

2770. Bogadek, Francis Aloysius. New English-Croatian and Croatian-English Dictionary. 3rd ed. enl. and corrected. 2 vols. in 1. New York: Hafner Publishing Co., 1949, 550 pp.

2771. Hammel, Eugene A., "Serbo-Croatian Kinship Terminology." KASP, No. 16, pp. 45-75.

2772. Hodge, Carleton Taylor. Spoken Serbo-Croatian: Basic Course. Vols. I-II. New York: Henry Holt and Co., n.d.

2773. Kadic, Ante, ed. Croatian Reader, With

Vocabulary. (University of California, Syllabus Series, No. 361.) Berkeley: University of California, 1957.

2774. Kotnik, Janko. Slovene-English Dictionary. 2nd rev. and enl. ed. New York: Heinman, 1952, 679 pp.

2775. Magner, Thomas F. Introduction to the Serbo-Croatian Language. Minneapolis: University of Minnesota, 1956.

2776. Prince, John Dyneley. Practical Grammar of the Serbo-Croatian Language. New York: Hafner Publishing Co., 1951, 218 pp. [New ed.]

2777. Sass, Charles, "Vuk Stefanovich Karajich." BA, XXVI, 144-146.

2778. Skerlj, Ruzena. English-Slovene Dictionary. 3rd rev. and enl. ed. New York: Heinman, 1953, 695 pp.

THE ARTS

2779. Bellow, Peter, and Anton Schutz, eds. Yugoslavia: Mediaeval Frescoes. Pref. by David Talbot Rice. Introd. Svetozar Radojcic. (UNESCO World Art Series, Vol. IV.) Greenwich, Connecticut: New York Graphic Society, 1955, 32 pp.

2780. Mestrovic, Ivan. The Sculpture of Ivan Mestrovic. Norman L. Rice, ed. Syracuse, New York: University of Syracuse Press, 1948.

LITERATURE

2781. Calder-Marshall, Arthur, "Notes on Yugoslav Journeys." YR, XXXV, 475-490.

2782. Dor, Milo, "Contemporary Yugoslav Letters." BA, XXX, 141-146.

2783. Kadic, Ante. Modern Yugoslav Literature. An Anthology with Biographical Sketches. Berkeley: University of California, 1956.

2784. Klancar, Anthony J., "Josip Jurcic, The Slovene Scott." ASEER, V, xii-xiii, 19-33.

2785. Noyes, George Rapall. The Life and Adventures of Dimitrije Obradovic. Berkeley and Los Angeles: University of California, 1953.

2786. Strelsky, Nikander. "Yugoslav Literature." Horatio Smith, Ed., <u>Columbia Dictionary of Modern European Literature</u>, pp. 881-887.

2787. Usmiani, Mirko A., "Marko Marulic (1450-1525)." HSS, III, 1-48.

FOLKLORE

2788. Cernkovich, Rudolph, ed. Piano Album of Yugoslav Songs and Dances. Nos. 1-4. Bradley, Michigan: The Editor, 1937-1945.

2789. Jankovic, Ljubica S., and D. S. Jankovic. Dances of Yugoslavia. Published under the auspices of the Royal Academy of Dancing and the Ling Physical Education Association. (Chanticleer ed., Handbooks of European National Dances.) New York: Crown Publishers, 1952, 40 pp.

2790. Lord, Albert B., "Avdo Mededovic, Guslar." JAF, LXIX, 320-330.

2791. _____, "Notes on <u>Digenis Akritas</u> and Serbocroatian Epic." HSS, II, 375-384.

2792. _____. "The Role of Sound Patterns in Serbocroatian Epic." Morris Halle, et al., comp., <u>For Roman Jakobson</u>, pp. 301-305.

2793. Parry, Milman, comp. Serbocroatian Heroic Songs. Ed. and tr. Albert B. Lord. Vols. I-II. Vol. I, Novi Pazar: English translations. With musical transcriptions by Bela Bartok. Pref. by John H. Finley, Jr. and Roman Jakobson. Vol. II, Novi Pazar: Serbocroatian texts. With Introd. and notes by the ed. Pref. by A. Belic. Cambridge, Massachusetts: Harvard University Press, 1953, 1954.

EDUCATION

2794. Roucek, Joseph S. Pre-War Educational Theory in Yugoslavia. Bridgeport, Connecticut: University of Bridgeport, 1956.

2795. Skendi, Stavro. "Education." Robert F. Byrnes, Ed., <u>Yugoslavia</u>, pp. 166-189. (East-Central Europe under the Communists).

PHILOSOPHY AND RELIGION

2796. Filipovic, Milenko S., "Folk Religion Among the Orthodox Population in Eastern Yugoslavia." HSS, II, 359-374.

2797. Jelavich, Charles, "Some Aspects of Serbian Religious Development in the 18th Century." ChH, XXIII, 144-152.

2798. Mestrovic, Matthew M., "Report on Yugoslav Catholics." America, XCVII, 584-588.

2799. Milivojevich, Dionisije. Persecution of the Serbian Orthodox Church in Yugoslavia. St. Sava Monastery, Libertyville, Illinois: The Author, 1945, 42 pp.

2800. O'Brien, Antony Henry. Archbishop Stepinac: the Man and His Case. Westminister, Maryland: Newman Bookshop, 1947.

2801. Pattee, Richard Francis. The Case of Cardinal Aloysius Stepinac. Milwaukee, Wisconsin: Bruce Publishing Co., [1953].

2802. United States. Library of Congress. Law Library. Yugoslavia: Churches and Religion. Digest-Index of Eastern European Law. Washington, D.C.: Library of Congress, 1951.

2803. Zebot, Cyril A., "Tito's New Drive Against Religion." America, LXXXVIII, 125-127.

SOCIOLOGY

2804. Anon. "The People." Robert F. Byrnes, Ed., Yugoslavia, pp. 71-89. (East-Central Europe under the Communists).

2805. Brown, Alec. Yugoslav Life and Landscape. New York: Ungar, 1955, 196 pp.

2806. Halpern, Joel Martin. Social and Cultural Change in a Servian Village. (Pre-publication Monograph, HRAF, 25.) [New Haven?], 1956, 619 pp.

2807. Mittleman, Earl Niel, "The Nationality Problem in Yugoslavia: A Survey of Developments, 1921-1953." DA, XVII, 2584.

2808. Raditsa, Bogdan, "Yugoslavia: Can Restless Peasants Make Good Soldiers?" Rept, VI, iii, 6-8.

2809. Tomasic, Dinko, "Nationality Problems and Partisan Yugoslavia." JCEA, VI, 115-125.

2810. Trouton, Ruth. Peasant Renaissance in Yugoslavia, 1900-1950: A Study of the Development of Yugoslav Peasant Society as Affected by Education. (International Library of Sociology and Social Reconstruction.) New York: Grove Press, 1952, 344 pp.

INDEX OF AUTHORS

Aaron, D., 1528
Abel, T., 2418
Acker, J., 2563
Adamesteanu, D., 1642, 2445
Adamic, L., 2542-3
Ady, E., 1858
Agard, F. B., 2515
Aizsienieks, A. P., 80
Akers, D. S., 1975
Alexander, M., 852
Allen, P. J., 2544, 2672
Allen, R. L., 498, 620
Alton, T. P., 2201-2, 2733
American Federation of Labor. International Labor Relations Committee, 499
Amery, J., 1106
Ames, E., 500, 1423, 2734
Anastasoff, C., 1063, 1074
Anders, W., 2079
Anderson, A. T., 1553
Andersons, E., 962
Andic, V. E., 1251
Andrews, T., 2405
Andriyevsky, D., 382
Andrusiak, N., 221
Anon., 1-2, 81-106, 199, 261-272, 326-333, 338-9, 383-8, 441, 501-539, 596-601, 621-626, 700-715, 722, 736-40, 744-7, 767-79, 829-32, 896-7, 1015, 1096, 1101-2, 1107-8, 1116-20, 1133-41, 1160, 1162, 1164-5, 1188-90, 1202-3, 1216, 1244, 1246, 1252, 1283, 1291, 1337, 1362-3, 1393-4, 1408-10, 1424-30, 1594, 1605-7, 1679-88, 1731-3, 1739-45, 1768-72, 1797-1801, 1847, 1917-8, 2080, 2114-20, 2153-9, 2203-11, 2286-7, 2406, 2428, 2460-2, 2486-91,
2518, 2534, 2545, 2649, 2735-6, 2804
Anthem, T., 1128
Antonoff, N., 1247
Aptheker, H., 1689
Arato, I., 1788
Arciszewski, F., 2177
Armstrong, H. F., 2673-4
Arnold, E., 1595
Arnold, G. L., 2675
Aronovici, Serge H., 2463
Arski, S., 2178
Ascoli, M., 2650-1
Ascom, B. B., 1142
Ashcroft, D., 1529
Assembly of Captive European Nations, 833-4
Augustinas, V., 947
Auty, Robert, 1292, 1460
Avakumovic, I., 3, 4, 2583
Avsenek, I., 2737-9
de Azcarate y Florez, P., 807

Babbitt, M., 1848
Backus, O. P., 968
Bacon, L., 627-9
Baczynski, W., 2226
Baerlein, H. P. B., 2519
Bagranov, T. S., 1248
Bailey, G., 1690, 1734
Bain, L. B., 1691-5, 2160
Bakken, H. H., 080
Bako, E., 5, 1896
Balbin, J., 2288
Baldwin, R. N., 649
Balodis, F., 963
Baltramoitis, C. V., 948
Baluta, J., 2259
Baretski, C. A., 2383
Barker, E., 1064
Barlowe, R., 1395
Baross, G., 1773

Barron, J. B., 748
Bartlett V., 107
Bartok, B., 1849
Bartos, M., 2652
Basch, A., 108
Basic, M., 2546
Bass, R. H., 602, 1171
Beamish, T., 109
Beck, C. F., 1338, 1364-6
Beck, J., 1981
Bedo, A., 1789-91, 1904
Beke, L. (pseud.), 1696
Bell, H. M., 1530
Bellow, P., 2779
Bellquist, E. C., 1568
Beltchev, K., 1217
Bemelmans, L., 110
Benes, E., 1293-5
Benes, V., 1296-7, 1396-7
Benet, S., 2384
Bennett, P. P., 1608
Bentley, A. M., 442
Benton, W., 334
Berg, M., 853
Berkman, P. L., 337, 782
Berle, A. A., Jr., 1697
Bernatsky, K., 1802-4
Bernolak, I., 1831
Berzinsh, A., 999
Beuer, G., 1253
Bialer, S., 2121
Bidwell, C. E., 2769
Bienenstok, T., 854-5
Bilaikin, G., 2584
Bilmanis, A., 949-52, 969-72, 987, 989-90, 1000-1, 1046
Birnbaum, I., 475
Bishop, R., 898
Bizonfy, F., 1832
Black, C. E., 49-50, 111-2, 222, 273-5, 297, 305, 323, 350-1, 374, 389, 411, 478, 583, 592, 607, 784, 920, 932, 1178, 1982
Black, R. E., 1367

Blackburn, E. C., 1983
Blair, R., 780
Blit, L., 856
Bloch, J., 2168
Blum, J., 223
Bobula, I. M., 6, 1833
Bogadek, F. A., 2770
Bohmer, A., 1517
Boila, R., 2464
Bolanowski, J. E., 2260
Bolek, F., 1919
Bolles, B., 352, 749, 1431, 2081-2
Bonatt, E., 1984
Bone, E., 1792
Bonifacic, A. F., 2585
Boray, A., 113
Borkenau, F., 276, 857
Borsody, S., 1643
Bossy, G. H., 2492-5
Bossy, R., 2535
Boswell, A. B., 1985-7, 2289
Boucek, J. A., 788
Bourgeois, C., 1047
Bouscaren, A. T., 390
Boyd, N. L., 1489
Bradac, O., 1473
Braham, R., 1746, 2465-6
Brandt, K., 603
Brannen, B., 2429
Brannen, P. B., 391
Brant, I., 1920-1
Brashich, R. M., 2740-2
Braun, C. E., 931
Bregman, A., 1922, 2122
Brewster, R. H., 1644
Briggs, L. B., 1411
Brock, P., 1298, 1988-93, 2123
Brodney, K., 2467
Brooke, M., 826
Brown, A., 2805
Brown, G. T., 2676
Broz-Tito, J., 2677
Bruckner, A., 2290
Brunauer, A., 1793
Brunauer, S., 1747, 1905
Brunner, E. S., 604
Bryner, C., 789
Brzezinski, Z., 277-9, 443, 2124
Brzorad, V. J., 476, 1432-4
Buber, M., 114
Buday, G., 1889
Budz, A. I. Jr., 2179
Bugelski, B. R., 2353, 2356, 2358, 2367, 2377, 2381
Buhler, N. V., 741, 1698
Burck, G., 150
Burczak, H., 2385
Burillianu, A., 2430
Burks, R. V., 1645
Burnham, J., 115
Busek, V., 477, 1254, 1283, 1285, 1338, 1365-6, 1375, 1389, 1423-4, 1428, 1433-4, 1444, 1447, 1455-6, 1458, 1497, 1510, 1518
Butler, A. C., 1065
Byrnes, R. F., 116, 117, 444, 2547, 2579, 2590, 2639-42, 2658, 2678, 2734, 2736-7, 2740, 2744, 2754, 2756-8, 2761, 2795, 2804

Cahnman, W. J., 353, 858
Cakste, M., 1002-4
Calder-Marshall, A., 2781
California, University of, 51
Callimachi, Annie-Marie (Vacaresco), 2446
Campbell, J. C., 354-5, 2447-8
Canada. Department of Mines and Technical Surveys, 2574
Cannon, C. W., 540
Capa, R., 1646
Capek, M., 1284
Caranfil, A. G., 2496
Carey, J. P. C., 803
Carlston, K. S., 356
Carlton, R. K., 650-1
Caro, J., 671
Carp, M., 2431
Caruthers, O., 1066, 2679

Cary, W. H., 1923
Cattell, D., 1647
Cech, E., 1491
Cecilia, Sister, 1519
Ceichners, A., 1016
Celovsky, B., 804
Central and Eastern European Conferences, 805
Cernkovich, R., 2788
Cesarich, G. W., 2548
Challener, R. D., 2653
Chalupa, V., 835
Chamblis, R., 1601
Chandler, A. D., 1994
Chase, T. G., 973
Cherne, L., 1699
Chevrier, B., 991
Christophorov, P., 1234
Chudoba, B., 118, 445, 1368
Church, H. R. J., 214
Chyzhevski, D., 723
Ciechanowski, J., 446, 2083
Ciurea, E., 2432, 2530, 2536
Clarion, N., 2680
Clark, V. R., 1608
Clarke, J. F., 52, 1179-80, 2586
Clippinger, F., 119
Clissold, S., 2587
Clucas, L. M., 447
Coblentz, G., 2681
Cockburn, J. H., 751
Coffin, I., 1700
Cohen, B. V., 899-900
Cohen, E. E., 295, 859, 863, 875-6, 878, 889
Colbert, J. L., 2743
Cole, T., 273, 275, 280
Coleman, A. P., 53-5, 2318
Coleman, M. M., 2319-21, 2330, 2354-5, 2386-7
Collan, A., 1596
Columbia University. American Language Center, 1834
Columbia University, Klub Polski, 1995, 2321

Index of Authors

Committee Against Mass Expulsion, 806
Committee for the Defense of Albania, 1121
Conover, H. F., 7, 8
Conrad, D., 2291
Constandaky, S., 2507
Contaski, J. K., 2390
Coon, C. S., 1109
Cooper, J. S., 2682
Co-ordinating Committee of American-Polish Associations in the East, 2180
Corbridge-Patkaniowska, M., 2261-3
Cornell, C., 121
Cornish, L. C., 2442
Cottrell, A. J., 1774
Council of Free Czechoslovakia, 1339
Cowan, L. G., 56
Cowherd, R. G., 448, 541, 752
Cox, H. B., 122
Craemer, A. R., 123
Cramer, F. H., 124
Crayfield, E. S., 898
Creanga, I., 2520
Cretzianu, A., 2430-3, 2464, 2470, 2472, 2476-7, 2479, 2485, 2497, 2499, 2509, 2530, 2536
Crisan, G., 2539
Crkvencic, I., 2748-9
Croog, S. H., 1602
Cross, S. H., 224-226
Csicsery-Ronay, I., 1897
Cushing, G. F., 1859
Czaplinski, W., 1996
Czapski, J., 1924
Czechoslovak Jewish Representative Committee, 860
Czubatyi, N., 2181-2

Dacie, A., 2588
Dall, R., 1369
Dallin, A., 392
Dallin, D. J., 393-4, 652
Dangerfield, R. J., 50, 52, 57, 132, 452
Dauzyardis, J. J., 953
David, P., 2407

David, V., 1255
Davies, R. A., 1925
Deacon, K. J., 605
Dean, V. M., 125, 281, 357, 395-6, 542-4, 1340, 1701, 2183, 2212-3, 2549, 2614, 2654, 2683-6
De Biro, E., 1609
De Bray, R. G. A., 672
Dedijer, V., 1129, 2687
Dellin, L. A. D., 1166, 1176-8, 1189-91, 1196-7, 1204, 1218-19, 1221, 1224, 1227-30, 1232, 1236, 1244, 1246
del Vayo, J. A., 901, 1299
Dennett, R., 449, 932
De Robeck, N., 1648
Deutsch, K. W., 478
Deutsch, L., 1482
Deutscher, I., 282, 397, 2125, 2161
Devlin, L. R., 1533
Dewar, M., 630
Dexter, B., 398
Diamond, S., 861
Dimitrov, G. M., 283
Diver, W., 1235
Djaparidze, D., 9
Djilas, M., 2615-6
Djordjevic, J., 2617
Dobos, I., 1735
Dobriansky, L. E., 450, 1702
Dolan, E., 2408
Dolina, J., 2214-7, 2744
Dolnytsky, M. A., 200
Doman, N. R., 545
Dombrovsky, A., 201
Dor, M., 2782
Dorosh, J. T., 10
Dougherty, J. E., 1774
Douglas, D. S. (Wolff), 2218
Douglas, W. O., 2618
d'Or, R., 399
D'Otrange, M. L., 2292

Dragnich, A. N., 2550-1, 2619-20, 2644, 2688-9
Drahomanov, M., 202, 790
Draskovich, S. M., 2690
Drizari, N., 1143-6
Drobnig, U., 340
Drohan, L., 1068
Duchacek, I., 479, 1256-7, 1341-3, 1435, 1510
Duker, A. G., 862
Dushinsky, E., 879
Dutkowski, J., 845
Dvoichenko-Markov, D., 2449, 2478
Dvornik, F., 227-230
Dwyer, F. X., 341
Dyboski, R., 1997
Dziewanowski, M. K., 1998-2006, 2126-8, 2162, 2219, 2409

East, W. G., 400
Ebon, M., 284, 2131
Eckersley, C. E., 2262-3
Eckstein, A., 1805
Economic Research Group, 546
Edelman, I., 126
Ehrenburg, I., 902
Ehrich, R. W., 1300-1
Eisenstein, M., 2394
Eisner, K., 1258
Eisner, P., 1492
Ekbaum, A., 606
Elias, T., 1525, 1926
Englund, E., 1573
Entwistle, W. J., 673
Eppstein, J., 1649
Era-Esko, A., 1531
Erickson, J., 231
Ervin, E. W., 2691
Estreicher, K., 2293
Ethridge, M., 932
Eulau, H., 1192
Evans, T. B., 335

Fabian, B., 863, 1610, 1748-9
Fahy, C., 900
Farrell, R. B., 2692
Fast, H. M., 2693
Fay, S. B., 401, 808-9, 1927, 2132

Fedynskyj, J., 1051
Feierabend, L., 607, 1344, 1436-7
Fejto, F., 1703-4
Fenton, W. N., 58
Feraru, L., 2521
Ferrell, R. H., 451
Fetter, J., 810
Fields, H., 2084
Filipovic, M. S., 2796
Fischer, G., 11, 1511
Fischer-Galati, S., 2434, 2443-4, 2450-1, 2463, 2465, 2468-9, 2492-6, 2513, 2518, 2531-2, 2537
Fisher, R. H., 402
Fisher, S. N., 921
Fizer, J., 59
Flaningam, M. L., 1438
Fles, B., 1474
Florinsky, M. T., 403, 480, 1650
Foa, B., 547
Fodor, E., 1533
Fodor, M. W., 127
Folejewski, Z., 2322-3, 2536
Folkman, A., 2085
Fono, L., 1835
Forst-Battaglia, O., 2007
Fotitch, A. C., 2552, 2655
Fox, P., 2410
Foye, I., 1548
Frankel, J., 2621-2
Frantisek, R., 1483
Free Europe Committee, 128, 129, 659, 754, 1052, 1193-5, 1220, 1249, 1370-1, 1611, 1705, 1750-1, 1775, 1807, 1898-9, 2129-30, 2220, 2395
Free Europe Committee. Mid-European Studies Center, 12, 13, 1814
Free Europe Press Research Staff, 14, 130, 131, 608, 660, 1048, 1110, 1509, 1612-4, 1752, 1808-9
French, R. M., 755
Friedman, O., 1345
Friedman, P., 864-6,
2086
Frumkin, G., 203
Fryde, M. M., 15, 2221
Fryer, P., 1706
Fugedi, E., 1900

Gabensky, I., 1220-1
Gabor, R., 1753, 1810-1
Gacki, S. K., 481
Gadourek, I., 1346, 1372
Gafencu, G., 2452
Galantiere, L., 452
Gallen-Kallela, 1532
Ganeff, V., 1205
Garbuny, S., 1005
Garthoff, R. L., 1707
Garvin, P. L., 1836
Gasiorowska, X., 2324
Gasiorowski, Z., 2008-12
Gayn, M., 2553
Gedye, G. E. R., 1615, 2554
General Assembly of the Church of Scotland, 750
Georgescu-Roegen, O., 2498
Georgetown University. School of Foreign Service, 60
Gergely, E. J., 1850
Gerson, L., 2013
Gervasi, F., 1534, 2694-5
Gibian, G., 1439
Gilbert, F., 482
Gimbutas, M. (Alseikaite), 232, 1181
Gingerich, W. F., 2087
Ginsburg, G., 811
Ginters, V., 1017
Glabisz, K., 2133
Gleitman, H., 1708, 1913
Gliksman, J., 661
Gluckstein, Y., 404
Goldbloom, M. J., 2696
Goldstajn, A., 2645-6

Goldstein, B., 2088
Gombosi, O., 1851
Gorczynski, W., 1967
Gordey, M., 1347
Gorka, O. A., 2014
Gorove, S., 1794
Gorynski, M., 2281
Goudy, A. P., 1968
Goure, L., 483
Govorchin, G. G., 2589
Gracalic, L., 2555
Graham, M. W., 358, 992
Graham, R. A., 756, 1167
Granick, D., 631-2
Grbic, M., 233
Green, B., 1837-8
Green, R., 1616
Greenbaum, J. J., 1913
Grindea, C., 2522
Grindea, M., 2522
Gronowicz, A., 2015, 2184, 2294
Gross, F., 132, 283, 285, 484, 781, 794, 836, 1928, 2419
Grosser, A., 485
Grzybowski, K., 342-3, 405, 548, 633, 2169, 2223-5
Gryziewicz, S., 2222
Gsovski, V., 16, 344-5, 359, 662, 757, 1209, 1517, 1904, 2412, 2539, 2647
Guins, G. C., 286-7
Gulick, C. A., 288
Gunda, B., 609
Gunther, J., 133
Guri, D., 204, 2697
Gurian, W., 134, 406, 414, 817, 1964
Gwozdz, J., 2133, 2170, 2412
Gyorgy, A., 289-91, 1617, 2471
Gyorky, B., 1811

Haberler, G., 549
Hadsel, F. L., 634
Hadsel, W. N., 292-3, 360, 407, 453, 903, 1259, 1348, 1440, 1535, 1776, 2656
Haggerty, J. J., 2745

Haiman, M., 17
Haines, C. G., 1080
Hainsworth, R. G., 205
Hajda, J., 1524
Halasz, A., 550
Halecki, O., 234, 235, 408, 486, 812, 1929-32, 1974, 1978, 2016-24, 2089, 2114, 2118-9, 2128, 2133, 2185-6, 2203-4, 2214-6, 2239, 2245, 2249, 2251, 2255-6, 2295, 2334, 2400, 2406
Hall, R. B., 61
Halle, M., 674, 694-5, 698, 1038, 1839, 2278, 2379, 2792
Halperin, E., 2657
Halpern, A., 2090
Halpern, J. M., 2806
Halpert, H., 1890
Ham, E. M., 1236
Hammel, E. A., 2771
Hammond, T. T., 2590, 2623-4, 2658-9
Hamp, E. P., 1147
Hanc, J., 1260
Handler, D., 588
Handler, M. S., 2625
Hannover, N. N., 867
Hans, N., 2396
Hansen, K. R., 635
Harkins, W. E., 18-19, 724, 1461, 1493-5
Harms, R. T., 1582
Harris, S. E., 551
Harrison, E. J., 974
Harsanyi, A., 236
Harsch, J. C., 135, 152, 454, 1261, 1933, 2698
Harvard University. Russian Research Center, 62-63
Hasluck, M. M., (Hardie), 1111
Haven, A., 2699
Hechinger, F. M., 1412, 2025
Heideman, B., 1554
Heikel, Y. S., 1596
Heisler, J. B., 1262
Heller, A., 1709
Helmreich, E. C., 1618, 1640-1, 1651, 1698, 1739, 1774-6, 1779, 1797, 1811,
1819, 1821, 1823, 1829-30, 1862, 1902
Hencken, H., 232
Henderson, L. W., 455
Hepner, B. P., 2026
Herling, A. K., 409
Herling, G., 1934
Herman, L. J., 410
Hertz, A., 716, 864
Hertz, F., 552
Herzog, E., 895
Hess, M. A., 456
Hessler, W. H., 1006
Higgins, M., 136
Hilton, H. J., Jr., 1812-3
Hindus, M., 1263
Hinshaw, D., 1536-7
Hnykova, M., 1461
Hodge, C. T., 2772
Hodgkinson, H., 2660, 2700
Hoffman, G. W., 206-7, 220, 2746
Hoffman, M. L., 636
Hoffman, S., 1710
Hogan, W. C., 2187
Hogye, M., 1777
Hollander, H., 1484
Holmes, O., 1130
Homonnay, E., 1778
Hook, S., 294
Hoptner, J. B., 137, 411, 2661
Horak, S., 1969
Horbaly, W., 1441
Hordynsky, S., 1970
Horecky, P. L., 20-23, 1462, 1475
Horm, A., 138, 993
Horna, D., 12
Horniatkevych, D., 2296
Horthy, A. N., 1652
Horthy de Nagybanya, N. V., 237
Horvath, P., 1653
Hostovsky, E., 1496
Howlett, F. S., 2747
Hrobak, P. A., 1264, 1463
Hrusovsky, F., 1265
Hubbard, G., 1175
Hughes, D. J., 2397
Huizinga, J. H., 1538
Hulicka, K., 1373, 1442
Hungarian National Council, 663, 813
Hunt R., 1374
Huot, L., 2626
de Huszar, G. B., 412
Hutcheson, H. H., 637-8
Hutton, J. H., 1111

Ifkonen, T. I., 1549
Ignotus, P., 487, 1754
Ileana, Princess of Rumania, 2453-4
Illyricus (pseud.), 2701
Infeld, L., 742
Inks, J. M., 2591
International Conference of Free Trade Unions, 1711
International Court of Justice, 361
Ionescu, G., 2472, 2499-2500
Ionnitziu, M., 2479
Ivic, P., 1069
Iwanska, A., 1935

Jaanlila, K., 46
Jaatinen, S., 1574
Jackson, J. H., 954
Jakobson, R., 238, 675-7, 725, 2325
Jankoff, D. A., 1222-4
Jankovic, D. S., 2789
Jankovic, L. S., 2789
Janowski, O. I., 814
Janta, A., 2091, 2297, 2326
Jarecka, L. (Llewellyn), 2027, 2388
Jaroslav, M., 1400
Jaska, E., 1018
Jasny, N., 610
Jaspers, K., 2298
Jaszi, O., 139, 413, 1302, 1619
Jedlicki, M. Z., 2028
Jedrzejewicz, W., 2029
Jelavich, B., 239, 1182-3
Jelavich, C., 24,

Jelavich, C., cont., 1182-4, 2592-3, 2797
Jelenski, K. A., 2299
Jessup, P. C., 1081
Jewish Labor Committee, 868
Jirasek, A., 1526
Joesten, J., 1555
Jofen, J. B., 678
Johnson, J. E., 449, 932
Johnston, M., 1210
Johnston, W. B., 2748-9
Joint Committee on the Economic Report, 553
Jonas, K., 1464
Jonas, P., 1712-3
Jones, B. D., 1224
Jones, D. D., 2092
Jones, R. A., 2134
Jones, S. F., 1714
Jordan, C., 2501-4
Josephson, E., 639
Josten, J., 1266
Judas, E., 1024
Juhasz, W., 758, 1901-3
Juldanic, S. G., 1654
Jurgela, C. R., 975-6

Kaasik, N., 140, 837-8, 1007
Kaczer, I., 1655
Kadic, A., 2773, 2783
Kadragic, C. S., 1131
Kaeckenbeeck, G. S., 2030
Kaelas, A., 955
Kajeckas, J., 1008
Kalhous, R., 1399
Kalijarvi, T. V., 1556
Kallay, N., 1656
Kalme, A., 1009
Kalnoky, H., 1904
Kaminsky, H., 1303
Kann, R. A., 240-1, 869
Kantonen, T. A., 1599
Kaplan, H. H., 2031
Kapustyansky, M., 488
Karasz, A., 141, 1620
Kardelj, E., 2627
Kardos, B. T., 25
Karolyi, M., 1657
Karpf, R., 1527
Kartun, D., 2702

Kasparek, J., 1413-4
Katalin, F., 1609
Kecskemeti, P., 295
Keefer, L., 2357
Keitt, W. L., 346
Kelleher, P. J., 1658
Kellen, K., 2616
Kelly, E. P., 1971, 2358
Kemeny, G., 554, 1815
Kendrick, A., 904, 1621, 2703
Kennan, G. F., 1304
Keramopoulos, A. D., 1070
Kerner, R. J., 791, 1267, 1945, 2594
Kerr, W., 142
Kerstein, E. S., 1936
Kersten, F., 1557
Kertesz, S. D., 362-3, 414, 442, 444, 451, 457-8, 466, 549, 644, 815, 960, 1100, 1174, 1256, 1546, 1622, 1659-60, 1755, 1779-80, 1907, 1931, 2441, 2551
Ketrzynski, S., 2411
Kierst, W., 2265
King, F., 905
King, W. B., 906
Kirchner, W., 977
Kirk, D., 208
Kirkconnell, W., 143, 1860
Kirkpatrick, E. M., 336
Kisch, G., 1305
Kish, G., 555, 611, 1082, 2575-6
Kiss, S., 1715
Kiviranna, R., 759
Klancar, A. J., 2577, 2784
Klausner, L. C., 144
Kliewer, D., 415, 1225, 2435
Klimas, P., 978
Knepfle, G. A., 2750
Koc, A., 2226
Kocvara, Stephen (also Stephan and Stefan), 1375, 1443, 1517
Koehl, R. L., 364, 1972, 2188

Koeller, H. L., 2751-2
Koenig, E., 1444-5, 2227-8
Kohn, H., 145-6, 792-3, 1268, 1306, 1376
Kolaja, J., 839
Kolarz, W., 147
Kolehmainen, J. I., 1583
Komarnicki, T., 2032
Komornicki, S. S., 2300
Komorowski, T., 2093
Konirsh, S. G., 1307
Konopczynski, W., 2033-4
Konovalov, S., 2189
Korab, A., 1937, 2135
Korbel, J., 2704-5
Korbel, P., 1313-14, 1377-81, 1513-4
Korbonski, S., 2094
Korduba, M., 2035
Kormendi, F., 1861-2
Kormos, C., 2436
Korosec, J., 2595
de Korostovetz, V., 753
Kos, F., 2556
Kosa, J., 1661-2, 1914
Kossar, L., 1696
Kostanick, H. L., 459, 816, 1071
Kostelski, Z., 2578, 2596
Kostrzewski, J., 2036
Kot, S., 242
Kotiuznski, A., 2229
Kotnik, J., 2774
Kotschnig, W., 664
Kott, J., 1938
Kovac, E., Jr., 1465
Kovach, F. J., 1908
Kovacs, I., 1816
Kovtun, E., 1497
Kowalczyk, L. S., 2230
Kracauer, S., 337, 782
Kramer, A., 2359
Kramoris, I. J., 726
Kraus, D., 1466
Kremenliev, B. A., 1237-8
Kridl, M., 2190

Kridl, M., cont., 2327-9, 2360-2
Krippner, M., 2557
Krumin, P. O., 1019
Kruszewska, A. I., 2330
Krynski, M. J., 2331
Krzesinski, A. J., 2191-2
Krzyzanowski, J., 2301
Krzyzanowski, L., 2332-4
Kubina, F., 1485
Kucera, H., 1467, 1497
Kucera, J., 1468
Kukiel, M., 2037
Kulikowsky, D., 2136
Kulischer, E. M., 209-10
Kulkielko, R., 2095
Kulski, W. W., 148, 211, 416, 2038, 2193
Kuncewicz, M., 2363
Kunz, J. L., 365, 1083
Kupcek, J. R., 1469
Kurath, G. P., 727
Kusielewicz, E., 2039-41, 2194
Kutas, E. R., 870
Kybal, V., 1308

Lach, J. J., 1482
Ladik, G., 1637
Laid, F., 1041
Landes, R., 871
Landy, P., 1716
Lane, A. B., 2042
Lang, R., 366
Lange, O., 2231
Langer, R., 2662
Laqueur, W. Z., 872
Laserson, M. M., 2043
Lash, J. P., 2706
Lasky, M. J., 1717
Lattimore, O., 1269-70
Lednicki, W., 64, 794, 2335-8, 2364-7
Lee, A. S. G., 2455
Lee, D. E., 907, 1211
Lee, L., 2368
Lehrman, H., 150-1, 1623, 1756, 2437, 2558-9, 2628
Leiser, E., 1569
Lelcai, T. J., 1663
LeNard, L., 1638, 1904

Lengyel, E., 152, 454, 556, 717, 1637, 1664, 1718-20
Lens, S., 2629
Leslie, R. F., 2044
Lestchinsky, J., 873
Leszczycki, S., 1973
Lettrich, J., 1309
Levytsky, O., 2045
Lewis, A. R., 243
Lewis, F., 1476
Lichten, J. L., 864
Linehan, J., 460
Lingis, J., 840, 1050
Lisinski, M. J., 557
Lithuanian Consultative Panel, 665
Lockhart, Sir Robert Bruce, 1271, 1310, 1349
Logan, M. Z., 2560
Logoreci, A., 1148
Long, G. W., 2663
Lord, A. B., 728, 2790-3
Lotz, J., 1839-40
Lowenthal, R., 153, 1721, 2707
Lubinova, M., 1486
Luca, R., 2523
Lucas, W. O., 154
Luciv, W., 2046
Lukacs, J. A., 367, 417, 929
Lukas, J., 461
Lukinich, I., 1665
Lundin, C. L., 1558
Lunt, H. G., 679-80, 1072
Luthin, R. H., 1666
Lutz, H. T. B., 1600
Lutz, R. H., 155

M. E., 1757
M. J. M., 1974
Macartney, C. A., 1667-8
MacCallum, T. W., 2266
Macek, V., 2597
Maciuika, B. V., 979
Maciuszko, G. J., 1624
Maclean, F. H. 2598, 2708-9
Macridis, R., 2710
Madden, H. M., 1669

Magner, T. F., 2775
Major, R., 1625, 1736, 1817
Maks, L., 1939
Malara, J., 2047
Maldek, J. V., 2753
Malinowski, W. R., 2048
Mamatey, V. S., 462, 1212
Mangone, G. J., 1084-5
Mann, K., 729
Mann, K., 1272
Mann, S. E., 1149
Mannerheim, C. G. E., 1559
Mannering, H., 2561
Manning, C. A., 65, 760, 795, 938, 956, 994, 1054, 1239, 2049
Marcinkowski, K., 2050
Marcovitch, L., 922
Mares, V. E., 1350-1, 1446-7
Margold, S. K., 558
Marinoff, S., 1240
Marker, M., 1097
Markham, R. H., 761, 2438, 2630
Markon, G., 2754
Markus, V., 1055
Mars, A. M., 2302
Martin, D., 2599, 2631
Martinet, A., 681
Martinoff, G., 1043
Marx, D., Jr., 640
Mason, J. B., 2195
Massachusetts Institute of Technology. Center for International Studies, 120, 428
Matecki, B., 641
Matejcek, A., 1477
Matejka, L., 1470
Mates, L., 2562
Matossian, M., 296
Matthews, W. K., 980, 1025-6,
Matthiessen, F. O., 1515
Matusevicius, K., 1010
Maudlin, W. P., 1975

Maurina, Z., 1027
May, A. J., 244, 489, 559
Mayda, J., 1400
Mazour, A., 1560
McClellan, G. S., 368
McLain, G. A., 1122
McVicker, C. P., 2711
Mead, W., 1574-6
Mehnert, K., 66
Mehr, S., 1448
Meissner, F., 1449-51
Mekarski, S., 2420
Melezin, A., 1285, 1978, 2443
Mellen, M., 2579, 2754-5
Mellon, J. E., 1262
Menges, K. H., 682-3
Merzbach, H., 684
Messing, G. M., 1150
Mestrovic, I., 2780
Mestrovic, M. M., 2600, 2798
Meyer, H. C., 212, 642
Meyer, L. L., 2141
Meyer, P., 874-9, 2664
Michalkowa, J., 2303
Michalowski, R., 2196
Michalski, 2280
Michener, J. A., 1737
Mickiewicz, A., 2369-70
Mieczkowski, B., 156, 2214
Mihanovich, C. S., 2585
Mikhailov, I., (Macedonicus, pseud.), 1073-4
Mikofsky, B. S., 685
Mikolajczyk, S., 297, 2051, 2197
Mileff, M., 1206
Milivojevich, D., 2799
Millhauser, M., 1030
Mills, C., 2339, 2371-3
Milojevic, B. Z., 26
Milosz, C., 880, 2304-5, 2340, 2374-5
Minc, H., 2232
Mindszenty, J. C., 1909
Minshall, R., 1151
Mirkovich, N., 2768
Mitchell, D. W., 463
Mitrany, D., 490, 560, 783
Mittleman, E. N., 2807
Moats, A. L., 2456
Moennich, M. L., 157
Mollenhauer, B., 2341
Molski, I. H., 2389
Montgomery, J. F., 1626
Montias, J. M., 1940, 2233-5, 2246
Moodie, A. E., 612
Moor, P., 1722
Moorad, G., 158
Moore, W. E., 213
Moravcsik, G., 1670-1
Moravec, F., 1311
Morawski, B., (pseud.), 159
Morawski, S., 2306
Morin, F. A., 160
Morison, W. A., 673
Moritz, J., 2712
Morley, C., 2052-4
Morris, B. S., 418
Morska, I., 2342
Mosely, P. E., 161, 464-6, 817, 940, 1086, 2713
Mostecky, V., 1516
Moudry, V., 1056
Mousset, A., 796
Mowrer, E. A., 162
Munteano, B., 2524
Muran, J. B., 1312
Murphy, C. J. V., 1941
Mylonas, G. E., 923-4

Nagel, D., 2505-7
Nagorski, Z., Jr., 841
Nagorski, Z. Sr., 2171, 2376
Nagy, F., 1627
Nagy, I., 1758-60
Namier, L. B., 163
Nandris, G., 2516
Nano, F. C., 419
Nasakowski, M., 1942
National Committee for a Free Europe. (See Free Europe Committee).

Neal, F. W., 2632-5, 2714
Nemec, F., 1056
Nemec, L., 1520-1
Nemes, J., 1761
Nenoff, D., 666, 1193
Neuberger, E., 2756-8
Neuenschwander, E., and Claudia, 1597
Neuman, D., 1057
Neumann, R. G., 298-9, 467
Newbigin, M. I., 214
Newman, B., 908
Newman, O., 1891
Newmark, L. D., 1152-3
New York Public Library, Slavonic Division, 27
Nicoloff, A. M., 1207
Nieburg, P. C., 557
Niemira, P., 881
Nodel, E., 981
Nogaro, B., 1818
Noli, B. F. S., 1112
Norman, D., 1098, 2508
Normand, S., 2563
Norwid, T., 164
Nosek, J., 1517
Nowak, F., 2055-6
Noyes, G. R., 2785
Nuttonson, M. Y., 215, 216, 1103, 1286, 2236, 2759
Nyaradi, N., 165, 561, 1781

Oatman, M. E., 1452
Obolensky, D., 939, 1478
O'Brien, A. H., 2800
O'Brien, F., 906
Odolozilik, O., 166, 245, 1313-18, 1382
Ogilvie, A. G., 167
Ogrizek, D., 1539
Ohloblyn, O., 246
Oinas, F. J., 1028
Okinshevich, L., 247
Okinshevych, L., 982
Okkonen, O., 1598
Olin, S. C., 1561
Olli, J. B., 1584
Opie, R., 369
Opocensky, J., 1319

Index of Authors

Oprea, A., 2523
Oras, A., 1011-2, 1029
Ordon, E., 2343, 2377
Orme, A., (pseud.), 1628, 1673
Ornstein, J., 67-70
Orr, C. A., 667
Orska, I., 2096
Orszagh, L., 1841-2
Ostovic, P. D., 2564
Oxenfeldt, A. R., 562
Ozanne, H., 420

Padev, M., 1196, 2636
Page, S. W., 983, 1013
Paikert, G. C., 818, 1782
Pajewski, J., 2057
Palickar, S. J., 1320, 1479
Pallo, A., 1562
Palmer, G. B., 1273
Paloczy-Horvath, G., 1674, 1723
Pandzic, B., 2601
Papanek, J., 1274
Papee, F., 2058
Parker, R., 819
Parry, M., 2793
Parts, A., 964
Pasti, B., 1892
Pat, J., 882
Pattee, R. F., 2801
Paulat, V. J., 563
Pawel, E., 2637
Peaslee, A. J., 300
Pech, S. Z., 1321-2
Pehrson, R. N., 1603
Pelto, P. J., 1563
Perenyi, E. (Stone), Baroness, 1058
Peselj, B. M., 347-8, 613, 784, 941
Pesina, J., 1477
Pesola, V. A., 1577
Peter II, King of Yugoslavia, 2602
Petroff, L., 1241
Petrovich, M. B., 797-8, 2059, 2603-4, 2638
Philipp, H., 2307
Philon, A., 1077
Pick, F. W., 984, 995-6, 1044
Pihkala, K. V., 1578
Pintar, J. I., 2565
Piotrowska, I., 2308
Pirinsky, G., 842

Pirkova-Jakobson, S., 1275
Pirscenok, A., 1498
Pisky, F. S., 1176, 1640, 1819-20, 2444
Platt, R. R., 1550
Plessia, R., 2509
Plicka, K., 1480
Pociecha, W., 2060
Poels, J., 2580
Polach, J. G., 564
Polanie Club, Minneapolis, 1943, 2390
Polisensky, J. V., 28
Polish American Encyclopedia, 2267
Polish Research and Information Center (N.Y.), 2421
Polish Roman Catholic Union of America, 29
Politzer, H., 1499
Pollack, S. W., 168
Pollock, J. K., 289, 301
Polyzoides, A. Th., 421
Ponikiewski, J. G., 422
Pool, I. de S., 302
Popoff, E., 1197
Popovic, K., 2566
Porskyj, V., 2061
Possony, S. T., 303
Poulos, C., 169, 565, 909, 1168
Pounds, N. J. G., 566
Poznanski, C., 2309
Pranspill, A., 1030
Presviteros (pseud.), 762
Preveden, F. R., 2605-6
Pribichevich, S., 2715
Pribram, A. F., 1675
Pridonoff, E. L., 2567
Prigrada, A., 370, 567
Prince, J. D., 2776
Proch, F. J., 2249
Prochazka, A., 1401

Pronin, D., 2237
Proudfoot, M. J., 843
Prunskis, J., 988
Przedpelski, B. J., 2398
Psathas, G., 785
Pundeff, M., 248, 343, 349, 799, 933, 1169, 1213-14, 1247
Puner, M., 2616
Purdy, C. L., 1481
Purre, A., 249, 957
Putnam, E., 1762

Quandt, R. E., 1226

R., 2138
Racz, G., 1821
Racz, I. B., 1763
Raczynski, E., 491
Radescu, N., 668
Radio Free Europe, Information and Reference Department, 844, 1123, 1276, 1629
Raditsa, B., 423, 2568, 2808
Radius, W. A., 371
Radl, O., 1500
Rado, A. R., 1402
Radovich, E., 910
Rand Corporation, 30
Rangeloff, G., 1227
Rank, G., 958
Rasmussen, C. B., 372
Raud, V., 959, 1020
Rawicz, S., 2097
Raymond, J., 170-1
Reddaway, W. F., 1968, 1985-7, 1996, 2007, 2016-7, 2023, 2028, 2035, 2055-8, 2060, 2062, 2064, 2070-2, 2141, 2289-90, 2295, 2300, 2313, 2407, 2410-1, 2415
Rees, E., 1724
Reese, E. A., 1579
Reich, N., 883
Reiner, P., 1403-4
Remenyi, J., 730-1, 1676, 1852-4, 1863, 88
Reshetar, J. S., 743
Revai, J., 304, 1764

Revay, J., 1059
Rey, L., 2344
Rezac, V., 172
Rezler, J., 1641
Riasanovsky, N. V., 424, 800
Ridder, W., 1765
Riggs, F. W., 2665
Ripka, H., 305, 492, 1277, 1352
Rislakki, E., 1544
Roberts, C. M., 173
Roberts, H. L., 31, 174-5, 373-4, 2473
Rodes, J. E., 2063
Rodin, G., 2760
Roditi, E., 1031
Rogers, L. S., 2607
Roheim, G., 1893
Ronimois, H., 1021-2
Rooney, E., 2422
Rosa, R. A., 306
Rosada, S., 2170, 2412
Rosdolsky, R., 614
Rose, W. J., 71, 1415, 1944
Rosenthal, G. S., 884-6
Rosu, G. G., 568, 2238, 2510-11, 2539
Rothfels, H., 425, 820, 2185
Roucek, J. S., 32, 176-7, 217-9, 468-9, 493, 801, 821, 911, 918-9, 930, 934, 1060, 1075, 1104, 1170, 1278, 1323-4, 1976, 2716, 2794
Royal Institute of International Affairs, 912, 1540, 2717
Rubenstein, H., 1471
Rubinstein, A. Z., 2439
Rudnyckyj, J. B., 2392
Rudzinski, A. W., 307, 2138, 2172, 2639-41
Rudzka, W., 2139
Rudzki, A., 569-72, 1453, 2239
Rumanian National Committee, 2474, 2533, 2538
Rusev, R., 1242-3
Rusic, B., 686
Rutkowski, J., 2064
Ryan, L. V., 1487

Saagpakk, P. F., 1032
Sadler, G. W., 763
Sadlik, J., 1383
Sahlman, S. S., 1585
Salvemini, G., 1087
Salys, A., 965
Sanborn, F. R. G., 1533
Sanders, I. T., 615, 942, 1245
Sarajas, A., 1586
Sass, C., 2065, 2777
Savery, F., 2310
Saygun, A. A., 1855
Schechtman, J. B., 822-4, 1977
Scheiber, A., 1894
Schenker, A. M., 2269-70
Scherer, P., 2271-2
Scherer-Virski, O., 2345
Scheynius, I. J., 178
Schimmerling, H. A., 732
Schlesinger, R., 308, 494
Schmalstieg, W. R., 687-8, 1033
Schmid, P., 1725
Schmidt, D. A., 1353
Schmitt, B., 1945
Schneiderman, S. L., 887
Schoenfeld, H. F. A., 1783
Schronkron, M., 2517
Schuman, F. L., 179, 375-6
Schuster, Z., 888
Schutz, A., 2779
Schwabe, A., 960
Schwarz, H. F., 1325
Schwarz, J., 1472
Schwarz, S. M., 426, 889
Schwelb, E., 1088
Schweng, L. D., 616, 1630, 1822
Scott, D., 1354
Sebeok, T. A., 689-90, 1587-8, 1843-4, 1895, 1915-6
Sebestyen, E., 1677
Seckar, A. V., 1488
Sedillot, R., 180

Semmes, H. H., 2173
Senn, A., 72, 691, 733, 1034-8
Serech, J., 692-3
Serech-Shevelov, Y., 2273
Seton-Watson, H., 181-183, 250-251
Seton-Watson, R. W., 1279, 1326
Setton, K. M., 1185
Shandor, V., 1061
Sharp, S. L., 184, 309-12, 573, 617-18, 1946-7, 2098, 2163
Shatzkin, L., 2088
Shaw, J. T., 33
Shayon, R. L., 470
Shearman, H., 1564
Sheean, V., 2718
Sheldon, R. C., 845
Shepherd, G., 427
Shepis, P. G., 1078
Sherman, H. J., 2198
Shimkin, D. B., 574
Shipkov, M., 185
Shipler, G. E., 2719
Shneiderman, S. L., 2164-5, 2240
Shotwell, J. T., 925, 2043
Shuster, G. N., 764, 1910-11
Shute, J., 1287
Sidzikauskas, V., 997
Siekaniec, L. J., 1919
Siekanowicz, P., 2241
Siemienski, J., 2140
Silberman, D., 495
Simonocic, K., 1495
Sipkov, I., 1198, 1208-9
Sirvaitis, C. P., 1049
Skala, H. M., 1384, 1454
Skendi, S., 34, 1079, 1096, 1099-1102, 1107, 1113-4, 1116-20, 1124, 1133-4, 1136-41, 1154-6, 1160-3, 2795
Skerlj, R., 2778
Skilling, H. G., 1385-8
Skrzypek, S., 2242-4

Index of Authors

Smal-Stocki, R., 825
Smith, C. J., Jr., 1565
Smith, H. M., 1948
Smith, H., 734, 1024, 1035-6, 1144, 1239, 1506, 1508, 1584, 2318, 2521, 2786
Smith, R. F., 2092
Smyth, H. M., 1089
Sobieski, Z., 2066
Soltan, C., 2099
Soltynski, R., 2311
Sommellius, T., 2581
de Somogyi, J., 186, 252
Sontag, R. J., 377
Sorensen, R. C., 2141
Soroka, W., 1416
Souckova, M., 1501-4
Soulis, G. C., 2608
Southard, F. A., 575
Spacek, A., 1489
Spencer, A., 1570
Spinka, M., 1327
Spitzer, L., 694
Spulber, N., 429, 566, 576-579, 643-4, 1228-9, 1254, 1283, 1285, 1338, 1365-6, 1375, 1389, 1423-4, 1428, 1432-4, 1444, 1447, 1455-6, 1458, 1497, 1510, 1518, 1823, 2245, 2512-4, 2761
Squier, R. J., 253
Staar, R. F., 73, 2142-7, 2413
Stan, A., 2440
Standard Oil of New Jersey, 1806
Standley, W. H., 2100
Stang, Chr. S., 695
Staniewska, A., 2067
Stanislawski, J., 2274-5
Stankiewicz, E., 1328, 2276-8
Stankiewicz, W., 2246
Starkie, W. F., 1856
Stavrianos, L. S., 926
Steanu, P. B., 313
Stedman, M. S. Jr., 2148
Stefan, A., 1062
Stepan, L., 1457
Sterling, C., 890, 1090, 2720

Stern, P., 1949-50
Sternberg, F., 2721
Steward, J. H., 74
Stillman, E. O., 1171, 1726
St. John, R., 2569
Stocker, C., 1589
Stoianovich, T., 936
Stokes, G., 1541
Stolz, G., 35-36
Stone, I. A., 471
Stone, I. F., 1091
Storm, W., 1355
Story, S., 1115
Stowe, L., 430, 1824
Straight, M., 187
Strakacz, A., 2312
Strakhovsky, L. I., 75, 188, 189, 224, 225, 226, 691, 827, 907, 920, 938, 1211, 1260, 1325, 1332, 1500, 1929, 2020-22, 2348
Stransky, J., 1356
Straubergs, K., 966
Straus, H. A., 2068
Strausz-Hope, R., 2570, 2666-7
Strelsky, N., 2786
Strem, G. G., 1857
Strode, N., 1542
Strong, A. L., 1951-2, 2247
Struve, G., 2199, 2346
Strzetelski, S., 1953, 2166-7
Sturc, E., 2753
Sturm, R., 846, 1389, 1505
Sturmthal, A., 580
Sturzo, L., 378
Stypulkowski, Z., 2101
Sugar, P. F., 1678
Sulkin, S., 1543
Sullam, V. B., 1092
Sulzberger, C. L., 190
Super, M. Low, (Ann Su Cardwell, pseud.), 1954-5
Super, P., 1956
Suranyi-Unger, T., 581
Survel, J., 985
Swan, M. W. S., 1571

Sweezy, P. M., 314
Swettenham, J. A., 961
Swiecicki, M., 2102
Swift, S. K., 1912
Sworakowski, H., 37
Sworakowski, W. S., 37
Sydoruk, J. P., 254, 255
Syers, K., 1957
Sylvain, N., 879
Szaz, Z., 2480
Szczesniak, B., 2414
Szmaglewska, S., 2103
Szoszkies, H. J., 2104
Sztachova, J., 38
Szumski, R., 669

Taborsky, E., 315, 582, 718, 1357, 1390-1, 1405, 1417-8, 2069
Tallgren, A., 1045
Talmadge, I. D. W., 1419, 2722-3
Tanner, V., 1566
Tappe, E. D., 2525-7
Tatarkiewicz, W., 2313
Taubert, H., 826
Taylor, A. J. P., 256
Taylor, E., 1727-8
Taylor, J., 2248
Tedesco, P., 696
Teleki, G., 220, 583
Tellman, D., 316
Tennenbaum, J. L., 891-2
Tennyson, H., 2724
Thomas, J. L., 2423
Thompson, C. L., 472
Thomson, S. H., 802, 827, 1329-33, 1958, 2200
Thurner, M., 943
Tihany, L. C., 39
Timiras, N., 2528
Tinley, J. M., 2762
Tobias, H. J., 40
Tobias, R., 765
Todorov, V., 1230
Tomasevich, J., 2763-4
Tomashevich, G. V., 2609

Tomasic, D., 317, 431, 786-7, 944-6, 2809
Tomaszewski, W., 2279
Tomkiewicz, W., 2070
Topolski, F., 2314
von Torne, P. O., 2070
Torzsay-Biber, G., 1791, 1795, 1904
Towster, J., 432-3
Tozis, J., 1076
Trzaska, E., 2280
Trend, H., 1458, 2249
Trinka, Z., 1334
Trouton, R., 2810
Tuleja, T. V., 257
Turkina, E., 1039
Tymieniecki, K., 2072

Ulam, A. B., 318, 2149, 2725-7
Uminski, J., 2415
Unger, L., 1093
United Nations. Food and Agriculture Organization, 2250
United Nations. General Assembly, 913-5, 1729
United Nations Relief and Rehabilitation Agency, 584
United Nations. Security Council, 1132
United States. Army Language School, 1157-9
United States. Army Map Service, 1288
United States. Bureau of the Census, 2582
United States. Congress. House of Representatives, 435, 1125, 1172, 1199, 1766, 2150-1
United States. Congress. House Committee on Foreign Affairs, 434, 2105
United States. Department of Commerce, 645
United States. Department of State, 191, 380-1, 1215, 1784, 2481
United States. Department of State. Division of Library and Reference Services, 41, 42
United States. Department of State. Office of Intelligence Research, 43, 76
United States. Library of Congress, 45
United States. Library of Congress. European Affairs Division, 46
United States. Library of Congress. General Reference and Bibliography Division, 44
United States. Library of Congress. Law Library, 670, 1250, 1406, 1522, 1796, 2175-6, 2416, 2482-4, 2540, 2802
United States. Library of Congress. Legislative Reference Service, 192, 585, 1126, 1173, 1358, 1767, 1959, 2475
United States. Library of Congress. Mid-European Law Project, 590, 653-8, 1398, 2643, 2648
United States. Office of Geography, 1105
United States. War Department, 937
Urban, J., 1960
Usmiani, M. A., 2787

Vagassky, V., 1380-1
Vaiciulaitis, A., 2529
Vailer, R., 1042
Vajda, P., 1631
Vajk, R., 1825
Valeanu, A., 1053
Valkenier, E., 496, 847, 1963, 2417
de Valpine, J. E., 1785
Vambery, R., 1632-3

Van Cleef, E., 967, 1551, 1552, 1580
Van Dyke, V., 473
Van Narvig, W. (pseud.). See William O. Lucas
van Schooneveld, C. H., 697
Vasiliev, A. A., 258
Vasiliu, M., 2539
Veedam, V., 848
Vegh, J., 1826
Veiler, R., 1042
Venables, T. M., 2765-6
Veniamin, V., 2485
Venster, S., 986
Vent, H., 436
'Veritas', 646, 1827-8
Verkko, V. K., 1604
Vernant, J., 849
Vettes, W. G., 259
Vincenz, S., 735
Viner, J., 647
Virski, F., 2107
Vishniac, R., 893
Vitols, H., 1014
Vlahovic, V. S., 193
Vogeler, R. A., 1634
Vosnjak, B., 194, 2668
Vucinich, W. S., 195, 474, 916, 1127, 1200-1, 1231, 1359, 2108, 2457, 2571, 2610-3, 2669, 2728

W. J., 586
W. V. H., 1978, 2251
Waddams, H. M., 748
Wadsworth, J. J., 1786
Wagley, C., 77
Wagner, A. M., 2347
Wagner, F. S., 719
Wagner, W. J., 2152
Waldrop, A. G., 1590
Wall, C. B., 848
Wallenberg, E., 2281
Wallenius, K. M., 1545
Wallis, M., 2315
Walsh, E. A., 437
Wandycz, D. S., 587
Wandycz, P. S., 78-79, 438, 497, 1420-2,

Index of Authors

Wandycz, P. S., cont., 2073-4
Wanklyn, H. G., 1289
Wankowicz, M., 2109
Ward B., 2767
Warfield, G., 1963
Warfield, H., 1963
Warne, C. E., 2252
Warren, G. L., 1738
Warvariv, C., 2075
Waskovich, G., 196
Wechsberg, J., 1280, 1459
de Weerd, H., 2076
Weinberg, S. S., 260, 1186
Weinreich, M., 698
Weinreich, U., 699
Weinryb, B. D., 879, 894
Weintraub, W., 1964, 2378-9
Weiss, E., 1845-6
Weisser, A., 720
Wellek, R., 1392, 1506-8
Weller, G., 2670
Wellisz, L., 2380
Wepsiec, J., 47
Werner, A., 721
Werth, A., 379, 917, 1094, 1281-2, 1965, 1979, 2253, 2572-3, 2671, 2729-30
Westfal, S., 2282-3
Wheeler, Bennett, J. W., 1335
White, L., 2731
Whitfield, F. J., 2348
Whitnack, D. S., 588
Whitney, A. H., 1591
Wierzynski, K., 2349

Wilbur, E. M., 2541
Willen, P., 319, 1635, 2732
Wilmot, C., 197
Winner, P., 766
Winslow, A., 1636
Winston, V. H., 589, 1177, 2254, 2755
Wiskemann, E., 828
Wittlin, J., 850, 1966, 2350-1
Wloszczewski, S., 2424
Wojcicka, J., 2284, 2400-3
Wojcicki, A. B., 2404
Wolanin, A. S., 29
Wolff, L., 2458
Wolff, R. L., 927, 1174, 1187, 2441, 2459
Wolska, H., 2393
Woolsey, L. H., 2110
Wren, M. C., 928
Wright, H., 2111
Wright, H. W., Jr., 648
Wszelaki, J. H., 591-5, 1232, 1829-30, 2255-7
Wuolle, A., 1592-3
Wuorinen, J. H., 998, 1546-7, 1567, 1572
Wyczalkowsky, M. R., 2753
Wynne, W., 1290

Xydis, S. G., 935

Yakobson, S., 439
Yohe, R. S., 1581

Young, E., 320
Young, R., 1787
Yurchak, P. P., 1336, 1490

Zagorov, S. D., 619
Zaborska, S., 2316
Zaremba, Z., 2425-6
Zarnecki, J., 2317
Zauertnik, R. J., 1095
Zawacki, E., 2285, 2381
Zawadzki, M. I., 2258
Zborowski, M., 871, 895
Zbyszewski, K., 2112
Zebot, C. A., 2803
Zenkl, P., 1407
Zenzinor, V., 283
Zgorzelski, C., 2382
Zielinski, H., 1980
Ziffer, B., 48, 2077, 2352, 2642
Zilinskas, Vl., 1023
Zinner, P. E., 321-2, 440, 1360-1, 1730
Ziverts, M., 1040
Zlatin, I., 1233
Znaniecki, F., 2427
Zoltan, R. M., 1696
Zubek, T. J., 1523
Zubrzycki, J., 851
Zukowski, S., 741
Zulawski, M., 198
Zurcher, A. J., 299, 323-5
Zywulska, K., 2113
Zyzniewski, S. J., 2078

Z
2483
B9

JUN 2 1970